The Merck Druggernaut

The Merck Druggernaut

The Inside Story of a
Pharmaceutical Giant

FRAN HAWTHORNE

WILEY

John Wiley & Sons, Inc.

Published by John Wiley & Sons, Inc., Hoboken, New Jersey.
Published simultaneously in Canada.

For general information on our other products and services, or technical support,
please contact our Customer Care Department within the United States at
800-762-2974, outside the United States at 317-572-3993, or fax 317-572-4002.

Wiley also publishes its books in a variety of electronic formats. Some content that
appears in print may not be available in electronic books.

For more information about Wiley products, visit our Web site at www.wiley.com.

Library of Congress Cataloging-in-Publication Data

Hawthorne, Fran.
    The Merck druggernaut : the inside story of a pharmaceutical giant /
Fran Hawthorne.
        p.   cm.
Includes bibliographical references.
    ISBN 0-471-22878-8
    1. Merck & Co.   2. Pharmaceutical industry—United States.   I. Title.
    HD9666.9.M4H39 2003
    338.7′616151′0973—dc21

                                                              2003000567

Printed in the United States of America

10 9 8 7 6 5 4 3 2 1

Contents

Acknowledgments

For all the people who are quoted in an article or book, there are always far more who don't appear by name, but whose assistance seeps through so many of the sentences.

Some of them I can't name even here, even in a mass listing that doesn't connect any names to any specific pieces of information. I can only thank them anonymously—the sales reps, factory workers, clerks, middle managers, and executives who work and have worked at Merck; the doctors; the reps from rival drug companies; the veterans from Madison Avenue; the relocation advisor; the consultants. I know that many of them were nervous about talking to me. They worried that they were revealing the secrets of a very secretive company, or that it might be hard for them to work in the industry if their names were made public, or that outsiders would consider the practices they described unethical. So I want to thank these people especially for being willing to share their information.

Even when it comes to those I can name, it's hard to single out anyone in particular; I feel as though I should cite every one of the 175 or so people I interviewed, because almost every one was so incredibly helpful. But a few definitely need to be mentioned.

- David Goetzl of *Advertising Age* (my former Crain Communications colleague), who helped me understand the peculiarities of prescription drug advertising.
- Bruce Booth of McKinsey, Don Drakeman of Medarex, and David Perlin of the Public Health Research Institute, who walked me through the process of drug discovery from microorganisms to genomics and patiently answered my elementary questions.
- Boyd Clarke of Neose Technologies, who not only spoke with me in depth about his years at Merck—and again and again over the months after our first interview, as I kept checking in for updates—but also took on the role of booking agent, putting me in contact with new sources every time he ran into another former Merck colleague.
- Guy Fleming of the PACE union, who may not have realized what he was getting into when he showed me around the Rahway plant, and similarly, Larry Naldi, the plant manager. (But what happened took me by surprise, too.)
- My agent, Susan Barry of the Swayne Agency, who made this whole project possible by putting me together with Jeanne Glasser at Wiley, and then calmed me down and

got me back on track so many times when I thought this would *never* work.

- My editor at Wiley, Jeanne Glasser, who had the great idea of doing a book on the pharmaceutical industry to begin with, and whose advice was always wiser than I realized at the time.

- My husband, Pete Segal, and my son, Joey Hawthorne, who were there for me even though I was hardly there for them for seven months, plus all the other family members and friends who had to put up with my obsession.

- All the friends and fellow journalists who helped in so many ways, by introducing me to sources, finding obscure clips and data, sharing child care, sharing their investment strategies, and debating the merits of the pharma industry—Jennifer Airley, Marian Baskin, Andrea and Alan Bloomfield, Matthew Boyle, Michael Cacace, Ann Cohen, Elizabeth Cummings and Steven MacBride, Anna Domanowski, Steve Gandel, Jan Koch, Debbie Majerovitz and Wrolf Courtney, Bethany McLean, Michael Peltz, Rebecca Reisner, Faye Rice, Portia Richardson, Mary Sisson, Vera Titunik, Barry Weinbrom, and Craig Winer.

- And everyone who was willing to take a few hours to talk with a complete stranger: Here is the result of your words.

Introduction

called Greg Reaves, one of Merck's top PR people, from the patio of my parents' house in California four days before New Year's Eve of 2001.

Did he remember how I'd told him, at Merck's meeting with Wall Street analysts a couple of weeks ago, that I was working on a big project involving his company? And I'd like to get together and talk about it with him? Well, I continued, the project was that I was writing a book about Merck.

"Do you know where I am now?" he replied, seemingly apropos of nothing. "I'm on the floor."

"You're on the floor in shock because I'm writing a book?"

"No. I'm on the floor trying to fix an electrical connection."

It was classic Merck. On the surface, what a refreshingly different kind of company, so egalitarian, so genuine. Even its suit-and-tie guys get down and dirty and do their own electrical work.

But we were on the phone, for Heaven's sake. I couldn't see what Greg was doing; whether he was truly looking for an electrical connection was as much a secret as the ingredients in the vials in Merck's labs. He could just be stalling for time while he digested the implications of "book." Still, if he was, it was a pretty clever stall—which, in executing a tough maneuver better than your average company, was also classic Merck.

There was a point during the writing of this book that my publisher and I seriously debated using the subtitle "The Last Good Drug Company." To many people, that might seem like a nonstarter, because for most of the world today, no drug company is considered good. They are greedy Godzillas, they charge impoverished grandmothers outrageous prices for medicines the grandmas can't live without, they spend billions of dollars on commercials to tempt us to buy expensive drugs we don't need, they try to muscle out cheaper generic rivals and keep their own drugs on patent longer than the law allows—all so that they can rake in the highest profits of any industry in America. And much of that litany (with the rhetoric toned down) is basically true. On the other hand, it is also true that these companies, by and large, produce socially beneficial products. They pour billions of dollars and years and years of effort into solid, sometimes groundbreaking research that can result in medicines that genuinely make people's lives better.

Whether the pharmaceutical makers are villains or heroes, Merck has traditionally been seen as a little better than the rest. It is, supposedly, more scientifically pure: It focuses on breakthrough R&D, not frivolous copycat drugs, and it doesn't try to keep generics off the market. It is, supposedly, more community-minded: When it stumbled upon a cure for river blindness, a horrible disease that affects millions of the poorest people in the world, Merck agreed to give the drug away for free. It is, supposedly, more ethical: It was never as extravagant as others in wining and dining doctors in order to get them to prescribe its drugs, and when public outrage built up over what looked suspiciously like quid pro quo's, it was among the first to declare that it would drop the freebies altogether. For a long time, it managed to accomplish all that while also being the biggest and most successful drug company in the world, doing what a business is supposed to do—making money and beating the competition. If you were going to write about the pharmaceutical industry—and as the subject of so much popular anger, it was a hot topic to write about—the obvious company to focus on was Merck. It was the example of what a good drug company could really be. When I first began considering taking on this project in the spring of 2001, Merck was still a star on Wall Street.

By the time the project was under way in late autumn, it wasn't.

Patients taking its newest blockbuster drug seemed to be suffering an unexpected number of heart attacks and other cardiovascular complications. Other blockbusters were facing competition from cheaper generic drugs, and its once-powerful pipeline of future products was only dribbling. Its earnings didn't meet Wall Street's forecasts. Its stock dropped and dropped. Later, with names like Enron and WorldCom tumbling all around, the "ethical" company even got caught up in its own mini-accounting scandal.

Now this would be a different book, not the last good drug company, but the struggles of a once-shining star.

In the end, this book is a combination of the books it might have been—an inspirational piece about an industry leader, a cautionary tale of a falling star, and something more: a what-if question.

Once upon a time, Merck seemed to prove that nice guys could finish first, that it could be a profitable business and a social service at the same time. Then both aspects fell apart.

"As a scientist, I love them, the idea that you only work on breakthroughs. But the economy has no respect for virtue," says Richard Evans, an analyst with Sanford C. Bernstein & Company, who argues that Merck needs to put more effort into uninnovative but profitable "me-too" drugs.

He may be right. The first priority of a business is to make an honest profit for its shareholders. I don't want to make Merck out to be some kind of crusading charitable foundation. A drug company is not, as Princeton Unviersity economist Uwe Reinhardt puts it, "a Catholic nonprofit hospital."

But the pharmaceutical industry isn't like any other industry. By virtue of what it produces—and the respect it demands for what it produces—it does carry some social service obligations. The public expects drug makers to be more ethical than the proverbial widget makers; prescription drug commercials prompt public outrage in a way that McDonald's ads do not. If the industry is ever to gain the public's trust, more companies will have to behave like the old Merck. In fact, Merck will have to behave like the old Merck.

Because of that—because of what Merck was and could be—I'll give Greg the benefit of the doubt on his electrical work.

1
In the Bull's-Eye

On a February morning, snow is falling lightly outside Kathy Maglione's fifth-grade classroom in the blue-collar town of Linden, New Jersey, some 10 miles south of Newark. Gianna, Amanda, and Raquel are in close consultation at a table near the back, huddled over a clear plastic funnel and some coffee filters, screen filters, disposable cups, and plastic bags. They are variously pouring gravel, salt, and diatomaceous earth—earth containing the ground-up remains of tiny aquatic organisms—into cups of water; then, they'll try to separate the ingredients again by pouring the mixtures through some kind of filter.

"I don't think the sodium chloride will go through this."

"Well, I don't want to use a coffee filter. The powder will go through it."

"Are you serious? This is grounded-up bones?"

"We're touching people's bones here?"

"The salt won't go through. It's too thick."

"It's not people's bones, it's animals."

Two months later and 30 miles away, on an unusually chilly late-April afternoon, a fleet of blue buses ferries several hundred shareholders across the wooded, dandelion-strewn sprawl of Raritan Valley Community College to the 2002 annual meeting of Merck & Co., Inc.

The mood in the purple and burgundy college auditorium is amiable and polite. Most of the questions to Raymond V. Gilmartin, the company's chairman, president, and chief executive officer, are on the order of, Why is my pharmacist always out of Timoptic eyedrops? or, Are you doing any research into obesity? The officially nominated directors are all approved; the unofficial shareholder resolutions are all defeated. Everyone nibbles melon slices and chocolate pastries.

The amiability is tinged with resignation, however. The past six months, for people who own pharmaceutical stocks, have been a long parade of bad news. Patents on numerous key products are expiring—five for Merck alone. Earnings at many companies are flat or falling, and even firms with good numbers are seeing their share prices slide. But it's not just the financials that are nagging at the people in the Raritan Valley auditorium. Every day some government official or consumer group in the United States is questioning something the industry does. Even as Gilmartin is fielding the queries on eyedrops and obesity, the chairman of the Federal Trade Commission is complaining to the Senate Committee on Commerce, Science and Transportation about the way pharmaceutical companies try to keep less expensive generic drugs off the market. Congress is considering an array of measures that challenge the industry from every angle, measures to allow cheaper drugs to be imported from Canada, to make it harder to block generics, to tighten the rules on clinical testing, to put more restrictions on advertising, and—the granddaddy of them all—to add prescription drugs to Medicare coverage, with the potential that would bring for regulating prices. State politicians, too, are pressuring the industry to lower prices by filing lawsuits and demanding discounts for their Medicaid programs.

Worse news—though the retired Merck scientists and secretaries in the purple auditorium don't know it—is yet to come. Within the next three months, there will be regulatory questions about their company's hot new arthritis drug and accounting questions about its Medco subsidiary, and their stock's value will plummet.

A onetime administrative assistant has stock options that will expire at the end of the year. "I might as well throw them out," she jokes bleakly, staring at herself in the ladies' room mirror.

"It's almost like pin-the-tail-on-the-donkey, which pharmaceutical company you buy," shrugs a former temp worker who lives in one of Merck's hometowns.

Sheldon Schwartz worked at Merck for 14 years in the 1950s and 1960s, rising from mailroom to marketing. Now he does industrial lighting, and he's worried about the implications of some of the news stories he's read. Why does one say Merck is going "back" to basic research? Hasn't Merck been doing research all along? Why doesn't Merck have more blockbuster drugs ready to replace the ones that are about to go off patent?

He's been going to the company's annual meeting for years. But this time, he says, "it's not the same."

Both these scenes are stories of Merck.

The first is the story Merck likes to tell the world—the Merck of the two legendary leaders, George W. Merck and P. Roy Vagelos; the Merck beloved by small investors; the Merck that discovered a treatment for river blindness in Africa and then handed out the drug for free. This Merck develops groundbreaking medications for tuberculosis, high cholesterol, osteoporosis, and AIDS. This Merck is also an upstanding member of the community. It provides child care for its employees. It gives away tens of millions of dollars.

In that fifth-grade classroom, Gianna, Amanda, and Raquel were part of a unique 10-year, $20 million project that Merck launched in 1993 to completely revamp the way science is taught in four New Jersey and Pennsylvania school districts, including the one where Roy Vagelos graduated from high school in 1947. With its own money plus $2.5 million from the National Science Foundation, Merck hired consultants, trained hundreds of teachers, sent some of the teachers out to Arizona and to Washington, D.C., for further training, bought new science materials, helped set up community science fairs to draw in parents, arranged professional evaluation, and essentially rewrote the curriculum for all the districts' elementary and middle school science classes to emphasize learning by doing rather than learning by text-book reading.

"If it weren't for Merck, this initiative would not have happened," said Dolores Maslo, the tall, elegant, perfectly coiffed director of science for the Linden public school district, as she showed off class after class on that snowy February morning. There was a glimmer of tears in her eyes.

That Merck certainly exists. However, it was the second Merck that looked to be the Merck of the twenty-first century—its labs struggling, its profits slipping, and under attack from politicians, consumers, doctors, other businesses, and insurance companies.

Of course, it was not alone. All the multinational pharmaceutical giants—collectively known as Big Pharma—were facing an overwhelming and unprecedented barrage of scientific, financial, and political problems, much of it their own fault. But that was just the point. Merck was supposed to be different from the rest. If even Merck couldn't come up with good drugs or win the public's love, then the industry really was in trouble.

To understand what was happening to the pharmaceutical industry as the twentieth century moved into the twenty-first, the best place to start is probably with the dollars. Politicians, employers, and patients saw general inflation rising only 3 to 4 percent, overall health care up 5 to 7 percent, health insurance premiums jumping 12 to 14 percent—and spending on prescription drugs soaring almost 20 percent. News stories showed grandmas forced to choose between food and medicine, or elderly couples taking turns filling their prescriptions each month because they couldn't afford two sets of pills. Then, in the same newspapers and magazines, the business pages reported that the pharmaceutical industry was raking in profits of 17 or 18 percent, making it the most profitable industry in the United States. The public connected the dots: *Big Pharma is making obscene profits from the pockets of starving grandmothers* . . . .

Overseas, the headlines were even worse. Millions of impoverished children were suffering from AIDS in Africa and Brazil. Lifesaving medication was available, but incredibly, the drug makers were charging the same $10,000 to $12,000 a year that they billed in the United States. Under the glare of publicity, the companies slashed their prices, to the point where they claimed they were just breaking even. The price cutting didn't do much for their image, however, because they seemed to be dragged kicking and screaming to do it.

Actually, there were plenty of drug companies eager to provide the most popular drugs cheap: generic drug-makers like Barr Laboratories, Inc. and Mylan Laboratories Inc.

The way it was supposed to work, under a 1984 U.S. law governing drug patents, was that the big pharmaceutical companies would do the research, discover the drugs, and get exclusive rights to market the products at their comfortable profit margins for, typically, 20 years. Then, the generic drug makers would get to jump in with copycat versions, selling for one-fifth or less of the patented drug's price. Health insurance plans would include financial incentives to encourage people to use the generics. At that point, the so-called branded companies would forget all about their old drugs and go discover new ones.

That was all very nice in theory. But when the crunch came—as a rush of blockbusters began to come off their patents like dominoes between 2000 and 2002, including such make-or-break names as the allergy pill Claritin and the antidepressant Prozac—the theory fell apart. Instead of simply kissing good-bye to their steady moneymakers, the industry desperately began looking for new ways to patent the old drugs in order to eke out another 6, 12, or 30 months of exclusive rights and keep the generics off the market. Anything would do: the markings on the pill, the color of the bottle it came in, or the chemical compound it produced in people's livers.

In their defense, the pharmaceutical companies pointed out that groundbreaking new drugs don't grow on trees, or even in too many test tubes. Experts argued about how much it really cost to discover the average new drug. Was it $200 million? $500 million? $800 million? Still, there wasn't much debate that it's a long, hard, expensive slog. Although the industry upped its spending on research by close to 70 percent (after inflation) from 1990 to 2001, the number of new drugs approved by the Food and Drug Administration (FDA) pretty much held constant, at around 30 per year, according to The Boston Consulting Group. In other words, more money did not buy more results.

Again, though, as with AIDS, the industry managed to pull the rug out from under its own defense. A sizable number of the FDA approvals weren't for new cures for cancer or other serious ailments; they were for questionable "improvements" to existing brands or the fifth cholesterol drug of the same type. Instead of focusing their millions of research dollars on cures that were needed, too many drug makers took the easy way out.

The mapping of the human genome was supposed to be the answer to Big Pharma's research problems. Yes, it had given the industry an important new tool, and computer modeling had made research faster and more efficient. But the study of genes was turning out to be even more complex than expected. There are something like 30,000 genes in the human genome, each of which can produce up to a dozen proteins, which in turn may (or may not) catalyze a reaction that will act on a particular disease. It could be 2010 or later before any products from genomics research would be ready for market—by which time a lot more patents would have expired.

And after all that, after struggling through those years of decoding and genomics research, what kind of product would the pharmaceutical labs end up with? Most likely a narrowly targeted niche drug that wouldn't make much money.

All of which meant that, even as the public was howling over obscene profits, the days of 18 percent returns might not be around much longer. For many companies whose hot-selling drugs had lost their patents, those days were already gone.

So if big new products were going to be sparse and the generic drug makers couldn't be blocked, the pharmaceutical industry turned to the other tried-and-true business strategy for pumping up the bottom line: marketing. From time beyond memory, drug companies had wooed doctors with everything from free samples to doughnuts to hard-to-get theater and sports tickets, hoping the doctors, in return, would prescribe their drugs. Then, in 1997 Big Pharma was handed a magnificent new weapon, thanks to changes in federal rules—TV advertising. The companies poured in a billion dollars, then two, then two and a half. They hired the best of Madison Avenue, who in turn brought in celebrities like Olympics skater Dorothy Hamill and erstwhile presidential nominee Bob Dole. The aim, Big Pharma said, was to "empower" consumers so that they would crack their doctors' omniscience and demand the brand-name medication they saw on TV. Unfortunately for the pharmaceutical world, it's hard to calibrate empowerment.

Pretty soon, people started asking a lot of questions, and the questions weren't necessarily, "Will you prescribe Vioxx for me?" AARP, the powerful lobbying group for seniors, warned that the ads might entice people to demand expensive medicine they didn't really need. Believers in natural health said American society relied too much on pills, anyway. Ethicists worried that there was something wrong about advertising serious medicine as if it were toothpaste. Consumer advocates said that all the money that was going into commercials ought to be used instead to keep prices down. Doctors weren't exactly thrilled to have their opinions challenged (or to waste nonbillable hours arguing with patients). Even the hoary old wining and dining of physicians came under so much attack that the industry's trade group, Pharmaceutical Research and Manufacturers of America (PhRMA), had to produce a code of conduct drastically curtailing all the freebies.

Popular culture was quick to latch onto the newest villain. In 2001, John le Carré came out with a thriller, *The Constant Gardener*, about a rapacious pharmaceutical giant that hides evidence of the fatal side effects of its TB drug and blithely kills anyone who threatens to reveal the truth. Within that same year, two other novels also featured greedy drug companies or overdependence on prescriptions. The hero of the 2000 movie *The Family Man*, in his soulless Wall Street incarnation before he discovers the True Meaning of Life, finds his greatest satisfaction arranging a multibillion dollar drug company merger

To Frank R. Lichtenberg, a professor of economics and finance at Columbia University's Graduate School of Business in New York who specializes in the pharmaceutical industry, the outpouring against the big drug giants wasn't all that surprising. "If their access to pharmaceutical products is limited by price or other reasons, people get upset," he points out. "That's testimony to the pharmaceutical companies' activity and their contribution to society."

And that was exactly the way the companies had always wanted to see themselves—contributing to society. They were the good guys, the purveyors, after all, of something that saves lives and improves health. In his speech in March 2002 to the PhRMA annual meeting, the lobbying group's president, Alan F. Holmer, even dared compare drug makers to the nation's newest heroes, the firefighters who risked their lives when the World Trade Center was attacked on September 11—because drug companies risk millions of dollars researching new cures that may never pay off. Typical lobbyist hype, of course. But Holmer could be confident he wouldn't be laughed off the podium by his members.

As things degenerated in the winter of 2001–2002, top executives from a big manufacturer brought one of their most vocal critics, Ron Pollack, executive director of a Washington, D.C.–based consumer group called Families USA, to their headquarters to explain what was going on. Pollack, in a backhanded way, actually sympathized with Holmer's point of view. "Here were people seated around the table who thought they were heroes," he later recalled. "They were finding the medicines that were cures for diseases. They thought they were on this great mission. They were profoundly perplexed and hurt that they were being vilified."

How could they be lumped now with the dregs of the business world, with the oil companies and the tobacco industry?

If the pharmaceutical industry was supposedly somehow a little more pure, a little better than the rest of the business world, Merck was the best of the best.

If the scene at the annual meeting could have taken place at almost any other pharmaceutical company, the scene in the fifth-grade classroom was Merck's alone.

Simply put, whether in terms of product or philanthropy, numbers or niceties, no other pharmaceutical company, and perhaps no other U.S. company of any sort, has ever had a reputation like Merck's:

- Number one on *Fortune* magazine's "Most Admired Companies" list for an unprecedented seven years in a row, from 1987 through 1993.
- The only company to stay on *BusinessWeek* magazine's annual ranking of the top 50 performers in the Standard & Poor's 500 index (based on sales growth, earnings growth, total return, and other bottom-line considerations) every year for the first six years running since the list began in 1997.
- The only pharmaceutical company to be included in the bellwether Domini 400 Social Index—a diversified group of 400 companies screened for factors such as product quality, employee relations, community relations, and environmental practices—when the index began in 1990 and for three years afterwards.
- The only pharmaceutical company, as of 2002, to make the National Association for Female Executives' roster of the top 25 companies for executive women each year since the list was launched in 1999.
- A perennial on *Working Mother* magazine's ranking of "100 Best Companies for Working Mothers," qualifying as one of the 10 best for 9 of the list's 16 years.
- The only pharmaceutical company to rate as one of *Fortune*'s "100 Best Companies to Work For" every year since the list started in 1998, and the only pharmaceutical company to qualify for the precursor list, initiated by veteran business writer Milton Moskowitz in 1984, for every year of its existence but one.
- The first pharmaceutical company to win the U.S. Commerce Department's Ron Brown Award for Cor-

porate Leadership, launched in 1997 to honor "companies that have demonstrated a deep commitment to initiatives that empower employees and communities while advancing strategic business interests."

- The only pure-play drug company in that icon of leadership and might, the Dow Jones Industrials.

By the mid-1980s, "Merck was both the Arnold Schwarzenegger and Mother Teresa of American businesses," journalist Barry Werth wrote in *The Billion-Dollar Molecule*, his 1994 book about the founding of a biotech company by a group of ex-Merck scientists.[1]

The double-barreled Merck reputation goes back at least to the 1940s and the discovery of streptomycin. Merck had agreed to provide facilities and staffing to a Rutgers University professor named Selman A. Waksman in return for exclusive marketing rights to any of his results. One of those results was streptomycin—a new, powerful antibiotic that could be used against tuberculosis. The potential market was millions of people, untold millions of dollars; it was like holding the patent on a cure for breast cancer. And Merck, in the public interest, waived its exclusive rights, handing over the patent gold mine to a Rutgers-based foundation.

Through the 1980s and 1990s, the company's research and development prowess was unparalleled in the industry. When Ernst & Young launched an index in 1993 to evaluate R&D spending, revenue, and other financial signposts among the biotechs, the standard it used for comparison was Merck. The company prided itself on creating entire new classes of treatments, on coming out with revolutionary drugs way ahead of anything else on the market, or even better, on being the only one on the market. It had the first or second significant products for cholesterol, hypertension, osteoporosis, asthma, and a class of pain medications known as COX-2 inhibitors, as well as certain broad-spectrum antibiotics. From the 1960s onward, it produced more breakthrough medicines than any rival. "It means something when someone says, 'We've just hired that R&D person and that person came from Merck.' That carries greater weight than if that person came from wherever," Edward Pittman, the investment analyst specializing in pharmaceuticals for the giant New Jersey public employees' pension fund, asserts. "They are the pharmaceutical company that many in the industry see as the quintessential R&D entity. Merck has become the benchmark for the whole biotech industry," says the chief executive of one of the largest of those biotechs, Don Drakeman of New Jersey–based Medarex, Inc., which genetically engineers mice to carry specific antibodies.

That's not all. *The Merck Manual*—a massive compendium of descriptions and treatments for probably every known human ailment—is a staple of doctors' bookshelves. Merck could boast of never having a drug recalled in the United States (unlike some other pharmaceutical makers it could name). It was the first company to volunteer under the 1983 Orphan Drug Act to manufacture a product that was desperately needed by only a handful of people—the drug industry's version of pro bono work. It was one of the first two companies to sign up with the Council of Institutional

Investors, a shareholder rights organization that investigates corporate management practices, back when "it was a very scary thing for a corporation to do," says Sarah Teslick, the group's executive director. Merck's sales tactics were seen as generally a shade cleaner than everyone else's, its attitude toward generics less hostile. AIDS activists considered it a little more willing to listen. As rivals mixed and matched into giant mergers—some of them more than once—from 1989 to 2000, Merck, virtually alone, held out. It was the biggest, the first, the one to beat.

Every day, staffers in Pfizer Inc's treasury office recorded the high, low, and closing prices of only two stocks, in a book that went back to the 1950s: their own company, and Merck.

And of course, there was Mectizan.

If there's one philanthropic act of Merck's that anyone knows about, it's the donation of Mectizan. Back in the 1970s, when Merck scientists were researching ways to fight parasites in farm animals, they accidentally realized that one of the compounds they were studying, ivermectin, might also be effective against a human disease known as river blindness. Transmitted by common black flies that breed in fast-flowing rivers, the disease causes chronic rashes, itching, and weight loss, as well as blindness. Millions of people in some of the world's poorest countries, mainly in Africa, were infected, with tens of millions more at risk. Up until then there had been no effective treatment. Merck's serendipitous find could have a potential market of over a hundred million people. And virtually none of them could afford to pay for it.

By its own admission, Merck originally hoped that someone else would cover the cost of producing and distributing the drug, which could run tens of millions of dollars annually until the disease was brought under control. The company sought out international health and development agencies, charitable foundations, and local and Western governments. When no one volunteered, there was a debate within Merck as to what to do. To donate Mectizan (as the drug was named) for free would not only eat into profits, but it could also open up the floodgates to demands from other charities for all sorts of freebies. A donation like that would go far beyond what any company had ever done. It's one thing to give away a few runs of an antibiotic that you manufacture anyway, as most drug companies do in some form or another; it's another thing to launch a new line solely for donation, and with no limit on how long you'll keep going or how much money you'll allocate.

But that's exactly what Merck did. On October 21, 1987, Roy Vagelos, then the CEO, declared that Merck would donate "as much Mectizan as necessary, for as long as necessary, to treat river blindness and help bring the disease under control as a public health problem." The company also worked with the World Bank, UNICEF, the World Health Organization, and more than two dozen other groups to set up a distribution system.

One former high-level manager who was in the executive meeting when Vagelos announced his plans still marveled at it years afterwards. "That was an extraordinary day. Roy flat-out said to a roomful of senior executives, 'We're going to do the right thing.' Most of us were thrilled." Ordinary employees called the CEO and wrote him letters saying, "I always thought we were a great company, but I never knew how great until now."

Interestingly, Vagelos, when I asked him why he made the decision to donate the drug, didn't mention the patients suffering from river blindness. He talked about "the people at Merck. The research people and how disappointed they would be if the drug never reached the people that would benefit." Merck was going to discover and produce innovative drugs, even if they were given away. Because great drug companies make drugs.

Of course, Merck has milked its Mectizan reputation for all it's worth. The lobby of its headquarters features a collage of Mectizan-related photos along with a sculpture of a boy leading a blind man—that is, a symbol of the kind of helplessness that Mectizan is supposed to end forever, which has become the program's trademark. "Any time you see someone from Merck, they're telling you that same story about Mectizan," harrumphs Daniel Berman, a Switzerland-based coordinator for the Nobel Peace Prize–winning international relief organization Médecins Sans Frontières (Doctors Without Borders). Nor is the giveaway a pure financial loss, since, as with most donations, the Mectizan program qualifies for tax credits.

Still, it's not every company that even has that sort of reputation to milk. It's not every company that takes as its motto: "We try never to forget that medicine is for the people. It is not for the profits. The profits follow, and if we have remembered that, they have never failed to appear. The better we have remembered that, the larger they have been."

For a long time, Merck had both, profits and popular acclaim.

But by the early twenty-first century, it wasn't going to be so easy for any pharmaceutical company—even Merck—to have either.

2
From Little Pharmacy to Big Pharma

The late seventeenth century was a smart time for an entrepreneur in the dying Holy Roman Empire to launch a medical business. Europe was going through a huge upheaval, both political and intellectual. The Thirty Years War—that century's version of World Wars I and II combined—had ended in 1648 with more than half the population of Germany wiped out. The then-reigning power centers of the Ottoman Empire, the Holy Roman Empire, and the Republic of Poland were collapsing, while Russia, Prussia, and Austria were steadily consolidating to fill the void. In England, Parliament would twice challenge its own monarchy, first beheading one king, Charles I, in 1649 and then throwing out another, James II, in 1689.

But if the old political order was losing its hold, Europeans were throwing their faith into a new form of order: science. Isaac Newton was decoding the basic laws of motion and physics, and William Harvey was delineating how blood circulates in the human body. Travelers were bringing back strange medicines—and diseases—from Turkey, China, Siam, and other exotic destinations.

In the midst of all this ferment, in 1668, a 47-year-old apothecary named Friedrich Jacob Merck took over one of the two pharmacies in the town of Darmstadt, 20 miles south of Frankfurt.

For the next century and a half, Merck was pretty much a family-owned drugstore. In 1827, however, Emanuel Merck—Friedrich's great-great-great-great-nephew—began trying to purify and manufacture chemical alkaloids, the basis of nineteenth-century medicine.

Back then there was no such thing as a pharmaceutical company. Pharmacists, in the United States as well as Germany, made their own medicinal compounds with ingredients bought from fine-chemical companies, many of them German. On the less reputable side, there were also hundreds of so-called patent medicines in the United States mysteriously claiming to cure everything from baldness to cancer to babies' teething pain. But even the legitimate pharmacists' drugs weren't necessarily safe. Because they were unregulated, they could be adulterated or diluted, or the wrong ingredients could be substituted—which was, in fact, what happened to American soldiers in the Mexican War of 1846 to 1848. Congress passed a Drug Importation Act the year the war ended that was supposed to ensure that drugs would be inspected for purity and quality at the port of entry to the United States, but it didn't do much good because it didn't set any standards and it didn't block the practice of appointing unqualified but politically connected customs officials. Between 1879 and 1906, a hundred more bills on food and drug purity would be introduced in Congress; all of them died.

By 1890, from its base in Darmstadt, E. Merck & Co. was exporting fine chemicals into this untamed American market and even had a small New York sales office. Not surprisingly, in light of the feeble U.S. drug regulations, problems developed—Merck labels were being illegally placed on other companies' chemicals—and Emanuel's son Wilhelm Ludwig, who ran the Merck fine-chemicals factory, decided that a family member needed to be on the scene. He sent his second son, George, then age 23, to New York in 1891 to join the manager there, a German-born chemist named Theodore Weicker. (Fourteen years later, Weicker and a partner would buy rival drug maker E. R. Squibb & Sons from the two sons of its founder—not the last time a Merck executive would jump to the competition.)

At first, George Merck merely ran the American branch of dad's export business. However, in that era of high tariffs, he figured it would make sense to start manufacturing his own supply. In 1900 he bought some 120 acres of swamps and woodland in Rahway, New Jersey, for a manufacturing plant, followed by a factory in St. Louis. Among his products were iodides, bismuths, morphine, and cocaine—the last two considered medicines at the turn of the century.

Like his ancestor Friedrich, George launched his business venture right at a cultural turning point. America was leaping into the industrial age. Just before George Merck arrived in New York, the first pioneering laws regulating corporations were passed—the Interstate Commerce Act in 1887 and the Sherman Antitrust Act in 1890—and the first major labor union, the American Federation of Labor, was organized in 1886. It was the era of the great consumer inventions and scientific advances, like the telephone, the phonograph, the light bulb, and x-rays, many of them invented by George Merck's neighbor, Thomas Edison. In 1906 Congress even finally passed the Pure Food and Drug Act, outlawing interstate commerce in adulterated or unbranded drugs. By the time Rahway was churning out its iodides and codeine, most of the companies that would be Merck's prime competitors a hundred years later were already in business, in some form or another, in the United States, England, and Germany, including Abbott Laboratories, Bayer, Bristol-Myers, Burroughs Wellcome, Eli Lilly, Pfizer, Smith Kline French, E. R. Squibb, and John Wyeth and Brother.

Then World War I broke out. In fits of anti-German hysteria, American orchestras stopped playing Beethoven, and hamburgers were renamed Salisbury steak. U.S. Judge A. Mitchell Palmer (who would later become infamous, as attorney general, for rounding up and deporting thousands of supposed radicals in the "red scare" of 1919 to 1920) declared that all German-owned chemical companies in the United States "will be thoroughly Americanized." That meant they would be confiscated by the U.S. government in the person of Judge Palmer, who had the authority in his position as something called the U.S. Alien Property Custodian to confiscate and sell what he considered alien property. Among those he zoomed in on was Merck & Co.

George Merck objected; he was by then a U.S. citizen with a growing brood of American-born children (even if he did tend to hire a lot of German immigrants). The government nevertheless took the 80 percent of Merck's 10,000 shares that were owned by the German parent company—George owned the rest personally—and put them up for sale.

The result: Merck went right back to George. On May 9, 1919, he outbid four rivals to buy back his own company for $3.75 million. He still wasn't totally in charge. He had to work under a trusteeship for 10 years, and his bankers, Goldman, Sachs & Company and Lehman Brothers, got 5,000 of the 40,000 new shares of common stock. However, Merck & Co. was now an American company. Meanwhile, the Darmstadt-based Merck KGaA still exists and in fact even has a U.S. branch, EMD Pharmaceuticals, but it has long been overshadowed by its far bigger offspring.

All this time, George was grooming his only son, George Wilhelm, to join him in business. After graduating from Harvard in 1915 with a B.A. (and a resume that included working on the *Harvard Lampoon*), the scion planned to go back to the family's native Germany for an advanced degree in chemistry. But instead, his father urged him, "Come on into the shop. The war will be over in a few months and then you can go and get your degree." The war, of course, lasted three more years; George W. lasted 42 more at the family firm.

If George Merck the elder officially created the American Merck & Co., George the younger created the conglomerate it would become.

Old-time employees remember George W. as a big, handsome, strong-looking guy. Historians, too, inevitably mention his size—six feet five inches, 250 pounds. It's almost a metaphor for the way he grew the company. In 1925, when he took over, Merck was a largely family-owned firm that made fine chemicals, recording $6 million in sales. By the time he died in 1957, it was a $188 million company, traded on the New York Stock Exchange, that had discovered Nobel Prize–winning medicines.

George W. Merck's most revolutionary decision was to branch beyond manufacturing and into research in the 1930s. For a drug company like Merck to say it was going to do its own research, back in those days, would be like a hot dog stand today announcing that it would be hiring the finest French chefs. Scientists at universities were the ones who looked in microscopes, mixed molecules in test tubes, and uncovered new cures. Drug companies were—well, they were mere sales agents, peddling what the real scientists had discovered (and probably some overhyped tonics besides). The American Society for Pharmacology and Experimental Therapeutics even refused to admit members who worked for private industry.

But George W. Merck didn't want to rely on professors' handouts. He would create labs that would be as good as and look just like those in the university. To do so, the company brought in respected academics like Max Tishler of Harvard and Alfred Newton Richards of the University of Pennsylvania. It set up a new pharmacological lab, the Merck Institute of Therapeutic Research, with its own board of directors.

Just like university professors, Merck researchers published their work in respected scientific journals and collaborated with others at academic institutions and nonindustrial research labs.

Merck plunged into the most cutting-edge research of the time—vitamins, sulfas (a precursor of antibiotics), antibiotics, and steroids and other hormones. In its labs, the TB cure streptomycin was discovered and the powerful hormone cortisone was first synthesized. During World War II, the government asked Merck, Pfizer, Squibb, and Lederle Labs to work jointly to speed up production of penicillin.

With medical knowledge still in its toddler years, it must have seemed as though every discovery was a miracle cure. Sulfa drugs knocked out gonorrhea, spinal meningitis, and childbirth fever. Streptomycin vanquished tuberculosis. Cortisone strode like a colossus over rheumatoid arthritis and was hailed as the cure for asthma, eczema, colitis, gout, poison ivy, baldness, and almost anything else that could afflict the human race. Even the duds were profitable: A sulfa compound that proved too toxic for use in humans against malaria turned into a hugely successful drug for chickens. As *Time* magazine gushed in an August 18, 1952, cover story on George W. and his company, in discussing their work on hydrocortisone, "A team of Merck chemists synthesized it after others had thrown up their hands and declared the job impossible. . . . Whatever its final place in medicine, there can be no question of its eventual value in probing the secrets of the human body."[1] In the ultimate proof of respectability, Merck-connected scientists won the Nobel Prize in Medicine

in 1950 and 1952 for cortisone and streptomycin, respectively—two of nearly two dozen Nobels that Merck would
claim a kinship with.

It was in that heady period of pursuing science for the
good of humanity that George W., in a speech at the Medical
College of Virginia at Richmond in 1950, coined what would
become the corporate motto about medicine being for the
people and not the profits. It's emblematic of Merck—or at
least, Merck's image of itself—that people actually remember this motto. Thirty years later, when C. Boyd Clarke came
to Rahway as a marketer, he would find the slogan tacked on
staffers' walls. Twenty years after that, after he'd been gone
from Merck for a full six years, Clarke could still quote it
almost word for word. So could employees riding on a Merck
commuter van in 2001 with a reporter from *Working Mother*
magazine, and employees showing the ropes to Dr. Charles
Hyman, a doctor specializing in anti-infective drugs, when
he came to work in 1997 in the regulatory division, and Dr.
Hyman himself, five years after that. Even hardened Wall
Street analysts cite it.

The other important change George W. brought to his
father's company was to expand and reposition it through a
pair of big mergers. Within two years of becoming president,
he engineered a hookup with another fine-chemical manufacturer, Powers-Weightman-Rosengarten, that more than
doubled Merck's size and added products like quinine. Then
in 1953 Merck merged with Sharpe & Dohme, a century-old,
$50 million Philadelphia-based drug company known for its
aggressive sales force, its vaccines, its sulfa drugs, and its over-
the-counter throat lozenges, Sucrets. The fact that George W.,

the son of the founder, the coiner of the motto, shaped his company through two powerful mergers would prove ironic: A half-century after his death, Merck would be almost the only pharmaceutical company not running around chasing a merger partner.

Then again, maybe George W's legacy is exactly why Merck avoided future mergers. There are indications that the Merck–Sharpe & Dohme linkup was somewhat of a shotgun marriage. True, the two partners—officially renamed Merck Sharpe & Dohme—enjoyed some obvious synergies. Sharpe & Dohme had a lot of experience on the biological side, whereas Merck's expertise was in chemicals; and Sharpe & Dohme's chairman and president had both worked at Merck in the past. However, Merck needed this match. The industry was changing: As drug companies increasingly made their own raw materials, Merck was losing the client base for its chemicals and synthetics. Its sales had been slipping for the past two years. Although it was three times Sharpe & Dohme's size, it wanted the smaller partner's marketing savvy.

The problem was that the two cultures just didn't mesh. Merck's research was miles above Sharpe & Dohme's in quality, and its approach to marketing far more low-key. Some Merck scientists weren't happy at being yoked to these new partners. In a sign of how awkward the pairing-up must have been, even the official (and therefore presumably whitewashed) Merck history, published in 1991, acknowledged some lingering family squabbles between Sharpe & Dohme's plant in West Point, Pennsylvania, and the Merckites in Rahway: "Seen from suburban West Point, the Rahway headquarters is the 'Emerald City.' From the New Jersey perspective, managers transplanted from Pennsylvania are part of a sales-oriented 'West Point Gang.'"[2] Molecular geneticist Keith Elliston, who worked at both places from 1986 to 1996, says that West Point was "almost like a separate company. I think they felt a little more second-class." Nearly 40 years after the merger, as part of a corporate branding effort that also included a new logo and trademark, the name was changed back to the original Merck & Co. The only vestige of the Sharpe & Dohme identity that remained was in the names of the international divisions.

Eventually, the merger also would help bring to an end the Merck family's control of its own namesake. The company became so big that in 1955 George W. decided he needed a CEO to provide some order and fresh ideas. It was a trend that was happening at other family-owned businesses in America, too, as professional managers began to take over from heirs. John T. Connor, a 40-year-old, Harvard-trained lawyer who'd been general counsel and vice president of the company, was appointed to the CEO job—though George W. stayed on as chairman and pretty heavily in charge until his death of a cerebral hemorrhage two years later. Two of George W.'s sons did stints at the firm; George Wall was a vice president and manager of offices overseas for 10 years during his father's tenure in the 1940s and 1950s, and Albert was a member of the board until the early 1990s and also held several management positions. But never again would a Merck run Merck.

Connor's 10-year reign is remembered mainly for three things. The scoffed-at Sharpe & Dohme researchers came up with a drug for congestive heart failure and high blood pressure called Diuril that became a big hit. As would be expected of the company's first professional top manager, Connor brought in such corporate tools as management by objectives and strategic planning. And in Washington, D.C., the industry came under a barrage of attacks for price-fixing. The Federal Trade Commission filed charges against Merck and four others, and after that Senator Estes Kefauver of Tennessee launched a set of hearings in his Subcommittee on Antitrust and Monopoly that would run for three years. Then Connor left to become President Lyndon Johnson's Secretary of Commerce, an achievement that some at Merck took a personal pride in, watching his swearing-in on TV.

With Connor's successor, the Sharpe & Dohme side of the merger took over—literally and figuratively. Henry W. Gadsden had been at Sharpe & Dohme for 12 years and was a vice president and director when the two companies got together. He then rose through the hierarchy postmerger, ending up as Connor's Number Two before becoming CEO in 1965. He was the classic tough SOB, a no-nonsense manager who could be so unyielding, says analyst Richard B. Stover, a senior vice president at Arnhold and S. Bleichroeder, Inc., that if the FDA asked for new data on a drug application, he might just as soon pull the whole thing. Yet, "people were fond of him, even though he was tough and gruff. He had grown up with the company. He really had a feeling for the people," recalls Simon Benito, who spent 25 years at Merck from 1974 to 1999 in a range of management positions, from CFO of the Spanish subsidiary to senior vice president of the vaccines division.

Philosophically, Gadsden was all Sharpe & Dohme, gung ho for marketing and expansion, with less interest in the scientific research that George W. had so proudly pioneered. By some reports, he at one point was pushing the company's researchers to come up with more consumer products, things like a quick-tanning lotion or a hair straightener. As even the Merck official history carefully put it: "In his view, Sharpe & Dohme's successful expansion before 1953 [the merger] could be attributed first to its skill in marketing new products of research, second to its ability to maintain its market share in existing products, and only then to its capabilities in production and applications research."[3]

However, Gadsden had another reason for being leery of emphasizing pharmaceutical research, beyond his natural affinity for marketing. After the bad publicity from the Kefauver hearings and the creation of Medicare and Medicaid in 1965, he figured that the drug industry would face increasing government regulation. Merck, he decided, ought to have a few fingers in other pies.

So Gadsden took Merck into industrial and agricultural chemicals, environmental controls, refrigeration equipment, water treatment, and kelp processing; he bought facilities in Canada and France. Sales nearly tripled, from $158 million a year to $457 million. But he overexpanded. He or his successors ended up bailing out of a number of acquisitions, including Baltimore Aircoil (which made equipment for refrigeration and industrial cooling) and several divisions of Calgon Corporation, a diversified chemical company.

The next chief executive, a staid, low-key lawyer named John J. Horan, spent 33 years at Merck pitching in from one trouble spot to another, from one job title to another. For instance, he helped tidy up the last remaining disputes with the onetime parent company back in Germany, forging an agreement that prevented the German Merck from using the M word in the United States. He also strategized on the company's defense during the Kefauver hearings. Moving to marketing, he revamped the sales force to make it more professional by, among other things, reminding reps to mention their drugs' side effects. As CEO from 1976 to 1985, he negotiated a deal to buy a majority stake in Banyu Pharmaceutical Company, a major Japanese manufacturer. In the mid-1970s, as the business world in general was slowly being forced to face up to its historic discrimination against women and minorities—both women and blacks at Merck organized advocacy groups—Horan ordered all senior executives to include affirmative action goals in their annual objectives. Their bonuses and other pay, he warned, would be tied to those objectives. It was also under Horan's aegis that Merck opened the first of the child care centers that would land it on so many "best" lists.

Most important, Horan put more emphasis back on the flagging research side. And to do so, he promoted a biochemist from the neighborhood named P. Roy Vagelos.

In the pantheon of Merck heroes, the first George Merck would of course be George Washington, the father of his company. George Wilhelm Merck might be Teddy Roosevelt, the patrician heir, big and hearty, pounding his company into the modern age and bursting with passion for higher ideals beyond merely running a business. And Roy Vagelos? It takes two icons to encompass the Vagelos legend: He's both Abraham Lincoln, the poor boy who made good, and Franklin D. Roosevelt, the charismatic leader who launched a multitude of blockbuster products and inspired his company to heights of greatness.

Roy Vagelos grew up in Westfield, New Jersey, just five miles away from the Merck plant in Rahway, and moved to working-class Rahway for high school. The son of Greek immigrants, he spoke only Greek until he started school. His parents had a candy shop, then a luncheonette, and young Roy did his share—sweeping floors, making deliveries, and cleaning tables. From Rahway, he worked his way through the University of Pennsylvania (Phi Beta Kappa) and Columbia University's medical school, with a summer internship at Merck's labs back in Rahway in 1951. At the National Institutes of Health, he did pioneering research into cholesterol that won him the American Chemical Society's Enzyme Chemistry Award in 1967. Then, at Washington University in St. Louis, he became chairman of the biological chemistry department. He went to Merck in 1975, and a year later he was running its research labs; nine years after that, he was CEO (beating out A. E. Cohen, head of the international division, and marketing executive John E. Lyons).

When Vagelos arrived at the old red-brick plant in Rahway that was then the company's headquarters, the great labs that had produced streptomycin and cortisone and vitamin B_2 were far behind in the newest molecular research and had nothing much in the pipeline. He revamped the research operation, bringing in hundreds of new scientists, creating a managerial fast track for them, modernizing the labs, and focusing on categories like cardiovascular treatment and his own specialty, cholesterol. He sought—and found, he says— "really better people who wanted to work in drug development." In his first five years as head of research, he increased the R&D budget an average of 17.2 percent a year (covering the years 1978–1983), up from just under 12 percent annually during Gadsden's tenure. He set up a crash program to ensure that half the new hires would come directly from universities. Many of them—including all the PhDs—he interviewed personally. Even after he became CEO, Vagelos would meet with the senior scientists who were hired, and he even reviewed clinical results.

Like George W., Roy Vagelos wanted the labs to have the feel of a university. To do that, he made publication in academic journals a criterion for promotion at the senior level. He gave scientists time to work on their own projects. "He didn't tell you what to do; he helped guide you to what you wanted to do. In terms of inspiring science, he was unparalleled," Keith Elliston, the geneticist who worked at West Point and Rahway, says. "There was incredible freedom to think and explore new ideas and pursue new options," adds Alaina Love Cugnon, who started as a researcher in immunology in the early 1980s, then worked on clinical trials for the heartburn drug Pepcid, and later became a manager in the human resources department.

"There was a kind of energizing of the company. We just began to work harder. We began to measure ourselves more intensely against the peer companies," recalls Boyd Clarke, the marketer who memorized the company slogan; he worked at Merck during the Horan and Vagelos eras, from 1978 to 1996, in a range of countries and jobs, including marketing in Canada, head of cardiovascular marketing and strategic planning in Rahway, and president of a joint venture in France.

It was common for people to work on Saturdays, and to stay until eight o'clock at night or maybe go home and come back again until midnight. Researchers would help out colleagues on projects they had no stake in, even pitching in with the most boring chores, such as injecting hundreds of mice with doses of whatever was being tested.

One reason Vagelos inspired the troops was that he met so many of them directly. He was one of those leaders with the common touch. He ate in the company cafeteria, even chatting with union workers—some of whom, after all, had probably been his high school classmates. As chief of research and even for a while as CEO, he drove his own Honda to work. If he needed information, he went to whoever might have it, grabbing managers he saw in the hallways, regardless of rank.

In the softer aspects, too, Vagelos remade Merck. The decision to produce and donate Mectizan was his, of course. He extended bonuses and stock options to lower ranks of employees and encouraged flexible scheduling. He named more women to higher-level jobs, including the general counsel and the chief financial officer. When managers were relocated, Merck gave them a bigger allowance and more perks than most pharmaceutical firms did (although not particularly more than top companies in other industries).

Merck would bring the employee and spouse to visit the new location, and if they didn't like it, they didn't have to move.

Merck even seemed to be ahead of the game politically. Health coverage was changing. The old Marcus Welby system of medicine, in which doctors prescribed whatever they thought best, was turning into something more like a discount megastore. Now health maintenance organizations and other managed care companies were making the prescription decisions, using insurance coverage as their leverage. To contain costs, they would pay for only the drugs on their approved lists, or formularies. To get their drugs on those lists, pharmaceutical companies had to give big discounts. Further propelling the trend, Bill Clinton was elected president in 1992 on a platform calling for health care reform. The entire medical industry hit the panic button, foreseeing price controls, government bureaucracy, and even more power going to the managed care companies.

Merck's answer was to buy a pharmacy benefits manager (PBM)—the middleman that employers hire to administer their prescription drug benefits. (Vagelos was also savvy enough to invite then-candidate Clinton to speak at Rahway during the 1992 campaign.) The theory was that the PBM could use its clout to persuade employers and insurers to substitute Merck products for rivals on their formularies. The era of sales forces pitching drugs one-on-one to physicians was over, Vagelos told Wall Street analysts. Other drug companies bought or tried to buy their own benefits managers, but Merck bagged what was then the biggest, Medco Containment Services. Once again, Merck was on top—so it seemed.

It was in many ways a company made in Roy Vagelos's image: intense, driven, loyal, scientifically brilliant, collegial, and arrogant.

In return, the company's image was incredibly important to Vagelos. When Keith Elliston proposed a multimillion dollar genomics project—it involved sequencing some gene fragments and publishing the data—the CEO asked a lot of questions about how it would work and whether it would meet Merck standards. Then, Elliston recalls, "he said, 'This can not in any way embarrass Merck.' He was very concerned about the image of Merck."

And it never stopped. At dinner parties, Vagelos's social conversation consisted of asking the Merck people what they thought of some news item that related to business. Three weeks before he retired in June of 1994, Vagelos and his wife, Diana, flew to Lyons, France, to help Boyd Clarke officially launch a new joint venture for vaccines with what was then Pasteur Mérieux Connaught. With the clock winding down on his tenure, "a lot of people might be doing victory laps," Clarke points out. But Vagelos wasn't letting go: Throughout the 40-minute drive from the airport, "he worked me over: how I needed to manage this organization, how I needed to control the headcount, how I needed to control the assets, how I needed to work it to make sure the kinds of standards we were used to were done."

The Vagelos Merck had its cracks, of course. Less charitably, his style could be described as micromanaging; if you had to wait for the chief of research to interview every Ph.D. who was hired, let alone every midlevel chemist, it could take a long time to fill a job opening. Indeed, the ultracentralization was a major reason Clarke left in 1996 to head a series of biotechs on the East and West Coasts.

Even Merck loyalists admit that both Vagelos and the company could be arrogant. You can hear it in Vagelos's voice—terse, unhesitant, with an undertone of impatience. There was a tendency among managers, some say, to think they had all the answers. According to one ad agency veteran, Merck executives would regularly make impossible demands, like calling at five o'clock on a Friday to order a 400-page report by Monday. "It was, 'We're the most admired company in *Fortune*. You should be honored to be our ad agency.'"

And as *Fortune* magazine kept anointing Merck the most admired company in America year after year, 1987, 1988, 1989, seven years in a row through 1993, employees partly started to expect the accolade and partly felt almost panicked about maintaining it. "I was surprised when we were voted most admired" the first two times, Vagelos admits in one of his less arrogant moments. "After we were 'most admired' two years in a row, you start saying, 'Oh my God, what if we're not most admired [next time]?' Then you become anxious about it."

But mainly—at least until the last couple of years—the Merck method worked.

One after another, the company's scientists spit out more than 10 major new drugs in the 1980s and 1990s and launched research on a dozen others. Most of the blockbusters that would put Merck on the map began under Vagelos's leadership, when he was either head of research or CEO: Mevacor and Zocor for cholesterol, Vasotec and Prinivil for hypertension,

Vioxx for acute pain and osteoarthritis, Pepcid for heartburn, and Crixivan for AIDS.

By the time Vagelos retired in 1994—mandatory at age 65—his company was the undisputed Number One in sales, size, and quality of its marketing force. Rivals measured themselves against it. *BusinessWeek* magazine, in a 1987 cover story, called it "The Miracle Company." True, the entire industry was under intense political and financial pressure, but Merck was still seen as the star of a dimming constellation.

The reputation spread among doctors, scientists, marketers, and outside vendors who dealt with the company. "The sales forces love it when you're bringing new, exciting products to market, a half-dozen products that become billion dollar products in a half-dozen years," points out an executive who spent more than 15 years at Merck before, during, and after the Vagelos era. "Physicians will talk to people who are detailing [marketing] from a company like that. People wanted to work there." Pharmacists who ran small, independent shops—and who had little love in general for the drug manufacturers that favored big, bulk purchasers— saved special praise for Merck because it was the only one that set no minimum size on orders, and it was generous regarding returns. "We needed one bottle of a $3 item, they sent it to us," recalls James R. Schiffer, the Brooklyn-accented owner of Jim & Phil's Family Pharmacy in the multiethnic Sunset Park neighborhood of New York City. By the way it listened to its employees and tried to be sensitive to their concerns, says one advisor on transferring and relocating executives, who has worked with Merck for almost 20 years, "Merck made us a better supplier."

"There was a sense," Alaina Cugnon the researcher-turned-HR manager, says of those glory days, "that we were doing something important. What we were doing was going to make a positive difference in people's lives. People really believed that."

It would be tough for anyone to follow an act that good.

Ray Gilmartin walked into the top job at Merck in 1994 with at least three strikes against him:

First, unlike every predecessor going back to George Merck, he was an outsider. He hadn't spent a single day working at the company; he didn't have the network or know the corporate culture.

Second, he was the choice of the board, not Vagelos. For that matter, he was at least the second choice: Vagelos had been grooming a "dream team" of insiders, including executive vice presidents Jerry T. Jackson, Francis H. Spiegel, Jr., and John L. Zabriskie and—the presumed heir apparent—chief operating officer Richard J. Markham. It was only when those plans fell through and Markham left abruptly for never-explained "personal reasons" after less than a year as COO, that the board looked outside.

Third, unlike Vagelos, Gilmartin wasn't a scientist; he wasn't even from the pharmaceutical industry. He was a Harvard MBA.

True, Gilmartin had been at Becton, Dickinson and Company, a manufacturer of medical devices and diagnostic systems, for 18 years, ending up as its chairman, president, and CEO. However, to people bred in the pharmaceutical industry, medical device companies are a lower order of being, just the way academic researchers used to view drug companies. A Lou Gerstner may jump from Nabisco to IBM, or a Paul O'Neill from International Paper to Alcoa, but the pharmaceutical business is so technical and complex, so dependent on knowing the regulatory ropes, that you really have to come from inside in order to handle the top job effectively, management experts say. "Maybe if they served on the board of directors for a number of years"—which Gilmartin didn't —"and they're very bright, they might be able to switch industries," muses William W. McCutchen, Jr., an associate professor at Baruch College's Zicklin School of Business in New York (who himself might qualify for a CEO job, since he spent 17 years at Eli Lilly and Company). "I think it would be extraordinarily difficult," he adds.

It also was Gilmartin's misfortune to be in charge just as the health care paradigm was changing again. And, to be fair, to clean up the mess Roy Vagelos left behind in his last two years in the form of a brain drain and Medco.

In 1992, under the pressure of managed care and what looked like imminent government controls, Merck had decided to downsize by offering early retirement to anyone 50 years old who had 25 years at the company (a relatively easy threshold, considering the long-term loyalty of the staff). Scientists with a combined hundreds of years of experience bailed out, many going to rival firms. Altogether, more than 2000 people departed, costing the company $775 million in incentives and a punch in the gut to morale. "Merck had never done anything like this before. People never felt the company would encourage them to leave,"

Simon Benito explains. "The people who remained never felt the same afterwards." On top of that, within six years of Vagelos's retirement a cluster of other important managers also left, including Richard J. Lane, head of human health for North America; general counsel Mary M. McDonald; Michael M. Tarnow, executive vice president of Merck-Medco; Dr. Roger Perlmutter, executive vice president for research and development; Alfred W. Alberts, the longtime head of biochemical regulation and probably Roy Vagelos's closest colleague at the company; and the entire dream team.

Moreover, the purchase of Medco, now renamed Merck-Medco Managed Care, was turning into a major mistake, maybe Merck's worst. The margins were tiny—typically no more than 5 percent—and the quick-service mentality was foreign to Merck's corporate culture. There was also an inherent conflict of interest between Medco's obligation to scout out the best deals for its customers and its presumed imperative to push Merck drugs. A lot of people at Merck were upset at the way Vagelos seemed to be nevertheless latching onto this supposed new philosophy of health care. And the company almost froze in shock at the short-lived possibility that Medco's chief, Marty Wygod, would replace Vagelos.

Whatever justification there had been for owning a PBM, it disappeared completely after President Clinton failed to get his health care plan through Congress and the power of the HMOs eroded. Consumers rose up in howls against the restrictions of managed care. Doctors regained some influence over prescriptions, and then TV advertising took the decision-making over the heads of HMOs and doctors alike, straight to the patient. As Medco dragged down both its margins and its clean image, Merck finally announced—to some industry snickering—that it was spinning off the subsidiary in a public offering in 2002. Then it was revealed that Merck had booked as revenue $12.4 billion that Medco never actually received. No matter that Merck offset the same amount with expenses or that this was common practice among PBMs. Following a slew of corporate accounting shocks in the past six months, Merck was seen as another business crook.

If Vagelos had left Gilmartin some messes, however, he also left behind the best legacy in the business: his research labs. For the next five years, Merck lived off that inheritance. But the last of the Vagelos blockbusters, the arthritis and pain drug Vioxx, rolled out in 1999; then Vioxx was hit by a report in the prestigious *Journal of the American Medical Association* in the summer of 2001 indicating that it (and other drugs of its type) might increase the risk of heart attacks. Less than a year after the Vioxx bad news, Merck pulled the application for regulatory approval for Vioxx's second-generation successor, Arcoxia, in the United States, first saying it was going to add an application for Arcoxia to be used for a rare spinal condition, then admitting that the FDA wanted more data on the drug's effectiveness and cardiovascular safety. (Merck planned to resubmit the application in late 2003.) Five other blockbusters, meanwhile, lost their patent protection. Of course, the company had plenty of projects in the works; it promised to file or launch 11 new medicines and vaccines between 2002 and 2006, including products for AIDS, diabetes, and depression. Within one month in late 2002, it got approval for a new cholesterol drug and announced promising test results on a cervical cancer vaccine. To many skeptics, however, not much seemed big or imminent. (The cervical cancer vaccine, for instance, while a scientific breakthrough, might never be a big money maker—and still had years of tests and approvals ahead before it could hope to hit the market.) It was the reversal of the virtuous cycle of the Vagelos days, when great products led to high morale, happy sales reps, and admiring doctors. "As we felt more and more pressure because several products were going off patent and we didn't have a new blockbuster, the mood deteriorated among many people," says one midlevel manager who left in the early 2000s. "The stock was falling. The stock options were not worth as much."

The stock plunged from nearly 100 at the end of 2000 to the 40s in the summer and early fall of 2002. Merck unexpectedly announced in June 2001 that it would miss its earnings for that year, then followed up in December with the shocker that its earnings for the next year would be flat. On Wall Street, the pressure grew to seek a merger, even as archrival Pfizer swallowed up Warner-Lambert Company, then Pharmacia.

By 2000, Merck was no longer the biggest drug company in the world. By 2002, it was just twelfth on the *Fortune* "Most Admired Companies" list.

The supposed industry leader when it came to community service couldn't even win the ultimate community service bid—a government contract to produce 155 million doses of smallpox vaccine pronto in the aftermath of the September 11 terrorist attacks and the follow-up anthrax scare.

For Merck, it was as though someone had knocked a bottle of pills off the shelf while the cap was loose, and all the contents were tumbling out. Vendors and employees said Merck didn't care about its people the way it used to any more. Researchers said they didn't have the academic freedom they used to. Rival companies still looked up to Merck, but for many of them it was only one of the best. It was no longer on a pedestal by itself.

Quietly, inevitably, the mutterings began about Gilmartin. He wasn't showing leadership. He should have gotten more research going sooner into new drugs. He should have bitten the bullet sooner in warning investors of weak earnings. He should have dumped Medco sooner. He should have been more forthcoming about the potential side effects and problems of Vioxx and Arcoxia. He was being arrogant to think Merck could survive without a merger partner. He didn't make people *want* to discover great drugs, the way Roy Vagelos did. He had inherited the best drug company in the world, and he had frittered it away.

One Merck executive asked colleagues at Becton Dickinson what the reaction had been to Gilmartin's switching over to Merck. "When Gilmartin left Becton Dickinson," they answered, "the clock started moving again"—that is, the company had been stuck in the mud under Gilmartin. "I see Ray as an in-box guy. I see him calling balls and strikes. I don't see him changing the direction of a company whose direction needs to be changed," says Richard R. Evans, a senior research analyst specializing in drug stocks at Sanford C. Bernstein & Co. in Manhattan.

In truth, there is something homespun and uninspiring about Ray Gilmartin. He's almost universally called "nice," even "super-nice." As a manager, he does not have a reputation as an aggressive take-charge type. The most positive description is leadership by listening, encouraging others to talk—"facilitating," in biz jargon. The negative description: weak.

To many investors, the problem went even beyond uninspiring leadership—it was that Gilmartin had downright misled them. "Wall Street has finally said, 'We don't believe these guys any more,'" says Rick Stover, the Arnold and Bleichroeder analyst.

Of course, it's much too simple to say that everything was great under Roy Vagelos and everything went wrong under Ray Gilmartin. Whether Wall Street likes the choices he's made or not, give Gilmartin credit for sticking by Merck's principles. He put the company's efforts into research instead of playing patent-extension games. He stood up to the Street's merger pressure. And he did—if belatedly—pull the plug on Medco. Nor is that Harvard degree merely a wall hanging.

It's important, too, to remember the timing. When Gilmartin took over, the industry was still terrified that President Clinton would pass some sort of health care reform. Managed care and its formularies were gaining strength. Big Pharma was just picking itself up from a stock collapse in the early 1990s. "He was not dealt a particularly good hand," Simon Benito says sympathetically. What the Becton Dickinson people might see as stopping the clock—lack of innovation—Dr. R. Gordon Douglas, vice president of Merck's vaccine division from 1991 to 1999 (and Benito's onetime boss), calls much-needed stability in the midst of turmoil.

"Gilmartin was a very stabilizing influence at the time he came," Dr. Douglas says. "He's a Harvard MBA, he knew what a CEO needed to do—articulate the mission and core values, and keep doing it."

And Gilmartin, with his experience in marketing to corporate and hospital clients at Becton Dickinson, was seen as the perfect CEO for a world in which drug companies would sell to other corporations via HMOs. It's just that the world didn't turn out that way,

Undoubtedly, a lot of people have to share the blame for what's happened to Merck, and some things are no one's fault. It was Roy Vagelos, not Gilmartin, who made the decisions to offer early retirement and to buy Medco. It was under Roy Vagelos, not Gilmartin, that Merck fell off the "Most Admired Companies" list, but then again, that was during the heyday of the Clinton health care reform, a time when all pharmaceutical companies were slipping in public favor. One reason Merck lost its ranking as the largest drug company was that so many other companies merged. If a flurry of executives fled, it's hardly surprising that people who were passed over for CEO wouldn't stick around. For that matter, if Gilmartin was such a lousy choice, why didn't Vagelos have a better successor lined up?

Vagelos is very careful when talking about the new management and what's happened to his company; "I can't comment on that" and "that's not a fair question" are answers he uses a lot. He claims he "was not part of that process [of selecting Gilmartin]. It was a board process." But he admits he joined in on the decision to look outside for a CEO "for obvious reasons. The inside candidates were not quite ready. All the top people at Merck were considered, of course." Once he left, he turned down an invitation to stay on the board. "Initially, I saw Ray Gilmartin a couple of times, he wanted to talk about some things. Issues at the company." But that ended by 1997 or so.

Would Merck have been better off with a scientist-CEO like himself? "It was definitely an advantage" being one, Vagelos says.

Is this the same Merck he used to lead?

"That is the question. I don't know the answer to that. The stock price is a bit down. The news would say they don't have an adequate pipeline; I don't like to hear that." What Merck needs is new products, and the annual report shows "some very good things, some very interesting things." But R&D takes a long time.

Then, very pointedly, in talking about his Mectizan decision, Vagelos says, "If you're going to be a research company and be as successful as Merck"—pause—"was"—pause—"you have to take some giant steps."

But if it was no longer Roy Vagelos's Merck, that didn't mean it had to be a disaster. The pills could be put back in the bottle.

If some top guns had left, Merck by virtually all accounts was still able to bring in highly rated scientists to its labs, including Peter S. Kim, a respected biologist from the Massachusetts Institute of Technology, as the second in command of research (later promoted to the top R&D job). If Merck didn't seem to be touting any new products, well, that was the pharmaceutical industry, which hates to talk about drugs still in the early stage. If Wall Street was kvetching, well, that's what Wall Street does at the slightest breath of wind. Merck regularly continued to make the various "best" lists, albeit perhaps at lower rankings. It was still a colossus, with a workforce of 78,000, $48 billion in sales, and a presence in nearly three dozen countries around the world. Employees still worked long hours, still quoted the company motto, still enjoyed perks like on-site child care and pickup and delivery of their dry cleaning—and still walked around with the air of knowing they were the best. Merck had survived dry spells before.

The drug business is notoriously fickle. All it takes is the next set of test results, or the next edict from the FDA—maybe Merck's new cholesterol drug or its cervical cancer vaccine. Things could change, too, with Peter Kim now in charge of research. Merck insisted that earnings would be growing by double digits again in 2003. What mattered was whether Merck still had the brainpower in its labs and the fire in its belly.

3

Off the Cutting Edge

No one is galloping down the halls shouting "Eureka," or even staring especially intently at a test tube. On the second floor of Building 800 (Basic Chemistry Process Research), inside the Merck compound in Rahway, New Jersey, it's as sedate as a purchasing manager's office.

The floor is laid out in three rings. First is a series of small offices marching one after another along the outer wall. Then comes a light-filled hallway. Along the inner core, the third ring is a line of individual labs, each housing two short aisles crammed floor to ceiling with shelves, bottles, beakers of all sizes, and other instruments. A clicking sound comes from a lab doing antibiotics research; "Somewhere Over the Rainbow" wafts out from one working on mutagens (chemical or physical agents that cause genetic mutations). In most of the labs there are one or two scientists—only a few in white coats—measuring, pouring, or reading. With pale beige walls and carpeting in the hallway, the office doors mostly open, and a large window looking into every lab, the overwhelming feeling on the floor—surprisingly, for the hub of a deeply secretive pharmaceutical company's deepest secrets—is of light and a lack of secrecy.

These labs are the heart, brain, and soul of Merck. In rooms like these, at Merck and other pharmaceutical companies, researchers have come up with pills for high cholesterol, high blood pressure, osteoporosis, asthma, heartburn, prostate troubles, and arthritis. And in rooms like these, they hope to find the magic answer for schizophrenia, diabetes, cancer, Alzheimer's disease, obesity, AIDS, and whatever else human beings suffer from. There's no point being a drug company if you're not going to discover drugs.

In the realm of these labs, Merck has long considered itself the king.

Other manufacturers might merge with competitors in order to add new drugs to their pipelines. Not Merck. Merck does its own research, and it doesn't need anyone's help.

Other manufacturers might come out with the fourth or fifth beta-blocker for high blood pressure, even if it couldn't be first. But not Merck. Merck makes discoveries, not just drugs.

"For us, 'breakthrough' isn't a slogan—it's our focus. We develop medicines that offer novel approaches to disease treatments; help large patient populations; and are effective, well tolerated, and convenient," Ray Gilmartin told the annual meeting in 2002.

To the rest of the industry, Merck seems to have some sort of magic touch with the FDA. Its drugs generally get approved faster than those of rival manufacturers. It has never had a product recalled in the United States. "That is unbelievable to me," says Dr. Susan Hendrix, a gynecologist in Detroit who is also a paid consultant to Merck and several other big drug makers. "That means they spend a lot of time before they take it to the person, making sure it's safe and effective. There's no other company that hasn't had any drugs pulled from the market."

Fiercely competitive—especially against Pfizer—Merck drives its scientists hard to keep its crown. "If others got approval in a year, we'd do it in nine months," says Charles Hyman, the anti-infective drug specialist who worked there in the late 1990s. "We always criticized Pfizer by saying that a lot of what they did was me-too drugs, or that they licensed-in," notes Gordon Douglas, the former vaccine division chief. "Our image of other companies," says Boyd Clarke, the veteran marketing executive, "was that they might be interested in pursuing things that were simply commercial opportunities. Our self-image was breakthrough science."

Adds Dr. Douglas, "They [at Merck] believe in themselves. They know how to do everything better than anyone else. There's a great deal of confidence that the company has the people, the resources, and the facilities to do whatever it decides is the best course of action."

However, around the late 1990s, the rush of innovation started to trail off. Merck and the industry as a whole seemed to be having a harder and harder time coming up with big breakthrough drugs—drugs that were significantly different from what was already on the market, that worked better, that had fewer side effects, that targeted ailments that had had no cure before this. Maybe that's why Building 800 was so quiet.

Producing a new drug has never been easy. Early human societies probably tasted (and spat out) a lot of herbs before they found which ones worked for cramps, and which for a stuffed nose. In modern days, a drug company will consider maybe 10,000 molecules and test 5,000 in order to get one marketable product—and that will take 12 to 15 years.

These are, after all, powerful substances that are expected to invade the human body and change what cells or proteins are already doing. They are fighting Mother Nature. The odds against them are tremendous—think of trying to reverse the direction of a hurricane or a river. And if the drugs are strong enough to succeed, then they could be strong enough to also knock down other bodily functions unintentionally in the process, to create side effects, in ways that could be dangerous.

Unleashing this power starts with scientists screening hundreds of thousands of molecules against the diseases they've chosen to focus on (more on that later in this chapter). Interesting ones go into preclinical testing on animals. If those results seem promising and safe, a company files an investigational new drug application with the FDA, which launches it into a strict series of increasingly larger and more demanding human tests. In Phase I clinical trials, lasting maybe a year, the company tests the would-be drug for safety on several dozen healthy people. Phase II trials focus on effectiveness and side effects over the course of about two years, using one 100 to 300 people who have the disease, measured against control groups of patients taking other drugs or a placebo. Finally—assuming all has gone well so far—the drug-to-be moves to Phase III trials. Still studying effectiveness and side effects, this phase can involve several thousand patients in clinics and hospitals over three or more years, also compared with control groups. (When there's no other treatment and the disease is life-threatening, the FDA might speed up the process, giving approval after small trials and no control group.) At the end, the company files a new drug application. Actually, that's not the end: Even after the drug is on the market, the FDA monitors it for adverse reactions and long-term effects, and the manufacturer may keep staging tests—informally known as Phase IV—to try to add approved uses or remove warnings from the label.

It took Merck more than 25 years all told to produce a chickenpox vaccine, Varivax, that the FDA approved in 1995. Vaccines are, admittedly, among the most difficult of drugs to manufacture, because they are typically a form of the agent that causes the infection. Every batch has to be grown in a cell culture, and, as with all living things, the quality of the cultures can be inconsistent. "Growing [vaccine] viruses in cell cultures is almost like growing tomatoes in your garden. Some years they're great. Some years they have worms. You have to control all the variables," explains Gordon Douglas.

The chickenpox vaccine was especially sensitive to temperature. "We couldn't make it consistently with a high enough quantity," Dr. Douglas recalls. "Every time we did a study, the research people would say, 'We found a better way to make the virus.'" Which meant it was no longer the same virus that had been previously tested. Which meant a new round of tests. "I wasn't very happy, because I knew it was going to delay us." Dr. Douglas would have turned down the revised trials if there had already been a product that was fit to license, but there never was. It finally took a new computer-controlled robotic technology to carry out the process of making Varivax in large enough, reliable batches. "There were newspaper reports, every year for the first few years I was there, that we were going to get this vaccine approved," Dr. Douglas says wryly—now. (It was approved exactly four years after he took over the division.)

Talk to almost anyone who has ever worked there, even the harshest critics of the Gilmartin era, and he or she will soon start to gush about the incredible caliber of the staff at Merck. Ask Roy Vagelos the secret of the company's success during his tenure as CEO from 1985 to 1994, and he replies, with no wasting of words, "It had better people." Of course, that's a cliché. The trick is picking these great people.

Merck tries to find its scientists young, at universities, rather than at other companies. "We always felt that if you hire the best people off an academic environment and give them a challenge, you could keep them for a long time," says Steven M. Darien, who retired in 1994 as senior vice president of human resources. (He should know something about keeping people: He stayed at Merck for 30 years.) New college graduates can also be paid less than veterans, but that doesn't seem to be Merck's main motivation. Most important, the company wants to mold the new hires in the Merck style, before they're contaminated—that's a word several people use—by another pharmaceutical culture.

Although students don't have long résumés, Vagelos says that in hiring, "I looked at their performance as postdoctoral fellows and tried to figure out if they were interested in drug development, whether they had been inventive. Because of my relations with the academic group"—his own prior experience at the National Institutes of Health and at Washington University—"we were able to reach back into the graduate schools. We knew who to talk to. They felt secure in talking to us." Ray Gilmartin doesn't have those connections, but instead he began building a $100 million research center near Harvard Medical School that was expected to lure junior faculty from Harvard and other Boston universities.

For these new recruits—especially when Vagelos headed research and then the whole company and to a lesser degree now—going to Merck is almost like still being in academia, but with more money to spend. In the Vagelos days Merck researchers were given an extraordinary degree of academic freedom. Their basic job was a kind of scientific drudgework, doing the first-stage molecular screenings. However, "if you spent 25 to 50 percent of your time doing screens for new compounds, the rest of the time you could spend on [independent] research," recalls Keith Elliston, the molecular geneticist who cofounded Merck's gene indexing project in the mid-1990s and later established its department of bioinformatics (that's a process of using math and DNA to tackle biological problems). If all the spare time in their workweek still wasn't enough, Al Alberts—Vagelos's long-time research colleague—would tell his staffers, "the labs are open 24 hours." And the researchers came.

"We had wonderful people. So long as they were innovative and wanted to work on drug discovery, I didn't care what they did. I just wanted to know what they were doing. When I saw them, we would talk through the ideas," Vagelos says. Further encouraging this independent work—which some called "back-pocket science"—researchers could put their pet ideas on the agenda for the program review that senior research managers held every month at a Merck-owned farm-house. If approved, the ideas would become official Merck projects. (Of course, "most of them were turned down," Alberts points out.)

The system tightened up around the time Vagelos retired in 1994. Elliston attributes it to politics, as outlined in a speech by Dr. Bennett M. Shapiro, the head of worldwide basic research at Merck's division of Worldwide Licensing and External Research. With the industry under heavy public criticism and President Clinton's health care reform leading the agenda in Congress, it was more important than ever to have concrete results, to show what wonderful things the drug industry did for humanity. Merck would now put more emphasis on churning out product. There would be less time for independent basic research. To Alberts, meanwhile, the change had more to do with the way the personality dynamics at the research labs were altered once Vagelos was gone and there was no one left with the scientific, institutional, and historical authority to overrule Dr. Edward M.

Scolnick, the brilliant and overbearing head of research. "You have a man in charge of research who is very smart. He's throwing out ideas. People would jump [to pursue his ideas]. Instead of ideas coming from somebody down below, the ideas came from on high."

Whatever the cause, the result was that "you had to account for all your time. You had to spend more time screening, you had to be working on drugs," Elliston says. "For some of the individual scientists, the loss of independent research took away some of their individuality. That's a little bit disheartening."

By most accounts, Merck scientists got some of their academic independence back after a few years. In part, that was because molecular screening became more efficient. Using robotics, one senior scientist could run a project with a group of technicians, freeing up other scientists for their own work. In addition, Dr. Scolnick had been constantly at odds with his Number Two, Roger Perlmutter, so probably things just relaxed all around after Dr. Perlmutter went to Amgen in January 2001.

Today, the research milieu is somewhere between the glory days and the tight days—freer than at other drug makers, but less freewheeling and more bureaucratic than at most biotechs. "Research is big enough that they can let someone work on something for a couple of years before they decide it's a dead end," Dr. Douglas says. If a project does seem to be a dead end, "your support will be cut off faster than the [National Institutes of Health] would cut it off. But if you have a good idea, you can gain resources to go after it much more quickly."

Like university researchers, too, Merck researchers schmooze at obscure scientific meetings. This is more significant than it might seem, because these sessions are where cutting-edge ideas are picked up. "Other companies won't let people go. That's why [Merck] can attract people, giving them the scientific freedom, the fact that they're allowed to go to meetings and talk to scientists," says Judy Hedstrom, a former consultant with McKinsey & Company and now the senior vice president of corporate development at Alteon Inc., a biotech in Ramsey, New Jersey, that focuses on cardiovascular disease, aging, and diabetes. "They're masterful at going to scientific meetings, seeing a poster of a new idea, chatting up the guy, then taking it home and turning it into something," she adds. The only catch, according to Al Alberts, is that "the travel budget was always tight." Sometimes he'd ask marketing for extra funding.

Merck's blockbuster arthritis drug Vioxx, in fact, got its start at a lecture, according to a story in the *Asian Wall Street Journal* in January 2001. At a medical conference in Montreal in 1992, Peppi Prasit, then a medicinal chemist at Merck, noticed a display from a Japanese company about a painkiller that supposedly didn't upset the stomach but that, unfortunately, wasn't chemically appropriate for people. Prasit knew that Merck was looking for a painkiller without stomach problems. So he went back to his lab and started to concoct it.

Dr. Scolnick's retirement at the end of 2002 probably won't alter Merck's basic approach to research, but it will mean a significant change in leadership style. His successor and former deputy, Peter Kim, is considered more easygoing and is expected to allow the staff more independence. Some observers think Kim may even be able to attract smart young scientists who didn't want to work for the intimidating Dr. Scolnick. In terms of pure science, Kim has a solid reputation as a biologist and a big interest in cutting-edge genomics— where the whole industry is headed anyway. He had already been playing an increasing role in the research operations, including recruiting top scientists in diabetes and neurology. One extra twist is that Dr. Scolnick is back at the lab bench, doing research on mental illness. Will be be providing helpful guidance to Kim? back-seat driving?. Or will he really stick to his test tubes?

One of the most famous and least understood aspects of Merck's R&D culture is its teams. Under Vagelos, research was organized into project teams, centered on a particular product and led by a "champion." Since even a company as big as Merck can't pursue every interesting molecule its scientists discover, Vagelos says he tried to make sure the teams' agendas were realistic. "I encouraged them to focus on smaller numbers of projects. To have enough critical mass [of people] to have it done in shorter than a lifetime," he says. But the teams purposely did not get their own budgets. The champion had to persuade other specialists—chemists, biologists, and marketers—to contribute from their own resources.

Over time, the teams expanded to as many as 50 people, with members from basic and clinical research, toxicology, marketing, regulatory affairs, and quality standards and maybe some lawyers. The entire team for one major drug, according to a midlevel manager who worked on it for several years in the late 1990s to early 2000, would have four-hour meetings at least every month (with some people joining in by videoconference) and then break into smaller groups for "lots" more meetings, to discuss everything from the newest clinical studies, to the FDA, to the competition. There were also all-day get-togethers a couple of times a year. It was a heavy schedule of meetings, but "that was what was fun about working in our industry. It's all teamwork," the manager says.

When Gilmartin took over, he added a superstructure of what are called worldwide business strategy teams, consisting of people from the manufacturing, marketing, regulatory, and research sides, possibly joined by others from finance and PR. The teams—which can range in size from eight to a dozen members—are organized by class of drug, or by product if it's a major one like Vioxx. A core group, at least, meets once a month. Except for manufacturing, the members are all staffers working on the particular product or class. (Manufacturing is treated differently because there's too much shifting of which products are made at which plants to have any consistent representation.)

The idea is for the group members to work with each other from the very earliest research in order to devise a long-range strategy and coordinate all the aspects of development. "What Gilmartin tried to do, with a certain amount of success, was to break down the divisional silos. It got the teams talking together," says Simon Benito, the former international and vaccines manager. When should a manufacturing plant be geared up to move from the pilot stage to full production? Did anyone check how the chickenpox vaccine interacts with the 19 other toddler inoculations? "That's the kind of thing that a researcher may forget," Gordon Douglas explains. "You need the interaction with marketing. [Marketing people are always asking], 'What's the ideal label I want my drug to have? What studies do I need to do [to get that label]?' They're thinking about that three or four years before it gets to the market."

Within the teams, that theory seems to be succeeding. "In the very beginning, organizations were reluctant to share information across lines. There was some apprehension," one midlevel operational manager admits. Eventually, that manager adds, the skeptics realized that the teams "made their job easier. They had information when they needed it." The Vioxx team's ultra-efficient coordination cut that product's launch time by five or six weeks, according to the *Asian Wall Street Journal* article. And the midlevel manager says it was helpful to have a team that could do strategic marketing analysis.

But it doesn't take a Harvard MBA to know that trying to coodinate so many players from such different cultures could make even a professional juggler panic. There can be turf wars, culture clashes, and new layers of bureaucracy. Especially, the idea of letting marketing in on the research process, though a growing trend industrywide since Vagelos's day, raises a lot of hackles. Consumer groups fear that researchers will be pressured to tilt their findings in order to justify the widest possible uses on the label. The industry has always pointed to its wall between marketing and research as proof of its ethics; now, this wall seemed to be breached.

Dr. Douglas, who left Merck in 1999 but still keeps in contact with people there, points to one potential turf problem: Middle managers—say, a marketing head for a particular country or a plant manager—might be on the team, "but if the boss wasn't in on it and they come up with a strategy he didn't buy into, it wouldn't happen." "You need a champion," agrees Benito—and under the Vagelos system, he says, good ideas could more easily get one.

Other insiders complain that the teams are more talk (and talk and talk and talk) than action. From what Al Alberts hears, the big problem is bureaucracy—which has grown throughout the industry in any case since the 1990s. In the old days, if a scientist had a new idea, "it would have been a couple of people, you'd argue your case," Alberts says. But now the scientist has to wait for the strategy team's monthly meeting and prepare a formal presentation. "If the genesis is in a committee, a project will tend to get squashed," Benito worries.

The advantage of bureaucracy, though, is that any project gets a thorough review. One reason Merck hasn't had products killed by the FDA is probably that it kills them early itself.

A company has two basic choices if Phase I or II results are questionable: It can push ahead anyway, hoping that it might be able to fix the problem or that further tests will show that the worrisome results were only minor side effects. Alternatively, it can dump the project. That second approach "is one that I think Merck pioneered: Study a lot of patients early, this is where you'll find a problem. Spend most of your money in Phase II, broadly screen—and periodically kill your early calls," says Hedstrom, the former McKinsey consultant. As part of that approach, she adds, Merck includes more people in Phase II trials than most other companies do. Merck might not give up on a project completely, if there seems to be some promise, but it will go back a step and drastically redesign the drug or the trial, Alberts says.

Merck's quick trigger finger could mean losing out on a promising drug that might have been salvaged. On the other hand, it builds a no-recall reputation and gives investors like Edward Pittman, the giant New Jersey public pension fund's pharmaceutical analyst, more faith in what does emerge. "It's very rare for them to have a Phase III project that's unsuccessful. They seem to be very careful about what's required before they advance into later stages of development," he says. "I have greater confidence that something in their Phase II is going to make it."

All this effort—the salaries over 12 or 15 years, the clinical trials, the lab equipment, the overhead, the cell cultures and test tubes and other supplies—costs money. The big mystery is how much.

More than $800 million per drug, counting the cost of failures as well as successes, asserted at least two reports done in 2001 by consultants with industry connections—and happily touted by the drug makers.

Ridiculous, consumer groups retorted, citing a study by The Global Alliance for TB Drug Development that claims it takes just $76 million to $115 million to develop a drug for tuberculosis.

"You are not ever to know" the true cost, says Uwe Reinhardt, an economics professor at Princeton who specializes in health care.

A report by Joseph A. DiMasi, director of economic analysis at Tufts University's Center for the Study of Drug Development—the one most often cited—came up with an average cost of $802 million, which was more than double the $231 million price tag in Tufts' previous study, back in 1987 (after adjusting for inflation). This time around, DiMasi analyzed 68 drugs chosen at random from a data base that Tufts has been maintaining since 1972 and that DiMasi says contains roughly 90 percent of the drugs that get into development. Then he asked the companies that made those drugs how much they spent per year to develop the products.

Critics hit on several points. Only $403 million of the $802 million is attributed to what drug companies actually pay out in cold cash; the rest consists of what's called opportunity cost, or what the money could have earned in the stock market had it not been spent on research. Another complaint is that Tufts' calculation doesn't subtract the billions of dollars of taxpayer-subsidized basic research undertaken by government scientists at the National Institutes of Health, research the companies would otherwise have to do themselves before they even had a disease target to test against. Most controversial are the Tuft Center's ties to Big Pharma, which, to skeptics, color its conclusions. Not only does DiMasi's information on expenditures come from the industry, but so does 65 percent of the center's funding. Ray

Gilmartin even spoke at the press briefing when the report was officially released.

DiMasi—tall, soft-voiced, and bespectacled, with thinning gray hair—seems almost too passive to be the center of such controversy. Until he gets into the topic. Then his face grows stern, and hints of annoyance fleck his Boston accent.

"If [the critics] knew how hard it was to get this information out of the companies, they'd get the sense that [the companies] were being honest," he says. "The companies know what they're spending [per drug] now in a couple of [late-stage] therapeutic areas, but a lot of early-stage research isn't on particular compounds, so early data has to be aggregated." In other words, the individualized data he's asking for are so hard to come up with that the industry doesn't even have the time to manipulate the numbers. Besides, DiMasi adds, to some degree he can double-check the manufacturers' honesty. "If you do a very, very careful analysis of PhRMA's [the industry trade group] annual survey of member firms, what drugs get approval, you can get a range of what you expect the outcomes to be in." He also insists that he isn't beholden to the drug makers, despite the funding they give to Tufts. "They don't get to review the projects or tell us what to do." As for including opportunity costs, he points out that that's standard economic practice; the pharmaceutical industry's are so high, he says, because the period of lost opportunity is so long.

Using a different method but raw data also supplied by the industry, The Boston Consulting Group calculated a cost extraordinarily close to DiMasi's: $880 million. As Peter Tollman, vice president of the firm's biopharmaceutical

R&D business, explains, the information comes from interviews with 40 to 50 pharmaceutical companies, biotechs, and academic institutions, including Pharmacia Corporation; Roche; Bristol-Myers Squibb Company; Aventis; Biogen, Inc.; Harvard, and the Massachusetts Institute of Technology. All have a relationship of some sort with Boston Consulting—they might be clients or the alma maters of Boston consultants, or they might have provided advice to Boston at one time.

In its interviews, the firm asked each company or college to go through the process of drug development step by step. "We looked at all the activity it takes: How long does each activity take? How much does it cost? What is the failure rate? What does it take to identify a target? To validate a target?" From that, Tollman says, Boston Consulting put together "a model of what it takes to discover a drug."

James Love, director of the Ralph Nader–founded Consumer Project on Technology in Washington, D.C., is one of the angriest of the consumer advocates. To tear apart the high cost estimates, he focuses on human clinical trials, by far the most expensive part of the R&D process.

DiMasi had come up with a price tag for human trials of $282 million per drug (out of the $403 million in actual research costs), by using a generous definition of trial-related expenses—"everything that the firm spends after initial human testing begins." Thus, in addition to the direct trial costs, he also included things like additional research on dosages and "overhead related to not only the specific drug but also to the infrastructure that is in place for an ongoing concern."

Love, meanwhile, interviewed the outside institutes that are sometimes hired to conduct trials. He also looked at what companies claim as expenses on their taxes when they take an R&D credit for so-called orphan drugs (the drugs for serious conditions that affect only a small number of people). His conclusion: A typical trial costs $2,000 to $7,000 per patient. If a series of Phase I, II, and III trials involves maybe 3,300 patients, that would bring the cost of clinical trials to between $6.6 million and $22.1 million—way below DiMasi's figures.

However, while $6.6 million or $22.1 million may get a drug to market—which is as far as DiMasi went—it may not actually encompass enough trial costs. That's because of the follow-up studies that companies conduct, even after the FDA has given their drugs the go-ahead, which can involve hundreds or thousands more people and cost tens of millions of dollars. For instance, years after Zocor came on the market, Merck ran a five-year test on 20,000 people to study the drug's potential benefit for various groups of high-risk patients not included in the existing labeling. Richard Stover, the Arnhold and Bleichroeder analyst, says that these sorts of studies can actually be more valuable than the drugs themselves because of the wide-ranging knowledge about conditions and symptoms that's gained. The studies can also reveal unsuspected side effects.

For its part, the TB Alliance interviewed outside research organizations that Big Pharma might hire to conduct the early-stage animal trials. Its data on human trials came partly from the experience of staffers who used to work in the industry and partly from government institutions that run trials in the developing world. But the group's $76 million-to-$115 million estimates cover only the cost of development and trials, not the research that leads to a promising molecule to begin with—all those thousands and thousands of screenings. Nor does it take into account the opportunity costs. Also, warns Joelle Tanguy, the alliance's director of advocacy, the numbers are specific for TB research, which could be different than for other diseases.

Gordon Douglas claims he doesn't know how much it cost to finally develop the chickenpox vaccine, or any other vaccine he worked on at Merck, because he never totaled them up by product. "You pay for the marketing, research, administrations, and all other costs as the costs are incurred, and therefore they are expensed against current sales," he says.

To determine their annual budget, managers from Merck Research Laboratories, the company's giant R&D arm, meet once a year in a weeklong retreat. As Dr. Douglas describes it, someone from each grouping—they're organized by drug or by a broader franchise area such as hypertension—explains the studies his or her particular group wants to do and how much money it would like. The others challenge the speaker: Why do you need to do this study? How many subjects do you need? "You fight for resources. It's a zero-based budgeting process," Dr. Douglas says. At the end, the research chief totals up the requests, announces how much money is actually available, "and then you start cutting, a little bit out of here, out of there."

The industry has been notoriously unwilling to open its books to outside inspection. However, when drug companies want to emphasize how much effort they put into research, they will conveniently manage to calculate a dollar figure.

News stories have reported that Merck spent over $1 billion to develop Crixivan, one of the protease inhibitors that revolutionized the treatment of AIDS. According to a *Wall Street Journal* article in May 2002, Pfizer plowed $71 million into a "youth drug" before abandoning it after more than a decade of research and testing. Moreover, each company's overall R&D expenditure is listed in its annual report, and the industry is happy to brag about how much all of them devote to research in total—more than $30 billion in 2001, PhRMA, the trade organization, claims, some five times as much as the average U.S. industry.

Richard Evans, the Sanford Bernstein analyst, argues that that's still not enough. He says the drug makers are putting an average of just 12.9 percent of sales into R&D when they should be doing 17 percent—and Merck, at around 11 or 12 percent, is even below average. Not much of a crown for the king of research. (Arguably, by cutting off projects early, Merck could be using its resources more efficiently than others. Maybe.)

To put those numbers into even sharper perspective, the biggest companies spend two to three times as much on marketing and administration as they do on research, according to the consumer group Families USA, which analyzed data from annual reports for 2000. Alan Sager, a professor at Boston University's School of Public Health, has done research showing that the number of staffers employed in Big Pharma R&D dropped slightly from 1996 to 2000 while the number in marketing jumped 59 percent, according to an article in the October 2002 issue of *The New Republic*.[1] Merck boosted its marketing and administration outlays in 2000 by 19 percent, to $6.2 billion, while increasing R&D by just 13 percent, to $2.3 billion. The ratio improved, but not the percentages, for 2001 (up 1 and 5 percent, respectively). For 2002, the company expected to buoy R&D by $240 million to $340 million, or around 12 percent.

While spending gobs of money does not, of course, guarantee gobs of terrific new drugs, skimping on R&D outlays probably does guarantee a skimpy pipeline.

Merck and the others would undoubtedly need to spend more. Because finding new breakthrough drugs—as opposed to simply "improving" drugs already on the market—was getting harder and costlier all the time.

Partly, it was that the diseases being pursued were less well understood and more complex than in the past, which meant they'd need a lot of research. In the early 1990s, according to a January 2001 study by Lehman Brothers and McKinsey, researchers could find 100 references in the scientific literature for the average drug target. When Merck came out with its cholesterol blockbuster Mevacor, basic information about the enzyme it targeted had already been known for almost 30 years. But by the time of the Lehman-McKinsey report, with researchers still unraveling mysterious conditions like Alzheimer's, the average target had just eight scientific references.

Adding to the cost and effort, the new targets required longer, more expensive clinical trials. An antibiotic, like Merck's earliest discoveries, works quickly (or else it doesn't work at all). But the areas that were now dominating R&D—cardiovascular disease, Alzheimer's, cancer, Parkinson's, AIDS, anxiety, and depression—are slow, degenerative ailments. Not surprisingly, DiMasi found that the number of procedures involved in clinical trials rose 27 percent from 1990 to 1997 for Phase III, 90 percent for Phase II, and 120 percent for Phase I. Other experts have estimated that the number of people enrolled in research studies tripled, to 20 million, from 1991 to 2001. Finding so many people was hard, too.

In addition, the FDA was getting tougher. It has always been the ball in a game of ping pong, with the industry and some patient advocates urging it to push drug approvals out faster, and other patient advocates and medical experts saying it's not taking enough time to make sure the drugs are safe. From 1993 to 1998, the agency cut in half the median review time for what's known as a standard drug—that is, one that isn't a breakthrough and doesn't get high-priority consideration. Coincidentally or not, a high-profile series of drugs were then withdrawn from the market in the late 1990s and early 2000s. (None of them were Merck's of course; they included Bayer's cholesterol drug Baycol, Pfizer's diabetes drug Rezulin, and Janssen Pharmaceutica's heartburn drug Propulsid.) So by the early 2000s, burned by the bad press, the FDA was taking more time and demanding more backup in order to approve new-drug applications. For cancer drugs, the agency now was more likely to want proof that a new product actually extended life, not just that it shrank tumors—data that would take a lot longer to accumulate. The biggest shock to the pharmaceutical world came in December 2001, when the regulators turned down a colorectal cancer drug, Erbitux, from ImClone Systems that its celebrity-partying CEO Samuel Waksal had been touting as a sure bet. (Waksal later pleaded guilty to several charges related to insider trading.)

Most important of all, science itself was changing the way drugs are discovered, screened, and put into the body.

In its most elemental definition, a disease occurs when something in the body malfunctions. Heart attack: The walls of a coronary artery become too clogged with fatty deposits, blocking the flow of blood to the heart. Cancer: A mutated cell replicates out of control. Infection: A virus overcomes the body's immune system. To get the body back to normal, scientists try to find a molecule that will intercept the malfunction. If the disease is caused by the behavior of an enzyme, the molecule could block the enzyme, modify its behavior, or block the receptor it attaches to. In pharmaceutical talk, that magic molecule has been known as a compound. To the public, it's a drug.

Traditionally, scientists found molecules in the microorganisms that live in soil, sludge, ground-up plants, and the like. Penicillin, famously, derives from mold; Merck's big anticholesterol statins are fungus-based. In the lab equivalent of an assembly line, researchers screened hundreds of thousands of molecules against the disease target—say, a cholesterol receptor. (This was the screening that Merck scientists had to do before they could go off on their independent research.) Companies kept libraries of these compounds for possible use against future targets. When they found one that seemed to block the target or the process,

they chemically synthesized it. Things speeded up a bit starting in the early 1990s, with the advent of robotics for faster,
or high-throughput, screening—the industrialization that
allowed Merck's scientists to do independent research again.
By then, too, compounds were increasingly being made chemically rather than derived from natural products.

The growing understanding of genomics and proteomics,
topped by the decoding of the human genome in 2000,
promised to bring the most dramatic change to the drug
R&D process. Now scientists could hope to pinpoint the disease target more exactly by comparing genetic sequences in
patients with and without certain diseases until they found
mutations common only to those with the disease. At least in
theory, a company could then synthesize a molecule specific
to that target, which would mean fewer side effects.

Various forms of chips—gene, protein, and chemical—
were expected to speed up the screening even faster in what
was called ultrahigh throughput. The gene chip was the first
to hit the labs: A glass wafer, as tiny as a thumbnail, and
embedded with thousands of genes, it could compare the
patterns of thousands of other genes in just days, or hundreds of thousands in a few weeks. A computer-aided technology known as in silico testing let researchers match
different molecules against diseases to see where the molecule might attach to block the disease process. Some drug
companies were even substituting computer modeling for a
few clinical trials on live animals.

Eventually, this should make producing a new drug a lot
faster and more efficient. All told, The Boston Consulting
Group estimated that the new technology's greater produc-

tivity could lop $300 million and two years off the cost and time of discovering a drug.

That, however, was in the future. For the short run, the new science actually had the potential to make drug discovery harder. The Lehman-McKinsey report predicted that "genomics threatens to increase not only the overall associated R&D costs but also the average cost per new chemical entity," or drug.

The biggest problem was the explosion of data. Before the genome was mapped, the industry had identified only about 500 disease targets in the body. Thanks to genomics, researchers now estimated they would find 5,000 to 10,000. Yet discovering the right molecule to match against a target, whether there were 500 or 5,000 targets, was still what it had been in the days of fungus and mold—"a crapshoot," as Al Alberts puts it. Slow, tedious trial and error. "One thing the industry has learned is that drug development is like looking for a needle in a haystack. If you make the haystack"—that is, the number of targets—"bigger, the needle is harder to find," says Elliston, the former cofounder of Merck's gene indexing project, who later went on to launch a biotechnology company in Maryland called Viaken Systems, Inc. that specializes in information technology.

Nor did the problems stop once a molecule was identified. By some estimates, eventually 30 percent of all drugs would be so-called biologicals, or large-molecule drugs, rather than the traditional small-molecule, or chemical, kind. It's a lot more complex and time-consuming to make something biological than chemical. The would-be drugs have to go through a multistep process of growth, culturing, and purifying, rather than a much neater chemical reaction. These kinds of drugs, moreover, can't simply be swallowed the way traditional pills are, because the stomach acid would destroy them before they reached the bloodstream. Manufacturers have to find ways to inject them.

And even while they were investing in and setting up the infrastructure for this new type of research, companies would have to continue spending on old-style R&D to build up their pipelines in the near term, says Viren Mehta, a managing member at Mehta Partners in Manhattan, a small money management and advisory firm that specializes in pharmaceutical and biotech stocks. That would mean double-spending for the foreseeable future.

Big Pharma faced yet one more technology-related problem: The more precise focus of genomics could allow manufacturers to make drugs tailored to patients with a particular genetic mutation, a process known as pharmacogenetics or pharmacogenomics. Roche and Genentech, Inc., for instance, found that breast cancer patients who shared one certain genetic variation—maybe one-fourth to one-third of all those with breast cancer—responded best to their drug Herceptin. Other companies started looking for genetic ways to determine which cholesterol and asthma drugs might be most effective for which cholesterol and asthma patients. As this detective work is refined, manufacturers might no longer be able to market their one big cholesterol drug to all the 38 million Americans at risk for coronary heart disease, diabetes, and other related ailments.

Instead, target groups of maybe a few million patients each would be able to choose a particular drug, personalized for their genetic form of the disease. The trouble is that those markets are simply too tiny for big companies to bother with. A $48 billion company like Merck needs blockbusters that sell $500 million or $1 billion a year.

Just as all this was happening in the labs, small biotech companies like Elliston's Viaken Systems and Don Drakeman's Medarex were bursting onto the scene. Because the two trends emerged more or less concurrently, it was easy to get caught up in the assumption that they went together, and therefore, biotechs would take over the world from Big Pharma. Certainly, the biotechs have the standard advantages of the upstarts in an industry where technology is changing dramatically: flexibility, lack of bureaucracy, an entrepreneurial spirit, less pressure from investors, and stock options to offer to promising scientists. A $300 million, targeted genomics drug isn't too small for them. Moreover, some of them have a solid base of knowledge, having worked in the genetics area as far back as the 1970s and 1980s. As the big companies' pipelines of new drugs petered out, the biotechs seemed to be bursting with potential products. Ernst & Young's biotechnology index shows how the little guys have grown: In 1993, the biotech industry had total sales of $5.9 billion and 79,000 employees. By 2000, those numbers had jumped to $25 billion and 174,000.

"Genomics is going to be the death of blockbusters. We're going to end up with more products, and each is going to be more effective," brags Don Drakeman. (Founded in 1987, and with a $1.3 billion market capitalization, his monoclonal-antibody company, Medarex, is one of the veterans of the biotech field.) "For us, a product that could sell $300 million a year, that would be a wonderful thing to have. I think they're [Big Pharma] going to have to change their thinking."

Slow down, Don. Biotechs like Medarex can't match the big guys' marketing muscle, their skill at getting through the regulatory hoops, their experience conducting clinical trials, their manufacturing facilities, and the resources they could pour into R&D if they wanted. Nor, as the rejection of ImClone's cancer drug shows, do biotechs necessarily have the magic touch when it comes to drug development itself. "Small biotechs do not have the critical mass to develop. The sheer quality of people big companies attract is still larger than biotechs can attract. Good scientists want an environment where they can prosper—resources, camaraderie," says Vijay B. Samant, who was chief operating officer of Merck's vaccine business until 2000 and now runs a gene therapy company in San Diego, California. Besides which, as the stock market has proved, start-up companies with lots of brains and no track record or profits have a sad tendency to collapse.

So if neither side could beat each other, then they would join, forming alliances in which they shared the costs and profits of developing new drugs. The opener, by most accounts, came in 1993, when SmithKline Beecham plc paid $125 million for access to the human gene sequence data and technology of Human Genome Sciences, Inc. The fees paid to the biotechs rose higher, and the profit-sharing became less lopsided, as the years went by. Millennium Pharmaceuticals signed deals with Monsanto, Bayer, Aventis, and Abbott Laboratories between 1997 and 2001 for, among other things, drugs that target inflammation, obesity, and diabetes. Vertex Pharmaceuticals Incorporated (formed by a group of ex-Merckers) and Novartis AG agreed in 2000 to an $815 million hookup in which Vertex would essentially discover and do early tests on drug candidates, Novartis would be responsible for development and manufacturing, and the two would comarket some of the offshoots. Bayer and CuraGen Corporation topped the billion dollar mark in 2001 with an agreement to jointly discover, develop, and promote molecules for treating obesity and diabetes. Even in straight licensing deals, the terms were getting more generous. Where a biotech might have been happy with an 8 percent or 9 percent share of the profit in the early years, by 2002 it was getting 15 percent to 16 percent, said Rahul R. Jasuja, a researcher at Techvest, LLC, a small brokerage in Manhattan.

Merck didn't ignore the outside world. For all its talk about doing its own research, it had licensed plenty of drugs from other discoverers in prior years, including the heartburn megadrug Pepcid, the big hypertension sellers Cozaar and Hyzaar, and the osteoporosis blockbuster Fosamax. Under Gilmartin, it dropped out of joint ventures with E. I. du Pont de Nemours and Company and AstraZeneca Group but set up a partnership with Schering-Plough Corporation that developed a key cholesterol drug, Zetia. As genomics and biotechs entered the picture, it took every opportunity to brag about its acquisition in 2001 of Rosetta Inpharmatics, a company based near Seattle that develops tools and software for analyzing gene functions—which really was a coup, because it was expected to help Merck identify drug targets more quickly. Merck also bought SIBIA Neurosciences, a San Diego, California, biotech specializing in neurological research, in 1999. Among other deals, just in 2001 and 2002, Merck gained access to a genetic database from Deltagen, Inc. in Redwood City, California, and signed a deal for Artemis Pharmaceuticals of Germany to create customized, genetically engineered mice. Gilmartin told analysts, at the company's annual get-together in December 2001, that he was looking for licensing deals with "labs or small companies in the field we have chosen to be in," mainly genomics. Senior scientists were told to look out for potential deals.

But relying too much on outsiders goes against Merck's corporate culture. Why should the king of research need any help from princelings?

Well, it didn't. "Merck has far less than anyone else" in terms of collaborations of any sort, says Roger Longman, a managing partner at Connecticut-based medical-business publisher Windhover Information Inc. According to the company's Strategic Transactions Database, Merck arranged just 62 in-licensing deals, in which it gained access to other companies' technology, from 1991 through May 31, 2002. By contrast, Pfizer, GlaxoSmithKline, and Novartis—which rank first, second, and fourth among the pharmaceuticals to Merck's third in the *Financial Times* Global 500—had 135, 186, and 105 deals, respectively. (In fairness, those three companies' totals include deals done by rivals they subsequently acquired. But then again, it's hard to find a drug maker that hasn't merged, and in Pfizer's case, the numbers don't include any from Pharmacia, which it announced that it was buying after May 31.) Anyway, biotech executives like Drakeman and Kenneth I. Moch, the CEO and president of Alteon, also say they don't see Merck doing as many joint arrangements as other pharmaceutical giants. ("That's okay," shrugs Moch, whose firm focuses on compounds for cardiovascular treatment, aging, and diabetes. "I don't live or die on one company.") "We're very rigorous" in seeking alliance partners, Gilmartin advised the analysts. "We have tough standards, especially on the safety side."

When Merck does reach out, its licenses tend to be for early-stage technology, not late-stage drugs. Many times, these are technologies that rival Big Pharmas are also licensing, which means Merck doesn't gain any unique advantages. At one meeting in 2001, Longman remembers, Ed Scolnick declared that Merck would not want to rely on outsiders for essential capabilities and therefore, even if it signed biotech deals, it would duplicate any processes in-house.

It's Merck in a nutshell, the nexus where confidence bleeds into arrogance.

By trying to go it largely alone, Merck could miss the chance to pick up important, cutting-edge discoveries made by other companies. But the only way to keep its own research muscle in shape is to exercise it.

Can Merck do it all? "Merck's science has not been fundamentally passed by the biotechs. I think Merck does some of the best science in the industry, basic and clinical," says

Boyd Clarke, who's seen both sides, as a Merck executive for 18 years until 1996 and as the chief of a string of biotechs since then.

Retorts Longman: "If you think that only your own research is worth supporting, then you are probably fooling yourself."

Whoever is doing the research, the real issue is: What's the research for? Just what sorts of drugs are all that money and brainpower going to come up with, anyway?

The Drugs of Tomorrow

Mevacor, which Merck brought out in 1987, was as close as a pharmaceutical company could get to the perfect product. It targeted a serious and widespread problem—high cholesterol, which can lead to strokes and coronary heart disease—so it was a great service to humanity. There was no other prescription treatment, so it had a huge market to itself. The condition was chronic, so people would need to keep buying the pill for years. And it was a malady that affected middle-class Americans, so they could afford an expensive drug.

For a while, from the spring of 1999 until the summer of 2001, Merck's Vioxx looked like another perfect drug. A chronic and widespread condition (osteoarthritis). A condition that tends to worsen with age (think of all those Baby Boomers hitting their fifties). A condition suffered by middle-class Americans with health insurance. A condition without any other prescription treatment (there were plenty of inexpensive nonprescription pain relievers, but they all had a tendency to lead to ulcers and gastric bleeding). To Merck's strong annoyance, Monsanto actually beat it to market by less than five months with a similar antiarthritis prescription pain reliever, Celebrex. But Vioxx's launch, in the spring of 1999, was roundly hailed as a masterpiece of catch-up.

Unfortunately for Merck, however, when researchers re-analyzed existing data, they found that Vioxx and Celebrex (known as COX-2 inhibitors because they block production of an enzyme called COX 2) seemed to increase the risk of heart attacks. Later came reports linking Vioxx to a few cases of meningitis and raising questions about whether Vioxx and Celebrex slowed the healing of bone fractures. Finally, in the spring of 2002, the FDA approved new labels that allowed Vioxx to claim it was safer on the stomach but warned of higher cardiovascular risk (and essentially the opposite indications for Celebrex). All that, for a couple of drugs that were no better at easing pain than the cheaper nonprescription alternatives, like aspirin or Motrin, that had long been for sale in any drugstore.

If the obvious reason for a drug company's existence is to produce new drugs, it's less obvious just which drugs or diseases to focus on. Ray Gilmartin didn't just tell Merck's annual meeting in 2002 that "we develop medicines that offer novel approaches to disease treatments." In the rest of the sentence, he also noted that the company aims to "help large patient populations." What Merck and the other Big Pharmas really want are drugs that offer novel approaches while bringing in sales of $500 million to $1 billion annually, year after year after year for 20 years, or until their patents expire. In other words, choosing diseases to target is not just a matter of helping suffering humankind, but also a business decision.

For starters, the drugs should treat conditions that are chronic and serious—chronic enough that people will need to keep taking the medication indefinitely, and serious enough that they won't dare stop. "One of the old saws of the pharmaceutical business," points out Don Drakeman of Medarex, the New Jersey biotech specializing in monoclonal antibodies, "is that, while it's good to have a pill that cures the disease, it's better to have a pill you have to take every day."

These should also be conditions suffered by a significant number of people who can afford to pay for coverage, to wit, middle-class Americans with health insurance. Companies "are willing to put dollars where most people are affected," says Debbie Hart, executive director of the Biotechnology Council of New Jersey, Inc. (which, despite its name, actually counts plenty of Big Pharmas among its 130 members). Does that mean diseases that strike the well-off? "That's the natural inclination."

There are other considerations. Of course, the disease targets have to be scientifically feasible. Merck has traditionally said it wants drugs that can be taken orally, just once a day—that is, convenient drugs. And never underestimate the indirect influence of celebrity endorsements. When actor Michael J. Fox talks about how he copes with Parkinson's disease, or *Today* show cohost Katie Couric discusses her colonoscopy, it prompts a flurry of public discussion, a rush to the doctor's office for tests, and political pressure on Congress and the National Institutes of Health (NIH) to put more money into researching those conditions. The drug companies aren't immediately affected, since they don't rely on direct federal funding. But they can sense the potential market, and they will pick up research leads from the NIH.

All these criteria, at least for the foreseeable future, are most likely to come together in two types of drugs: those that target the lifestyle of the middle class, and those that target the aging (and vanity) of the Boomer generation. That means drugs for conditions like high cholesterol, osteoporosis (a severe loss of bone mass), Alzheimer's, asthma, high blood pressure, depression, anxiety, allergies, arthritis, obesity, baldness, and erectile dysfunction (a.k.a. impotence), plus the Holy Grail of medical research, cancer.

Alternatively, if the research isn't going well or the FDA approval process seems too onerous, companies can forget about novel approaches altogether. They can just fiddle with what's already on the market, maybe churning out a marginal improvement to a hot blockbuster.

Where were Merck's mighty research labs in this picture? As of the early 2000s, Merck had strong products on the market already for some of the most important ailments, including osteoporosis, cholesterol, high blood pressure, and arthritis, and was known to be working in key areas like depression, AIDS, diabetes, and obesity. True to its claim to do breakthrough science, the research was mostly on new approaches (in the case of cholesterol, obesity, and depression) or entirely new markets where there were no existing products (vaccines for AIDS and for human papillomavirus, or HPV, a sexually transitted disease that can lead to cervical cancer). Merck reportedly had patented more new compounds than any other pharmaceutical company between 1996 and 2002. There were not a lot of me-too drugs in the pipeline. All that is just the way the king of research should be.

But most of the innovative work was still in the early stages, years away from the pharmacists' shelves, which meant it could fall through. Others were nice enough products, but hardly blockbuster potential. In one of the jazziest areas of drug research—cancer—Merck's name hardly cropped up at all outside of the HPV vaccine.

Of course, no company can hit every hot market. "One, two, three [big drugs] will be plenty," says Viren Mehta, the money manager who specializes in the drug sector. And every pharmaceutical maker likes to keep plenty of secrets in its labs until it has to file with the FDA, so Merck might have some golden prospects hidden in Rahway. (The industry is so super-secretive, in fact, that at the PhRMA annual meeting— the kind of shindig that in most businesses is considered an occasion for mass journalist-source schmoozing—only five reporters are allowed.) Still, on top of the disappointing news on Vioxx, Wall Street worried that Merck didn't have enough power in its pipeline, especially for the near term.

What's also pushing the search for new drugs, beyond any desire to help humanity, even beyond the marketing considerations, is a ticking clock called patents and a hungry generic-drug industry.

As with other intellectual discoveries, those who develop original drugs get a monopoly for a limited amount of time, during which no one else can copy the product. After that period of patent protection is over, any company can, in theory, make a generic version of the same drug. Since they didn't have to invest the $200 million or $800 million or whatever it costs to research a new compound from scratch, these generic-drug companies should be able to sell their versions for a lot less than the brand-name originals. However, through the early 1980s this rarely happened, because the generic-drug companies by law had to repeat virtually all the clinical tests that the original drug had gone through, in order to prove safety and efficacy—a task that just didn't make it worthwhile. Brand-name drug makers were no happier with the patent situation back then. The patent clock started running before they'd finished developing the drug, yet development was taking longer and longer. The actual time they had to enjoy their market monopoly slipped from nearly 12½ years in the 1970s, to barely 8 in the 1980s.

Thus, in 1984, Congress concocted what was supposed to be a grand compromise, the Drug Price Competition and Patent Term Restoration Act, more commonly known as the Hatch-Waxman Act, after its main Senate and House sponsors (Senator Orrin Hatch, a conservative Republican from Utah, and Congressman Henry Waxman, a liberal Democrat from California). Generic makers would no longer have to repeat all the tests, as long as they could prove that the active ingredient in a particular product was released and absorbed at roughly the same rate as the active ingredient in the original, a standard known as "bioequivalency." Further speeding things up, they could file all their applications and gain approval in advance, so that the day the patent expired, their drugs could be right on the shelf. Big Pharma, meanwhile, got several opportunities to stretch out the patent life: There was a basic extension of up to 5 years, to a maximum of 14 years, on top of which a company could add 30 more months by challenging a generic maker's application, and 3 years beyond that if it got approval for a new usage to the label (though that last extension is only for the new usage).

That wasn't the end of the patent saga. Over the next decade and a half, Congress continued to fiddle in various ways, most of which ended up handing the big companies more years of market exclusivity. The 1992 Prescription Drug User Fee Act hiked the application fees that the industry pays to the FDA, with the money earmarked for efficiency measures to speed up approval of new drugs, which meant the drugs could be on the market sooner, earning far more than the cost of the higher fees. (That was the main reason FDA approval times had dropped from 1993 to 1998. Although review times started inching back up in 1999, they still didn't reach the original level of two and a half years.) In 1994, to conform to international rules adopted under the General Agreement on Tariffs and Trade and the World Trade Organization, the United States altered the patent term to 20 years from the date of application, rather than 17 years from the date it was granted. Then, in 1997, the Food and Drug Administration Modernization Act granted manufacturers a further six months of so-called pediatric patent exclusivity if they tested the drug on children. And in 1999, the Patent Term Guaranty Authority Act required that companies must be compensated if there were delays of over three years in processing their patents.

In theory, then, Merck and the other drug makers could get at least 23 years to rake in all they can from their blockbusters (minus whatever time they've spent on R&D). But after that, they'd better have a spanking-new drug ready, because the generics would be undercutting those whose patent had expired. And since it famously takes an average of 12 to 15 years to discover, test, and produce a marketable drug, the drug companies need to be working on the next generation of blockbusters almost as soon as they file the patents on the old set. That, claims Roy Vagelos, is what he did for Merck. "At the time I left" in 1994, he says, "there was an adequate pipeline to run the company for five or six years," including Vioxx, Fosamax for osteoporosis, and Crixivan for AIDS.

Merck would need that pipeline. It was approaching the 20-year mark since Vagelos first came to Merck and revamped the research labs. The parade of blockbusters he had launched would soon start marching into their patent walls, one after another. Between 2000 and 2002, patents were due to expire on Vasotec and Prinivil (high blood pressure), Pepcid and Prilosec (heartburn), and Mevacor.

The American lifestyle of the late twentieth and early twenty-first centuries is the best friend the drug makers could have asked for. You could take a roll call of middle-class suffering: allergies, anxiety, asthma, cancer, depression, heartburn, high blood pressure, high cholesterol, sexually transmitted diseases. (After the attacks on the World Trade

Center and the Pentagon, there was also a revival of interest in vaccines against smallpox and antibiotics that could counteract anthrax.) Diabetes and obesity were reaching epidemic proportions; asthma was one of three leading causes behind a surge in prescriptions among juveniles. The number of people taking cholesterol medication was expected to triple. The ailments have a mix of causes, of course, some of them genetic, some unknown. But in part, they are the product of a world with too much pollution and stress, and a way of living with too much rich food, junk food, smoking, drinking, casual sex, and couch-potato TV watching. And whatever the cause, the suffering is serious.

By the first years of the twenty-first century, Merck obviously had its finger at least partly on the pulse of this lifestyle. With asthma drug Singulair already Number One in that market, the company filed an application to expand its use to hay fever. Its Cozaar and Hyzaar combined dominated the world market in high blood pressure medications, although Novartis's Diovan had passed Cozaar in the United States and AstraZeneca had a new competitor drug that the FDA had certified as more effective. Phase II trials of what could be the first vaccine for human papillomavirus showed optimistic results in a test of nearly 2,400 young women in 2000–2002. As glowing front-page news stories trumpeted, none of the women treated with Merck's vaccine developed infections or precancerous tissue, whereas 41 of those who got placebos reported some negative symptoms. Meanwhile, a possible diabetes drug was heading into Phase III. There was also promising progress on a groundbreaking vaccine for AIDS and on a method for quickly screening potential anthrax drugs.

On the cholesterol front, Mevacor lost its patent in late 2001 (and four generics rushed in within two days). Zocor, its successor, was a major hit for Merck—it accounted for something like one-third of the company's drug sales—and new studies indicated that it might help treat multiple sclerosis and prevent and treat heart attacks even among people who didn't have elevated cholesterol levels. But there was no denying the frustration that it was running second to Pfizer's Lipitor, and its U.S. patent would expire in 2006. The big hope was Zetia, the drug developed in partnership with Schering-Plough, that took a different approach than Zocor, Mevacor, and the other so-called anticholesterol statins. Instead of reducing the level of low-density lipo-proteins, or "bad" cholesterol, in the liver, Zetia would keep that cholesterol from being absorbed in the intestine (while not blocking the absorption of vitamins and fats). When taken in combination with a statin, it drastically lowered "bad" cholesterol levels without severe side effects. In October 2000 Zetia was approved in the United States and also in Germany (under its generic name ezetimibe), the first step toward marketing throughout the European Union. Moreover, an all-in-one Zetia-Zocor pill was in chemical trials, with the goal of filing for FDA approval in late 2003. There were just two catches: Until the combination pill was on the market, there was the risk that Zetia could spur demand for Lipitor and other statins as much as for Zocor. And Merck would have to share the profits with Schering-Plough.

Besides cholesterol, the other area with big earnings potential for Merck was mental health. While Merck was a laggard in the field, it could expect a warm welcome if it could produce a solid new drug for depression or anxiety, because the old faithfuls like Prozac and Valium have serious side effects: Depending on the drug, they can cause dry mouth and drowsiness, diminish sexual activity, become addictive, and take weeks to kick in.

Merck, not surprisingly, announced that the central nervous system—not just mental health, but also memory, Alzheimer's disease, even appetitite—was going to be a prime focus for its labs. To upgrade its brain-related brainpower, there was the acquisition of SIBIA Neurosciences, the San Diego biotech, and Merck also poured money into its neuroscience lab outside London. According to published reports, between 1996 and 2002 it quadrupled the number of researchers working on the brain, to 800, and boosted spending 10-fold in five years. In late 2001 it created a new position, executive vice president for neurosciences, bringing in one of the stars of academia, Dr. Dennis W. Choi, the head of neurology at Washington University School of Medicine in St. Louis—proof, apparently, that Merck's research reputation still had drawing power

For the mental health area, Merck had two candidates: an anxiety drug, the so-called GABA-A (gamma-aminobutyric acid A) agonist, which was in Phase II testing, and—supposedly a favorite of Dr. Scolnick, the longtime research chief—substance P antagonist, a potentially innovative treatment for depression.

Homing in on a brain chemical (substance P) that had never before been associated with depression, the compound apparently managed to avoid the worst side effects of other antidepressants. (Not only that, it also seemed to inhibit nausea and vomiting, so the FDA in late 2002 put it on a fast track for approval for that narrow use for chemotherapy patients under the brand name Emend.) When the future anti-depressant drug moved into large-scale human trials, however, it hit trouble. The original compound had "problems with [long-term] consistency," Dr. Scolnick conceded, and the researchers had to try a new approach. The trials were complex to design. As the testing process dragged on, investors and advertisers started muttering that something was wrong with the drug, and even Dr. Scolnick had to acknowledge, at the company's meeting with Wall Street analysts in December 2001, that "there's been a lot of speculation and mystery as to where we are." He claimed, however, that the problems were solved. In any case, Merck assigned a top marketing liaison to the compound, and in the 2002 annual report the substance P antagonist was listed among "filings expected in 2003 through 2006" as an antidepressant.

In heartburn and ulcers, Merck had been perhaps too early: Its patent on Pepcid ended in 2001. AstraZeneca, its co-marketer for Prilosec, was fighting to stave off generic versions, but by 2002 AstraZeneca had basically abandoned that drug in favor of the very slightly improved, next-generation Nexium, in which Merck had a smaller share.

The big hole in Merck's labs was cancer. Finding a cure for cancer has become a cliché, the symbol of the ultimate scientific achievement. Especially sought after are treatments for the four most common cancers—breast, lung, colon/colorectal, and prostate. No one, as the 1990s moved into the 2000s, was anywhere close to "a cure." But other drug companies had been chipping away at small pieces of the goal for years, devising drugs that stopped the spread or eased the pain of various tumors. One of the earliest was Taxol, in the 1990s, which blocks cancer cells from dividing by interfering with the cells' skeletal structure. Discovered by government scientists at the National Cancer Institute and licensed to Bristol-Myers Squibb, it was approved for ovarian, breast, and certain types of lung cancers, as well as Kaposi's sarcoma, which can affect AIDS patients. AstraZeneca, Pharmacia, and Roche and Genentech (in a joint venture) also had breast cancer drugs. Altogether, according to PhRMA, the industry trade group, 712 cancer drugs were in development as of 2001, most frequently for lung, breast, colon, prostate, or skin cancer.

The star of oncology was probably Novartis, which in the spring of 2001 got fast FDA approval for its drug Gleevec for a rare type of leukemia. Gleevec also seemed to work for a rare intestinal cancer. What had the pharmaceutical world so excited was the way the drug was able to precisely target cancer cells, by blocking certain hyperactive proteins from sending out aberrant signals. That could mean fewer healthy cells harmed and thus fewer side effects. For a while, a hot runner-up was AstraZeneca, whose innovative cancer product, Iressa, also targeted cells precisely and was approved in Japan in 2002 for a kind of lung cancer. However, hopes dimmed when AstraZeneca later reported that Iressa in combination with chemotherapy did not seem to keep patients alive any longer than chemotherapy by itself.

And Merck? Well, its scientists were working with the Netherlands Cancer Institute on a technique they hoped would help determine whether tumors that spread throughout the body have different genetic patterns from those that don't. Moreover, Vioxx might have a second life as a cancer treatment; trials were under way to see if it and other COX-2 inhibitors helped shrink or prevent tumors involved in lung and breast cancer, and Celebrex had already been found to stop polyps from recurring in a rare form of colon cancer. There was also the potential human papillomavirus vaccine, of course, but that wasn't an approach that could be widely applicable to cancer research. Most cancers aren't caused by a virus and thus can't be treated with a vaccine. Nor is cervical cancer one of the big areas of oncology. Meanwhile, a much-publicized compound called L-778123 that targeted the protein ras—and that had gotten as far as Phase I and II trials by fall 2001 for use against several types of cancer, including lung and colon—had been abandoned because it failed to shrink tumors. What else Merck might be doing in the depths of its secret labs was unknowable.

But even allowing for some unheralded prospects, oncology was not exactly a field where the king of research could call itself a leader. It's the one failure that Roy Vagelos acknowledges about his stewardship. "I was disappointed that we never were really able to break into a major new drug for cancer. We never had the right idea. We didn't know enough about the biology of cancer at the time," he says.

Whatever ills the flesh is heir to, they get worse with time. Age 50 is one turning point: The birthday when AARP, the big lobbying group for the elderly, sends out membership cards to first-timers is also when doctors start to recommend colonoscopies to check for cancer of the large intestine and rectum and more frequent mammograms to detect breast cancer. In their early fifties, women generally enter menopause, putting them more at risk for cardiovascular disease, cholesterol problems, and osteoporosis. Most cases of breast cancer occur in women over 60. After age 65, Alzheimer's starts to become more common, and by 85, according to some estimates, it hits about half the population. The incidence of osteoarthritis multiplies 10-fold between ages 30 and 65. And all the diseases that are caused by accumulation or wear and tear have had plenty of years to worsen, whether it's the fat in the arteries, blocking blood flow to the heart, or bits of protein in the brain, causing Alzheimer's.

With some 76 million Boomers due to hit the magic age of 50 between 1996 and 2014, most of them vulnerable to multiple ailments, the drug industry was looking at riches beyond belief.

As the wave of birthdays rolled into its first decade, there were already drugs on the market for some of the major conditions, such as osteoporosis, high cholesterol, arthritis, and Alzheimer's. Merck, indeed, had very profitable toes in the first three camps, and their potentials were hardly tapped out.

Prospects for Fosamax, Merck's osteoporosis drug, blossomed after a series of reports starting in 1998 raised warnings about the risks as well as the secondary benefits of hormone replacement therapy (HRT) for women going through menopause. For half a century, women had been taking the hormones (usually a combination of estrogen and progestin) to combat the discomforts of menopause, such as hot flashes and mood swings. They knew that the hormones increased the possibility of blood clots, gall bladder disease, and breast cancer, but on the plus side, the therapy supposedly helped prevent or treat osteoporosis, heart attacks, stroke, and maybe even depression and Alzheimer's. As long as they were taking the treatment anyway for hot flashes—there really wasn't any other drug for that—they figured they might as well use it for all those other ailments. That calculus changed, however, as more and more studies questioned whether the hormones really helped with heart conditions, osteoporosis-related fractures, depression, and Alzheimer's. Research also found worse problems than expected with breast cancer, blood clots, stroke and heart disease. Spooked by the new doubts, women began limiting their HRT use to just the menopausal symptoms and abandoned it once the hot flashes were over.

Their rejection left a big opening for Fosamax to come in as an alternative, less risky treatment for osteoporosis. "That's the case we're going to face right now, especially [for] the women who stop taking HRT," promised Patrick Counihan, vice president of Merck's osteoporosis franchise business group. While other companies could also take advantage of the trend—Aventis and Lilly had osteoporosis products, and GlaxoSmithKline was working on two—Fosamax far and away dominated the market. A once-a-week version could help extend its patent life to 2018.

For the cholesterol market, Merck was counting on Zetia and Zocor. Arthritis, though, was a more depressing story. Targeting a market of anywhere from 21 million to 90 million Americans, Vioxx and its successor, Arcoxia, were supposed to be the blockbusters that would save Merck as patents on the older drugs expired. But the controversies—the potential heart problems and the debate over whether such expensive drugs were even needed—sent Vioxx sales plunging hundreds of millions of dollars below expectations. Nor was Vioxx ever able to catch up with Celebrex's head start, short though it was. Then, when Merck withdrew the Arcoxia application in 2002 to answer the FDA's questions on safety and effectiveness, profit prediction were set back even further. Making matters worse, Celebrex's successor, Bextra, was already on the market. (To be fair, Arcoxia was approved in many countries in Europe and Latin America.)

Merck argued that the apparent heart problems were overblown because Vioxx was being unfairly compared to another drug, naproxen, that was known to have heart-protecting benefits. But to Richard Stover, the Arnhold and Bleichroeder analyst, the questions about the COX-2 inhibitors' cardiovascular effects drowned out everything else. Merck, he argued, needed to do yet another study, a thorough, long-term, properly controlled safety trial of Vioxx, one that included people who had heart-related risks—a trial he said could cost $50 million to $100 million. Not doing so "risks the credibility of the organization."

Into the future, some of the most dramatic age-related research in the industry was taking place in the brain—unlocking the secrets of memory and the physiology of Alzheimer's disease. The research seemed to show that Alzheimer's is caused by a buildup of a protein known as beta amyloid (or variations of that name), which crowds out healthy tissue. Scientists were also focusing on a condition called mild cognitive impairment, a loss of memory that typically strikes in middle age and that might be an early warning of Alzheimer's. A few drugs were already on the market for mild to moderate forms of the disease, like Pfizer's Aricept, but there was plenty of room for more. By the early 2000s, some 4 million Americans were believed to be suffering from Alzheimer's, and if the trend continued, that could mean 14 million patients by the middle of the twenty-first century.

Merck was taking several tacks in looking at memory and Alzheimer's in its new labs in San Diego, in England, and in West Point, Pennsylvania, where the neurosciences star Dennis Choi was based. Scientists were studying whether statins like Mevacor or Zocor could inhibit beta amyloid's toxic effects or help the body get rid of the buildup. If that panned out, it would give Merck a big leg up, but test results with a rival statin on nearly 6,000 people in Europe in late 2002 were discouraging. Merck also said it was investigating other ways to slow down the formation of the beta amyloids. Its anxiety compound, the GABA-A agonist, might help increase alertness in regions of the brain that affect learning and memory and be useful in treating Alzheimer's. Two studies to see whether Vioxx, by reducing brain inflammation, might slow memory impairment had shown no effect, but Merck was still trying a third. Every now and then, the company let reporters into its British labs to show them what its rats were doing.

But again, all this was very preliminary. Indeed, Merck's memory-related GABA-A work was far behind efforts by GlaxoSmithKline, Johnson & Johnson, Pfizer, and a clutch of small companies that were already testing compounds on humans or expected to in the near future. For all the money Merck had poured into those labs in England since the 1980s, the only thing that had emerged was Maxalt for migraines. There wasn't a word about Alzheimer's or memory in its annual reports. Nor did Dr. Scolnick or Peter Kim mention those topics in their speeches on upcoming R&D at the 2002 annual meeting. It could just be Merck's typical secrecy—or it could be that there wasn't much going on. When one shareholder asked, Gilmartin essentially replied that any results were years off.

Boomers don't just want healthy bodies; they want 20-year-old bodies. There's big money to be made in drugs that could eliminate all signs of baldness, fat, wrinkles, impotence, and old age in general.

To be fair, these products are only a small part of Big Pharma's stable, and the companies don't always set out to make frivolous drugs intentionally. Propecia, Merck's anti-baldness drug, is simply a lower-dosage version of Proscar, its treatment for noncancerous prostate enlargement. (Both work by preventing the male hormone testosterone from being converted to another form, dihydrotestosterone, that enlarges the prostate gland and also signals certain hair follicle cells to become smaller.) Merck began looking into the dual-powered drug when doctors in the Dominican Republic noticed that men who failed to produce a particular enzyme never got prostate cancer—and never lost their hair.

Aventis's Ornidyl started as an anticancer drug, and then was discovered to work against sleeping sickness (a highly infectious disease that threatens millions of people in Africa, causing fever, itchy skin, hallucinations, and death). Only later did scientists learn that its precursor chemical might prevent the growth of facial hair in women. Most famously, Pfizer was actually researching a heart medication that it hoped would improve the flow of blood by relaxing the arteries, when it noticed that the medication also increased the flow of blood to the male genitals . . . . Voila! Viagra.

No doubt the most effort centered on obesity research. By the early 2000s, obesity had qualified as an epidemic, with some two-thirds of American adults classified as obese or overweight, along with a rising number of children—making it far and away the biggest potential drug market around. But this time, the industry wasn't necessarily appealing to vanity. Obesity can be a serious medical condition; people who are severely overweight are at risk for diabetes, stroke, high cholesterol, and heart disease.

Nor is the solution as simple as sticking to a diet. Drug makers were looking at the brain, bloodstream, and digestive tract for causes and cures. Among more than half a dozen hormones and brain chemicals known to affect appetite or weight, scientists had recently come up with two hormones that could be potential targets—ghrelin, which slows the body's metabolism, making it harder to burn fat, and PYY, which circulates in the brain and turns off the desire to eat. Amgen, the big California biotech, had an injectable hormone in the works that it hoped would lower fat levels. For its part, Merck was focusing on the brain's ability to regulate appetite, testing drugs that switch off hunger signals. In September 2002 it signed a $90 million licensing arrangement with DeCODE Genetics of Iceland to use the smaller company's genomics and genealogical research to seek out more targets for potential obesity drugs.

Still, clearly some R&D was going into areas that are hardly life-threatening. Bayer and Lilly rushed to come out with their own versions of Viagra. No one was interested in making Ornidyl, the drug for sleeping sickness, until its potential use in blocking facial hair was discovered. In the spring of 2002, to a mix of tut-tutting and fascination, Allergan of California began marketing Botox—essentially, a form of the poison botulinum that paralyzes facial muscles—as a cure for wrinkles. Some critics put Vioxx and the other COX-2's in this category of unnecessary drugs, seeing them as merely high-priced replacements for perfectly good non-prescription pain relievers.

Big Pharma likes to talk about how it makes products that save lives, points out Clay O'Dell, public affairs director for the Generic Pharmaceutical Association. Well, he adds, "it's one thing to say a new heart drug is saving lives. It's another when you're talking about Vioxx, Viagra, Prilosec, and Nexium. There's a big difference between drugs for the heart, and heartburn or impotence." O'Dell admits that the generic drug companies that belong to his organization will jump at the chance to turn out copies of Viagra and the rest as soon as their patents expire. "But we don't make the [life-saving] argument."

Merck, of course, would never call Vioxx an unnecessary or lifestyle drug. However, it apparently does have its standards. "Viagra," says Gordon Douglas, the ex-vaccines chief, "is not the type of product that Merck would traditionally pursue."

Actually, the American attitude toward medicine and health is a mass of contradictions. Americans eat more fast food than ever before—and also more food labeled "organic." They are bombarded with ads for Vioxx, Celebrex, and the rest on TV, and then comb the drugstore shelves for plain old vitamins and supplements that will perform miracles. If the Boomers are grabbing any drug that might make them young and beautiful, this is also the generation that went back to nature in the Sixties and Seventies, scorning preservatives in their food, polyester in their clothing, and chemicals in their bodies.

There is, in other words, a strong strain in American culture that talks about taking control of your own health through natural and nonintrusive means. Surveys by consumer magazines like *Prevention* and *Men's Health* in the late 1990s showed that some 22.8 million consumers relied on herbal remedies instead of prescription drugs, and that the use of herbal remedies, vitamins, and nontraditional treatments like aromatherapy were steadily rising. Another survey, this one by the American Hospital Association, reported that the number of hospitals providing alternative therapies such as yoga, acupuncture, and biofeedback almost doubled from 1998 to 2000.

Prescription drugs are a particular bugaboo because they represent the opposite of the whole natural/self-sufficiency trend. They are manufactured artificially. They can have serious side effects. They are expensive. And in order to get them, people need the intervention of the health care industry (a doctor and a pharmacist). So, as much as possible, natural health advocates first try diet, exercise, herbs, vitamins, soy, yoga, and the like. Or, if they have to take a "chemical" rather than an herb, they prefer to self-medicate with over-the-counter products. The drugs most easily replaced are ones for rashes and acne, high cholesterol, digestive complaints, depression and arthritis.

And what's so radical about that? It's standard medical advice to urge patients to change their lifestyle—go on a diet, get more exercise, throw out their cigarettes—even before popping pills for many conditions, most notably high cholesterol, diabetes, and heart disease. No less an authority than *The Merck Manual*, in its home edition, advises, "Generally, the best treatment for people who have high cholesterol or triglyceride levels is to lose weight if they're overweight, stop smoking, reduce the total amount of fat and cholesterol in their diet, increase exercise" and only after that, "if necessary, take a lipid-lowering drug" such as Zocor and Mevacor.[1] Exercise has been shown to help stave off osteoarthritis and also to promote blood flow to the brain, which could counteract the effects of aging on cognitive skills. A large study sponsored by the National Institute of Diabetes and Digestive and Kidney Diseases in 2001 found that diet and exercise were so successful in reducing the risk of developing type 2 diabetes (the most common kind) that the study was ended a year early, because there was no point waiting for clearer proof.

Even where medical treatment is called for, it doesn't have to be a prescription drug. By 2002, many doctors and health plans were becoming reluctant to prescribe or pay for expensive COX-2s for arthritis and pain if the over-the-counter standbys like ibuprofen could work just as well. For moderate depression, stress, and anxiety, therapy, psychoanalysis or even yoga could be as good as or better than an antidepressant. In fact, an analysis of drug company studies, released in the spring of 2002, seemed to show that antidepressant drugs worked no better than ordinary sugar pills.

Consider the medicine cabinet—if that's the phrase—of Paul Kaplan, a computer engineer in Long Island, New York, on a spring day in 2002. He was taking 3,000 milligrams of fish-oil concentrate daily for his cholesterol (he has what he calls a low-borderline reading) and had temporarily used cetyl myristoleate, a derivative of an unsaturated fatty acid that was first identified in mice, to ease stiff, swollen, semi-arthritic knee joints. When a relative had started losing large clumps of hair, he turned to softgel tablets of evening primrose oil, which works on the same principle as Merck's Propecia. Why not just get a prescription? "Why take drugs if I can do it through diet? All of the cholesterol drugs have side effects," Kaplan explains. And yes, his knee joints felt better and the hair stopped falling out.

"All of us should have in mind doing everything we can for our health, not relying on medicines as the only answer. We could do more with diet and exercise," advises Dr. Frank Williams, scientific director for the American Federation for Aging Research and a specialist in geriatrics.

Dr. Williams, by the way, gave this advice at the age of 80½, while striding the mile from the federation's office to his midtown Manhattan hotel. ("Can you walk that far?" he asked me before setting out.) He was still working almost full-time mentoring doctors at the University of Rochester hospital in upstate New York, and bicycling the six-mile round trip from home two or three times a week. He also took the stairs rather than the elevator at the hospital, worked out on a NordicTrack in his basement for 15 minutes most days, and kept to a low-fat diet.

People like Paul Kaplan and Frank Williams pose a direct, if small, threat to the pharmaceutical industry, one the industry has to treat delicately. So Merck, for instance, handed out pamphlets at its annual meeting entitled "You Can Control Your Cholesterol" and "Living with Osteoarthritis" that talked about losing weight, reading food labels, getting exercise, quitting smoking, reducing stress, using special tools, and changing one's lifestyle in other ways before getting to the point: "You May Need Medications."

But David W. Anstice, Merck's head of human health for the Americas, probably was closer to his company's true feelings when he described the potential market for Zocor and Zetia at the company's annual meeting for Wall Street analysts in December 2001. As he put it, "If you look at patients not yet treated with statins [the cholesterol drugs like Zocor]—they may be in dietary or exercise regiments—there are 24 million in the United States alone." In other words, diet and exercise is all well and good, but sooner or later those 24 million will be ripe for a prescription.

And Anstice had solid reasons to think so. It goes back to the contradictory American approach to health. For all the interest in natural living, there are also strong factors pushing Americans to the pharmacy, including basic laziness and health insurance policies that cover prescriptions but not vitamins.

Drugs, not diet, are still the automatic response in most cases. Some nutrition specialists complained that a special panel convened by the National Institutes of Health in May of 2001 put too much emphasis on statins for people with high cholesterol and too little on food. By the same token, it's a lot easier to rely on a magic pill than to stick to healthy eating habits. "Patients have the idea, 'I want to have that pepperoni pizza and tequila, so I'm going to demand my doctor give me Prilosec,'" says Dr. Jerry Avorn, an associate professor at Harvard Medical School whose specialty is the new field of pharmacoepidemiology, or the study of how drugs are used in a large population. Besides which, supplements and their ilk have plenty of problems of their own. Their claims can sound like the nineteenth-century ads for miracle elixirs in George Merck's day. A lot of their supposed benefits haven't been proved. And if prescription drugs' side effects are worrisome, things could be even worse with herbal remedies and supplements, which are far less regulated and which have been tied to dangerous conditions like liver ailments and even deaths.

They might be frivolous and unnecessary, but at least products like Viagra and Propecia were genuinely new chemical formulations that stemmed from substantial original discoveries. As scientific research becomes more complex, with larger clinical trials, more disease targets, and a more demanding FDA, the effort required to come up with any new drug, even a blockbuster like Viagra, can seem impossibly burdensome. Increasingly, some pharmaceutical makers are tempted to go for the easy income without trying to discover new targets—the fifth or sixth me-too drug of the same type, the line extensions, and most controversial, maneuvers that could extend the patents on their top-selling drugs. For instance:

- With the patent on its blockbuster allergy medicine Claritin set to expire in December 2002, Schering-Plough sued potential generics makers, claiming that they would violate a separate patent on the chemical compound (or metabolite) that is produced in the liver when the pill is swallowed.
- Bristol-Myers Squibb tried a similar "metabolite defense" three times in 1999 and 2000 for its antianxiety pill BuSpar, which was due to go off patent in November 2000.
- For its diabetes medicine Glucophage, Bristol-Myers took a different tack, seeking a three-year patent extension by combining aspects of three different laws (including the six-month pediatric extension, the three-year extension for new usages, and another legal provision concerning labeling).
- About to lose patent protection on Prilosec, Astra-Zeneca played for more time by contending that generics would violate its patent, not on the drug itself, but on the process for making the drug.

- Through a series of legal challenges and allowable extensions, Eli Lilly staved off a generic version of its blockbuster antidepressant Prozac for five years, until August 2001.

That's not all. Companies file so-called citizens' petitions challenging whether the generics are really bioequivalent or safe. They arrange deals with generic drug makers to keep copycat versions off the market. And when even the stalling tactics run out or they lose their lawsuits, many companies go to Plan B: They emerge with an "improved" version of the old blockbuster, dump all advertising for the original drug, and redirect their marketing firepower to persuade customers that they should switch to the new version rather than a generic copy of the old. Thus, Schering-Plough came out with Clarinex to replace Claritin, and AstraZeneca with Nexium as a substitute for Prilosec.

None of these generic-fighting tactics create one single new cure or treatment for any illness, except for possibly making some drugs available to children. The "improved" drugs, it's true, might have some advantage over their predecessors. Merck touts its weekly version of Fosamax as more convenient than the once-a-day pill, and most doctors agree with that concept. But other supposed improvements are highly debatable. The only known difference between Nexium and Prilosec, according to the press, is a slightly better healing rate in cases where the heartburn is so bad that the esophagus is eroded.

Yet these are the kinds of products, along with me-too drugs, that are increasingly filling the industry's pipeline.

Of all the new drug applications approved by the FDA between 1989 and 2000, by the estimate of the National Institute for Health Care Management (NIHCM), only one-third contained new active ingredients that could—even by a generous description—be considered innovative. (The pharmaceutical industry challeges the objectivity of the NIHCM, a nonprofit foundation, because it is heavily funded by the insurance industry, which has a natural bias toward low drug prices.)

Of course, the generic drug companies don't invent new cures either, but at least they charge less for their copies. For every month or year a generic is delayed, the prescription-buying public is paying millions to hundreds of millions of dollars in higher prices to the big manufacturers.

And for the amount the drug companies spend on legal fees, product research, and marketing to hold off the generics and switch consumers to marginally better brands, they could almost have discovered the legendary cure for cancer. AstraZeneca poured nearly $500 million into the first year of promotion for Nexium. By even the highest estimate, that's more than half the cost of developing the average new drug. By other estimates, $500 million could produce two spanking-new drugs.

"If the brand industry is so proud of its new drugs—and it should be," says O'Dell of the Generic Pharmaceutical Association, "then keep researching." Congress was so furious at Big Pharma's tactics that the Senate in the summer of 2002 passed a measure restricting how many times drug makers could use the Hatch-Waxman Act's automatic 30-month patent extension when they challenged a generic filing.

The pharmaceutical industry's approach doesn't come out of nowhere, however. Although the fight against the generics is first and foremost an attempt to keep the profits flowing, it is also part of a larger debate, spurred by the Internet, about intellectual property in general. The same issues of creativity versus public access that apply to medicine also apply to downloading digital music or films. The drug makers argue that they have put hundreds of millions of dollars into discovering these compounds, taken huge risks, gone down scores of wrong turns, and spent years of staff time, and they ought to enjoy the fruits of their labors. So, basically, does Hollywood. When patent and copyright laws allow corporate inventors to charge high prices for long monopoly periods, is that hurting consumers unfairly? But would the corporations still bother to research new drugs or produce new films if they couldn't make sizable profits from their work? Ironically, both the drug and entertainment industries got hit with hostile court rulings on the same day in February 2002. A federal district court threw out Bristol-Myers' metabolite defense, while the U.S. Supreme Court agreed to consider what had been a long-shot challenge to the constitutionality of a 1998 law that extended copyrights by 20 years.

Wall Street defends the me-too drugs and line extensions from a different vantage point: efficiency. When companies rely heavily on breakthroughs, as Merck claims to, "all of your research investment is as risky as it can possibly be. By definition, it's going to be sporadic output," says analyst Richard Evans. Companies need unexciting workhorses like weekly Fosamax and Nexium to provide some reliable income during the dry spells between breakthroughs, he argues. And after all, the "improvements" do offer some benefit to patients. Fellow analyst Richard Stover has a different problem with breakthrough drugs. They "have high promotional spending, so they're intrinsically not as profitable," he says. If you're the first one out in the market in a class of drugs, you have to educate the public and the FDA about the new treatment. You have to do all the original research on the target. Why not let someone else have the hassle, and still compete as a quick second?

The trouble with Stover's reasoning, however, is that somebody has to stop passing the buck and do the breakthroughs.

Merck may not always be the great pioneer it claims to be, but by all accounts, including that of the generic drug makers association, it is one of the few pharmaceutical companies that doesn't generally fiddle around with either court fights or meaningless improvements. "Merck is a company that really has tried to put more into R&D in new drugs than into legal strategy to protect old ones," O'Dell agrees. When its patent is up, it's up. Merck moves on to the next research. Its Medco subsidiary has a program that even encourages doctors to prescribe generics by handing out free generic samples (including some drugs that compete with Merck products). Reportedly, the company also let it be known—privately—that it could support some of the revisions to Hatch-Waxman.

Which is not to say that it didn't benefit nicely from Astra-Zeneca's delaying tactics and surprise victory in federal court in October 2002 on Prilosec, on which Merck gets 32 percent of the U.S. sales. Merck managed to rake in millions of dollars each month while letting AstraZeneca take the heat.

It has occasionally fought other patents, too. It delayed the introduction of Mevacor copies for about six months, first by seeking an extension, then by challenging the generics on legal technicalities. In November 2002 it won a district court ruling against two generic drug makers that had sought to overturn its extension of Fosamax. Back in the late 1990s, the joint venture DuPont Merck went from state to state trying to persuade legislators and pharmacy boards that a generic version of its blood-thinning drug Coumadin was not bioequivalent because Coumadin belongs to a class of "narrow therapeutic index" drugs whose dosages have to be carefully controlled. But all those are relatively mild stalling tactics, as these things go.

Ray Gilmartin has cited two reasons for not fighting the generics: First, the less that health plans spend on old prescription drugs, the more they have for the new ones Merck hopes to introduce. Second, Wall Street cares a lot more about what's next in the pipeline than it does about a few hundred million dollars of lost profits.

That approach wins Merck a lot of goodwill and may even give it a leg up in research, in the form of cash that it's not wasting on legal fights. But it also puts more pressure on the scientists in those labs in Rahway, England, San Diego, and Pennsylvania to come up with future blockbusters.

5

The Freebie Circuit

The doctor—call him an internist in a major American city—was nervous at first, smiling a little sheepishly, sitting stiffly in his living room chair, on a winter's day in 2002. But soon he was talking more fluently, and his smile turned halfway between smug and embarrassed.

"I get invited out to restaurants I could not otherwise afford" by salespeople from big pharmaceutical companies a few times a month, he shrugged, naming four upscale places in his city. The sales reps call and ask, "'Is there anything I can do for you? Do you want to go to the theater some evening?' I've let them know I prefer [classical music]. They say, 'I'll see what I can do.' The things I'm asking for are all very reasonable. I'm not asking for last-minute, front-row seats." On the drug companies' tab, he's seen "The Vagina Monologues," and Schubert, Wagner, Beethoven, and Mahler concerts. Along with several doctors, their guests, and the sales rep, he might go to two shows every six months, plus dinner. He figures it had to cost hundreds of dollars each time.

They never talk about medicine. "Obviously, it's all very informal. We just go there and enjoy."

Then, when it comes time to write prescriptions, "I try to give everybody a little piece of the pie. If I like the rep, they get a little more. Some of them have said to me, 'Two prescriptions a month would make a big difference to us.'" So he'll give that rep the extra business one month, as long as the rep's drug is basically the same as whatever else he might have prescribed. "Another company will get it next time."

Once, the internist recalled, he asked a rep for tickets to a particular show. The rep "never called me back. His drug [competes with] other drugs that are very similar, so guess what? He's not going to get many prescriptions from me."

According to the pharmaceutical industry, everything the internist described doesn't happen.

A lot of people in the business world—outside of pharmaceuticals—wouldn't bat at an eye at the internist's recitation. Every industry has to move its product, and most of them use gifts and glitz to some degree to do it. Sales reps the world over woo their clients with trinkets, expensive lunches, conferences in exotic locales, and skyboxes at ballgames. Do they really expect the clients to make their business decisions on the basis of these treats? Yes and no. It creates warm and fuzzy feelings. It creates opportunities to talk up the newest product (and talk down a rival). It can't hurt.

Thus, the pharmaceutical industry has traditionally showered its clientele—doctors—with everything from pens to free samples, pizza, football games, Broadway shows and hundreds of dollars in "consulting" fees. According to the most widely quoted surveys (from consultant Scott-Levin and market researcher IMS Health Incorporated), 80,000-plus drug sales reps spent around $16 billion in 2000 "detailing" doctors at their offices, at restaurants and shows, and at more than 300,000 formal meetings. These numbers represent a steady rise through the 1990s, dwarfing the $2.5 billion spent on consumer advertising and amounting to more than half of the amount the industry dedicated to research. The goal of all this expense: a few minutes face to face with a real, live doctor.

An argument could be made that the pharmaceutical industry has to rely more on client freebies than do most industries, or at least it did until 1997. Before that year, the kind of mass-market advertising that other businesses take for granted was strictly limited for prescription drugs, so hitting up the doctors in person was pretty much the only course open to a pharmaceutical company's promotion department. But medicine is a very fragmented, retail kind of market. Except for hospitals, it's hard to find any centralized locations with a large mass of potential customers; sales reps have to go from office to office. Physicians are also a very unusual sales target. They are busy, highly educated and often self-important. Their time is clocked by the minute. Their egos must be stroked. So what better way to reach them than with a nice dinner and tickets to a Knicks game?

To the drug reps and many doctors, all this was no big deal—it was the way the business world worked, and it was peanuts anyway compared with something like Wall Street's largesse. For that matter, about half of the $16 billion spent on detailing was the value of free samples, which arguably shouldn't count as frills.

However, to an increasing number of critics among consumer activists, politicians, health ethicists, and even doctors, by 2001 and 2002, this way of life was akin to bribery. In part the protests stemmed from the nature of the product. This wasn't toothpaste or sneakers being bartered for the price of a steak dinner. These were medicines that can affect people's health and even survival. Too, the outrage over drug marketing was part of a larger public fury at the pharmaceutical industry in general, especially its prices. Maybe prices wouldn't be so high if the drug companies weren't spending all those billions on pens and football tickets.

It was a level of outrage, in any case, that no other industry confronted. And Big Pharma had to appease that anger somehow.

Jessica Franklin (not her real name) has a bachelor of science degree in microbiology and medical technology. Tom Burr (not his real name) has undergraduate degrees in chemistry and biology and a master's in zoology. Casey Webber (also not her real name) has an undergraduate degree in biology and journalism and has finished the coursework for a master's degree in adult education.

Franklin, Burr, and Webber are not medical students or scientific researchers. They are or were sales reps for Merck through much of the 1990s and beyond.

In training for their jobs, Franklin and Webber each spent three months studying basic science, pharmacology, diseases, and the product lines of Merck and its rivals, and attended classes eight hours a day at a Merck regional center in the western United States. Only a small portion of that was sales training. When a major new product like the AIDS drug Crixivan came out, Webber got two more days of education. Depending on their background, Merck salespeople will come in as a medical rep, a rep I, or, if they have a master's degree and sales experience, a professional rep II.

The hiring process is similar elsewhere. To get her job at another Big Pharma company, Rebecca Dickinson (also not her real name) had to read the text *Basic & Clinical Pharmacology* and score at least 85 percent on a science test. Then she got six months of paid training, which included reading medical textbooks at home, role-playing with a mentor, and more tests. "I did more work in six months than I did in four years of college," she says.

This is not the image many doctors and consumers have of pharmaceutical reps. "You've got to understand the scorn that we physicians have for the drug reps in general," says Dr. Warden B. Sisson, a veteran neurologist in Fresno, California. "Usually they're fairly young people, they're dressed to the teeth, they come in your office, and they are going to talk to you about this drug. I just wish they'd go away."

The doctors' and consumers' image of pharmaceutical salespeople—pushy, sexy, flashy airheads—does have some basis in reality. All salespeople have to be a little pushy. And yes, Franklin and Dickinson are in their twenties and thirties. And yes, since the 1970s and 1980s, Big Pharma has hired a lot of young saleswomen, presumably to appeal to the mostly male medical profession. (Some old-timers from before the women's era refer to their predecessors as "detail men.") But the reps say they have to know what they're talking about, and be honest about their drugs' side effects, or physicians won't even let them in the door. Back in the late 1970s, when Boyd Clarke was a salesman for Merck, "I would run into doctors who would say, 'How useful is what you're saying? I know you're biased.' I would say, 'You know where my bias is right up front. I'm going to try and give you fair balance, but I'm going to tell you how my products will help your patients.'"

"I want them to use me as a resource," Dickinson says. "I know more about my products than they do."

To the degree that physicians don't throw all reps out the door, those from Merck tend to be seen as a cut above— better educated, more honest, and less pushy. Some of that is probably reflected glory from the company's research labs; doctors figure that the sales force has somehow absorbed the scientific expertise. Still, there are also valid reasons for the good reputation. "Physicians consistently rank Merck salespeople as being the most knowledgeable about the drugs. Merck takes the time to really educate the drug reps," points out Sean Brandle, a vice president at The Segal Company, a Manhattan benefits consulting firm. "With Merck reps," adds a New York City doctor, "you get a sense that they are definitely in control of the information. They know their stuff. Not all companies are like that."

Ward Sisson spares his Merck rep from his general dia-
tribe. The rep, he says, "doesn't bowl you over. He doesn't try
to throw the product at you. He dresses nicely, but not as if
he's coming for a spit-and-polish interview." Until Dr. Sisson
hurt his knees in 1998, he even used to play doubles tennis
with the rep—off-duty, he adds. They didn't talk shop, and
because they both belonged to the same tennis club, there
was no debate over who picked up the check.

In the 1980s, Merck dominated drug marketing the way
it dominated the whole industry. "When I was first hired in
[in 1987], and probably for the next five or six years, Merck
had the most reps out in the field," Webber says. And the
company kept expanding, shrinking each rep's territory or
product lines as it added more staff. If anything, one industry
veteran claims, Merck was too aggressive in using sexy sales
women. Then, in the early 1990s, Merck bought Medco, the
pharmacy benefits manager, and made its bet on managed
care. Predicting that prescription decisions would be determined more by insurance restrictions and President Bill Clinton's health care reform than by marketing, Merck shrank its
sales force. Meanwhile, Pfizer built up its marketing firepower to roughly double the size of Merck's.

Unfortunately, Merck guessed wrong. The Clinton reform
plan collapsed in 1994 of its own overambition and a no-holds-
barred negative ad campaign by the insurance industry, and
the Republicans grabbed control of Congress. As a result,
Merck had to scramble to catch back up. It added 1,000 reps
in 2001 and promised a further 500 in 2002—overkill, some
reps and analysts said—even as it cut marketing and administration expenses by the high single digits by consolidating

and pledging "accelerated operational-efficiency and work redesign initiatives."

A drug rep's territory is usually divided by geography and by medical specialty. Merck, by the late 1990s, also aligned its sales crews according to the categories in its worldwide business strategy teams. Thus a rep might handle all the drugs for diabetes, hypertension and cholesterol in a section of a large city, or the cardiovascular line for an entire small state. "Handle," of course, means calling on internists, cardiologists, pediatricians, or whichever doctors are likely to treat the conditions the rep's drugs are prescribed for. That's a lot of doctors—about 1,000 in Dickinson's urban territory. Naturally, the reps prioritize. To some degree, they'll try to cultivate new doctors, but mainly they'll spend time with the ones who give their company the most business, the ones Webber calls "high writers."

It's easy to find out who these high writers are: Almost every time a patient fills a prescription in the United States (and in some two dozen other countries), that sets in motion a whole system of trading information.

Most patients, and even many doctors, have no idea this is happening.

Market research companies buy prescription records from pharmacies and wholesalers (and, to a lesser degree, hospitals and doctors). "On every prescription, there's data about the prescription, the condition, the dosage, packet size, pharmacy, pricing, the doctor who prescribed it," explains Michael Gury, vice president of global communications for Connecticut-based IMS Health, which claims to be the largest of these information collectors. Then IMS and its ilk organize the information into a breakdown of which doctors are prescribing how much of which drug for what ailment.

The drug companies can use that breakdown to direct their sales efforts, Gury says. "If Dr. A is prescribing not much of your product or he's prescribing your competitor's product, that might be a target for you to go in or change his mind." Or perhaps the doctor is prescribing a drug for only one of its many approved indications; then the sales rep could point out the other potential usages. Gury says IMS gets data on billions of prescriptions from hundreds of thousands of pharmacies, and while he won't disclose what he pays for the information, some small local pharmacies say they've been offered a discount of $30 to $45 a month on their data processing in return for their prescription records.

No one bothers to tell the customers whose prescriptions form the basis of this whole business. But their privacy is protected, Gury insists, since his company never gives out any information that could identify individual patients. This is different from the more blatant practice—which has been publicized—of pharmaceutical companies paying pharmacies to go through their prescription records, then write or phone customers to urge them to switch to more expensive or newer drugs.

With the order data in hand, the sales reps try to visit the most prolific prescription writers—such as cardiologists and internists—once every three or four weeks. (This means office visits; it doesn't include conferences or dinner speeches.) For Dickinson, that's 250 doctors a month, or 3,000 a year.

Novartis reps make some 1,800 calls a year, according to a *Wall Street Journal* article in August 2002. Merck speeded up the pace from every four weeks to three weeks and then, by the time Webber left in December 2001 to work for a competitor, she says it had even gone to "hypertargets," requiring her to see the very top prescribers every week. At the same time, Merck was adding reps and carving up their territory again in some places into smaller and smaller niches. (All of which may be an indication that the analysts are right in saying the company overhired in rebuilding its marketing force and now has too many people with too little to do.)

The doctors set the tone for the visits: Is there a quota—no rep may visit more than once every three months? Must a rep make an appointment, or can he or she just drop by? And if it's drop-in, will the rep have to cool his or her heels in the waiting room along the patients? Some doctors and group practices have a flat ban on reps entering the premises or even lingering on the sidewalk at all. In the western states, the approach tends to be more casual.

They may stay five minutes or thirty minutes. Five minutes may not sound like much, but face time with a doctor is actually a vicious fight for advantage. Webber figures there are 100 drug reps covering the biggest city in her western territory. "Say 25 are in town at least on any given day. We all have the same high-writing targets. If the doctor could give each rep even three minutes, ..." There goes an hour and a quarter of otherwise billable time.

Under the strict eye of managed care, five unbilled minutes is a luxury. "Doctors are becoming more resistant. Before, you might be able to see them once a month or six weeks;

now it's every three months," says Burr, who's been a Merck rep for more than two decades.

And the hypermarketing and territory-slicing started to backfire. Too many reps were trying to see too many physicians too often. Scott Diamond (also a pseudonym), who left the Merck sales force in the early 2000s after several years, says he actually liked it better when he lost two large cities in his Montana territory and the number of doctors he was responsible for was cut in half to 100, because it meant less travel. But eventually, the overcrowding drove him out of the pharmaceutical business. "You'd go into the office at ten in the morning and you'd be the tenth rep that day. I felt I was bothering the doctors."

In that precious five minutes of face time, what's there to talk about—especially if the detailer just saw the doctor three weeks ago? A new clinical study always provides a good conversation opener—if the results are positive—but those don't happen every three weeks. So the salesperson might remind the doctor of old news, perhaps a secondary approved use. A competitor may have come out with a claim or criticism that has to be answered. (And if the claim is too strong to counter, talk about some other aspect of the competing drug, like its bad side effects.) By the same token, Franklin might explain why a claim Merck made for Zocor, based on clinical studies, can't be applied to rival Lipitor. Not every drug in the manufacturer's lineup gets mentioned, of course: In 2001 and 2002, doctors said that the Merck reps were especially aggressive with the new arthritis blockbuster Vioxx but didn't do much to push the hypertension drug Hyzaar. And reps won't waste their time on products that are about to go off patent.

Many doctors say that the reps do come up with nuggets of news worth listening to. "While it may have been slanted, you could take away some information that would keep you up-to-date," says Dr. Michael Delman, the senior vice president of medical affairs at Southside Hospital in Long Island, New York, who spent a quarter of a century in private practice in internal medicine, gastroenterology, and addiction.

But the best way to get the doctor's attention, marketers argue, is through the goodies.

"They say that cooking is the way to a man's heart," smiles Dr. Sisson. He may not much like most of the sales reps, but when they bring sandwiches, candy canes, and Easter eggs to his staff several times a year, "the food is, generally speaking, quite welcome."

Just as there is a hierarchy in how often a detail person will visit a doctor, so there is also a hierarchy to the quantity and quality of the freebies. At least, this is how things worked until well into 2002.

Virtually every doctor gets the lowest category of freebies— the notepads, coffee mugs, clipboard, and pens emblazoned with product names, as well as free samples and maybe educational tapes and videos. These are either so minimal, or the educational value is so unarguable, that they are the one giveaway everyone admits to. Even then, Franklin claims that Merck was on the cheap side, providing only Bic and Parker pens where other companies had classier brands. A little more rare and controversial are free medical supplies, such as stethoscopes, textbooks, or working models of the heart or kidneys, which could be worth a few hundred dollars.

Free samples are a different case entirely, the ultimate combination of medical value and brand-name promotion. Most doctors happily give them to patients, even if they're not the drug of choice, figuring this will help low-income and elderly people save money. "It's easier to know that the patient has his first several weeks' supply then and there," explains Dr. Russell Robbins, a Wilton, Connecticut, urologist and chief medical officer of an insurance software company. But the samples aren't totally without controversy: Some critics warn that too often they end up being used by the doctors and their friends rather than patients. And of course, once the free supply runs out, what brand name is the patient going to ask for?

The next rung up the freebie ladder is some sort of simple food in the doctor's office. It can be a box of Dunkin' Donuts every month for a New York City pediatrician, or Chinese food and deli sandwiches, also monthly, for the staff of 10 at Dr. Robbins's office. If it's lunch, the reps will generally stay for an hour to talk about their products. (However, there's no guarantee the doctor will be there to listen.) With all the clerical workers that physicians have had to hire to handle their managed care paperwork, the lunchtime crowd can easily reach 25 or 40. "If I had my druthers, I would only buy lunch for the doctors and nurses," Webber grumbles. "But I'm never going to say no to anybody who walks through the door. I think it's rude to do the [medical] staff and leave the receptionist at the front."

Hospitals and medical schools get particular attention. Drug companies like to catch doctors-in-training while they're still impressionable (also struggling enough financially that they really need the free meals). It's usually nothing big, just pens, pizza, and trinkets. Dr. Robbins remembers reps methodically making the rounds: lunch with surgical residents on Monday, medical residents Tuesday, orthopedists, urologists . . . .

Distinct from the drop-in meals are more formal luncheon and dinner programs, typically at hotels or medical clinics, underwritten at least in part by the drug companies. Big Pharma eagerly points to these sessions as proof that its interactions with doctors are indeed educational, not just pushing product. Actually, it's a lot more ambiguous—education with a logo. "Doctors know who's sponsoring it," Dr. Sisson says.

There are a range of variations on the basic meal-with-speaker setup, and a range of publicity the drug makers may get out of it. A pharmaceutical company may invite a group of doctors to a restaurant to hear one of its own scientists discuss how research is going on a new drug. One or several companies might chip in to underwrite a luncheon symposium with a scientific panel (and probably set up a little table on the side to hand out knickknacks and literature). Frequently, clinics ask their sales reps to foot the bill for a lunchtime speaker. At one AIDS clinic in a large northeastern city, drug companies pay for a weekly lecture series from September through June. That's an honorarium of $250 to $500 for the speaker, plus the speaker's travel costs, plus sandwiches or pasta for the audience, which could go as high as 75 people. In fact, when the funding started to dry up in the weakening economy of early 2002, the director admitted that he was "worried about maintaining our HIV education."

The speakers are respectable outside academics or doctors, never employees of Big Pharma, except for the talks that are clearly billed as an inside look at the company's products. They discourse on medical conditions and methods of treatment in general. When a third party like the AIDS clinic sponsors the program, the manufacturers may or may not even have a say in choosing who's on the podium. All that begs the big question, though: Does the speaker give a plug to the sponsoring company's drugs? Some will, some are under orders not to, and some will try to also talk about rival products.

At the AIDS clinic lectures, there are no marketing plugs. "We are very strict about that," the director says. He will make sure the audience knows who is sponsoring the programs, so that the speakers "won't push the drug company's product."

Lee Reichman, executive director of the New Jersey Medical School National Tuberculosis Center, has a different answer. Drug makers have sometimes paid the travel expenses and honorariums when he has lectured on TB around the world, and he boasts that "no drug company has ever tried to influence a talk that I've given." On the other hand, "I would not as a matter of courtesy zing a drug company that was sponsoring me." And he'll mention the company's product if it's something he'd be advocating anyway.

Merck, says Susan Hendrix, the Detroit gynecologist and consultant, is among the least pushy sponsors. When she does occasional speeches, "some companies will say, 'This is what we want you to cover. Mention all the good things you can about our product.'" But Merck does not interfere. "They'll say, 'These are what our goals are, this is the topic, do whatever you want.'"

The doctors on the podium aren't the only ones who can pocket some cash from these affairs. The drug companies may pay the doctors in the audience anywhere from $100 to $500 in "consulting fees" to participate in a discussion group for an hour or two afterwards. There, a rep will ask them about the drug or the disease: Who are the ideal patients for this product? What are the advantages and disadvantages of the drug? How could it be marketed better? (This "consulting" is not to be confused with the serious, ongoing consulting work that people like Dr. Hendrix do, in which she helps Merck and other companies plan their clinical trials and recruit patients.)

Of course, as with any industry and any business meal, the lunches and dinners are going to be held in quality hotels and restaurants, and the conferences are staged over several days at beautiful resorts. Says Dr. Hendrix: "You're not going to put them in Motel 6."

The really good meals, though—the ones at the three- and four-star restaurants—are the private dinners with just a few doctors, their guests, and the rep. In a big city, that could easily run $150 to $200 per person, including wine and drinks; among the venues are the ultra-trendy Danube and ultra-exclusive Jean Georges, both in Manhattan, and the steak chain Ruth's Chris. And this may happen several times a year. There may be no particular reason at all—simply a rep saying, "I'd like to take you to dinner, to talk with you more about our company and what we can do." If a regional sales manager came to town when Dr. Robbins, the urologist, was working near Albany, New York, the rep might take that manager and Dr. Robbins out to a nice lunch, just to schmooze. One New York City internist says his Merck rep was so aggressive about these meals that when the internist turned down a restaurant invitation, "he asked, did I want instead to get together at his house and he would have dinner brought in?"

It gets even better. Among the social events that drug reps have treated doctors to:

- Broadway shows, including such first-run hits as "The Producers"
- The U.S. Open tennis tournament
- Football games
- Hockey games
- Basketball games
- Whitewater rafting trips
- Wine tastings
- Performances at Carnegie Hall and Lincoln Center
- A round of golf
- Christmas parties

Once, Dr. Robbins spent a day at a dude ranch in upstate New York, courtesy of a big drug maker. Billed as "Family Fun Day," it included horseback jaunts and hay rides—plus a one-hour speech on the company's asthma drug.

Another doctor recalls a tennis clinic in Manhattan sponsored by one Big Pharma, where stars such as Tracy Austin gave out tips and posed for photos with the guests.

In the late 1990s, Merck arranged special Mother's Day binges in florist shops, where doctors could pick out flower arrangements. Merck would pay, but the doctor couldn't get away without a chat with a detail rep.

"They say, 'Are you interested in seeing any Broadway shows?' Or they might have specific tickets already. They try to find out what your interests are," the New York City internist says.

Okay, so there's no free lunch. The rep virtually always accompanies the doctor and squeezes in a little talk about products between innings or acts. (One exception is the big-city internist who likes classical music: If his request is too highbrow, the rep will probably just hand him a couple of tickets and bow out.)

Merck employees say—and some consultants, doctors, and rival salespeople confirm—that Merck never reached the top levels of generosity. It didn't do rounds of golf or rafting trips, no basketball or hockey tickets unless they were tied to an educational event, and it wouldn't pick up the tab for spouses. Al Alberts remembers one physician, whom Merck was paying as a "consultant" to fly out to a lecture, complaining to him, "I can only get one business-class [plane] ticket, while other companies will give me first-class tickets for me and my wife." The big-city internist says he might have lunch two weeks in a row with reps from the most aggressive companies, and probably a half-dozen dinners per year with the average company. And Merck? Only a few lunches and one dinner that he could recall in a recent year.

In fact, the reps have to stick to a budget. Dickinson in 2002 could spend no more than $10,000 in total—speaker programs, Knicks basketball tickets, you name it. That was down by half from the prior year.. Diamond, pitching Merck products in lower-cost Montana, spent at least $6,000 a year on lunches, candy, gift certificates and the like until 2002, plus easily $15,000 more on dinner programs with speakers.

For years and year, just as in any industry, doctors went to the dinners and pocketed the trinkets. But as the public complaints about this largesse started to grow, in the early 2000s, the pharmaceutical industry felt compelled to offer explanations—many of them common to other industries too:

1. *It doesn't exist.* "You can't do that. It can't happen," a veteran marketer at one major drug company says point-blank. He looks me straight in the eye; he seems sincere. But the big-city internist also looked me in the eye when he described exactly how freebies did happen.

A variation on this argument is that maybe some of the wining and dining used to happen, but it stopped long ago. The American Medical Association has had gift-giving guidelines since 1990, under which doctors are not supposed to accept anything worth more than $100, and only "modest meals" that are part of an educational function are allowed. "The reps are regularly reminded in refresher training," the veteran marketer insists. If some reps are piling on too many freebies, "they should report it." PhRMA, the industry trade organization, officially claims that "our intention [is] that our interactions with healthcare professionals are to benefit patients and to enhance the practice of medicine."

"We wouldn't just have a boondoggle," Clarke, the former marketer, says of his days at Merck.

Of course, most industry people add, there are always a few bad apples who will go overboard with perks. Maybe those are the ones taking the internist out to dinner and shows.

2. *It's all educational.* Sure, Merck would treat doctors to nice hotels and dinners, but it always included credentialed speakers and solid scientific information, this argument goes. "The scientific value of the meetings had to have preeminence," insists Boyd Clarke. (The former executive who spent more than 15 years at Merck notes that "I avoided islands" as venues.) And it's true—depending on how "education" is defined. Almost every event includes some shop talk, even if it's just a few minutes listening to the rep push his or her new product between periods at a hockey game.

3. *Doctors work hard and deserve a treat.* Casey Webber recalls an all-day program one Saturday in the late 1990s with seven speakers, each talking for an hour on a different disease. At the end of that, yeah, she took some doctors out to a minor-league hockey game. "If you had a certain amount of education, you could go out and have a little fun."

The basic argument is that doctors are so busy that the reps have to do something flamboyant to grab their five minutes. Or the only time the physicians have available to hear a sales spiel is after-hours, at dinner or a show. "It's almost fair," Dickinson says. "Doctors have obscene hours. We're taking them away from their families." For doctors who normally bill $300 an hour, a $100 or $200 "consulting fee" to participate in a one-hour focus group after a speech could actually be seen as a bargain.

It's not just that physicians work hard, some defenders of the freebies say, but also that the growing dominance of managed care has taken a lot of the fun and profit out of medicine. "I get what I can," the internist says bluntly. "The system has changed, giving control of medicine to the insurance companies, and screwed the doctors. I'm making now what I made 18 years ago. Ethical is not a consideration as long as it doesn't hurt the patient, as long as it's legal."

4. *The doctors make us do it.* After all, the doctors could just say no—and some claim they do. A muckraking web site, nofreelunch.org, was started in 1999. Medical students at several universities launched boycotts of sales-rep pizzas and pens. Dr. Delman, the medical affairs vice president in Long Island, says he has never been on a drug company outing and doesn't even go to the supposedly educational dinners.

But mostly, the doctors just take. In fact, they ask for more.

Sometimes it's only the little things, the notepads and sandwiches. "You see, in the offices, the staff treating reps like, 'What have you got for me today?'" grimaces Dr. Ira Bloomfield, an internist and emergency room physician for 20 years, mainly in Florida, and now chief medical information officer of a physician-hospital network in North Carolina. Sometimes the requests are more charitable: Franklin has been asked to donate $50 to $200 to a local baseball team or ambulance department, which she'll agree to, as long as it's "a valid program." The Northeastern AIDS program took in close to $15,000 by charging a group of reps $1,000 to $1,500 apiece to spend a day in the clinic. "They wanted to see how doctors in the clinic operate," the director says cheerfully. "This was a big moneymaker for the [program's educational] slush fund."

The demands escalate. The big-city internist once requested a shredder. (He got it.) Dickinson was at a pregame show for the New York Jets with a different internist, who brought his young daughter, maybe 6 years old. All of a sudden, Dickinson says, the daughter "leans over to me and asks, 'Will you buy me a T-shirt?'"

Even for a drug sales rep who doles out $10,000 worth of freebies a year, getting hit up by a 6-year-old is a bit much.

The most repeated justification—from both doctors and Big Pharma—is that all the wining and dining doesn't buy business. Which is hardly surprising: Would anyone want to admit that his professional recommendation can be had for the price of a basketball ticket? Or that he'd tell a patient that an arthritis medicine is better just because he likes the person who sells it? Besides which, any favorable impression from a dinner with Pfizer one week could just be wiped out by a dinner with Novartis the next. So the reps will say that they're simply building a relationship, and the doctors will say what the heck, they'll take the dinner if the reps want to waste a few dollars. "As long as the focus is on science and there is transparency in the nature of the sponsorship, to suppose that a professional like a physician is going to be fundamentally altered by a weekend in the Catskills—I don't get it," Boyd Clarke says.

"I sometimes wonder if some of the pharmaceutical companies are getting a return on their money," says Dr. Bloomfield of North Carolina. "It would be the absolute rare physician who is going to use a drug because someone is giving them a black bag. While they might accept the gift, they'll still prescribe what they feel is right for the patient."

In reality, several studies—including one by Dr. Avorn of Harvard in the early 1980s, another by the Cleveland Clinic in 1992, and a third by the consulting firm Scott-Levin in 2000—have shown that drug reps and their goodies do influence prescription decisions. In the Scott-Levin study, more than half the physicians attending events at restaurants and hotels said they intended to begin or increase their prescriptions of the products that were promoted at those events. The Cleveland Clinic study found that prescribing patterns changed significantly after doctors went to resort symposiums sponsored by drug companies, "even though the majority of physicians who attended the symposia believed that such enticements would not alter their prescribing patterns."

But even in reality, it's not as simple as, one dinner equals one prescription. Neither the gift givers nor the takers are stupid or naïve, and there are a lot of factors that go into a decision about what to prescribe.

Paul Reitemeier, a veteran of the burgeoning field of health care ethics, goes through all the back-and-forth. "Give me a break. If it didn't have an influence, [the drug companies] wouldn't do it." On the other hand, "I have great respect for physicians. I don't think they are the pawns of the drug companies." So what happens? "The fragility of the human mind is such that influence is not always obvious."

"It's not even conscious," adds Dr. Avorn of Harvard. "It enters their [doctor's] consciousness the way an ad does. They remember the name because it was on the napkin [at a lunch]. The doctor's heard about [a drug], he thinks he knows about it. It's no different from the way consumers choose anything."

Do the freebies and friendships influence them?

Several doctors take their time answering.

His good opinion of his tennis-playing Merck rep might be a "positive" influence, Dr. Sisson of California concedes, but it's also tied in with his high regard for the company and its products in general. However, Merck doesn't actually make too many drugs for his specialty, the nervous system. If anything, he continues, most reps affect him adversely: The more they push, the less he wants to prescribe their drug.

"The pharmaceutical reps come in. Did it have some effect? Personally, I don't think any," Dr. Robbins begins. But he goes on, "You might prescribe one antibiotic that day because they took you out to lunch, they had an antibiotic that was the same [as what he normally prescribes]. Then the next week another guy came around, you wrote his product."

Only rarely is there a correlation between perks and prescriptions as direct and intentional as the big-city internist's, and even he makes exceptions, including for Merck.

Although Merck isn't as generous as the rest, "their reps have been nice. They still get prescriptions."

A veteran doctor in the San Fernando Valley of Southern California says his prescription-writing habits changed in the early 1990s, when the AMA's ethics guidelines discouraged donations of free samples to physicians for their personal, long-term use. Merck stopped giving those samples, he says, but other pharmaceutical companies didn't. Therefore, he drastically cut back on his Merck prescriptions. "All things being equal, I will go with the company that's more forthcoming," the doctor says.

The physician who went to the tennis clinic with Tracy Austin says he'd definitely be more likely to prescribe drugs from the company that sponsored the clinic, assuming they were basically equivalent to other drugs on the market, because he had such a good feeling about the day. The problem is, he's not sure what company it was.

(When the freebies did influence their prescription decisions, obviously the doctors are too embarrassed to let their names be used in this book.)

Dickinson has one doctor in her territory who has a yearly party for his patients—and asks the drug reps to cover the $30,000 to $40,000 cost. When she refused, he told her, "Your company is not giving back to the community." Sure enough, as time went by, "we took a little bit of a beating" in his orders; she saw the drop in his prescription numbers from the market research firm that gets them from the pharmacies. Not that the doctor ever came right out and admitted the quid pro quo. When she asked why he wasn't prescribing her company's drug as much as he used to, he said that it didn't work for his patients, or that he really was prescribing it. "They'll give you every excuse in the book. You can tell by the detail of their answers if they really tried it."

To a certain degree, the extravagances were reined in during the 1990s, after the AMA issued its guidelines. Budgets were tightened, and some of the most outrageous perks were eliminated—frequent-flyer miles for writing a certain number of prescriptions, gift certificates at liquor stores, resort weekends with barely any educational content. Many reps claimed that they were glad to see things cool down, that they were tired of keeping up with the ℞ Joneses. "There are still companies that give more than I can possibly do. It's not worth your money to do it, unless you go above and beyond," frets Dickinson.

However, by the fall of 2001, with the public increasingly angry at rising drug prices, the old reforms weren't enough. The whole pileup of perks was looking more and more unseemly. On top of that, several drug-marketing scandals had broken out, most notably one involving TAP Pharmaceutical Products Inc. of Illinois (an offshoot of Abbott Laboratories and Japan-based Takeda Chemical Industries). TAP in 2001 pleaded guilty to conspiring with doctors in a scheme to overcharge government insurance programs for reimbursement for its prostate cancer drug Lupron. This incident was covered heavily by the press. Meanwhile, a number of states were considering bills that would curtail the tax breaks for drug marketing or make the companies reveal more about what they were spending. Indeed, Minnesota had had a law on the books since the mid-1990s that banned gifts worth more than $50 to doctors. In the summer of 2001, the AMA launched a big campaign to educate physicians about its decade-old guidelines; however, that backfired in part when it was revealed that Big Pharma was underwriting nearly $700,000 of the cost of this campaign against itself.

Anyway, the whole idea of pitching to doctors was starting to lose some appeal. As of 1997, the industry had another marketing weapon—direct TV advertising to consumers. And while HMOs and state Medicaid programs didn't have the clout some had predicted, they did limit somewhat doctors' ability to determine what drugs their patients took.

Merck had been arguably a less egregious player than most, with better-educated reps and a tighter lid on freebies. But the public didn't see it as any more ethical than anyone else. Then, in October 2001, Merck took the step most others were just dancing around. At its district marketing meetings, it told its sales reps that it was changing the rules—effective immediately. No more Broadway tickets, no more flower-shop binges, no more sporting events even if they were tied to an educational program—that is, no more of the freebies that former executives like Clarke and the 15-year veteran insist they never did anyway. "Essentially," says Webber, "you can't do anything that might give the impression that you might try to buy somebody's business." The reps could still treat physicians to meals, but only meals with a reputable speaker, or the kind of meals where the rep brought sandwiches into the doctor's office and talked about Merck's products.

Webber and her colleagues had mixed reactions. They worried about how they would compete with their free-spending rivals. "On the other hand, you know it's the right thing," she says. Burr, the twenty-year Merck veteran, says he's glad of the change, because "there's less pressure for us to do these stupid programs." One manager suggested that more companies might well follow Merck's lead, so it would all even up.

That manager was right. The public pressure finally forced even PhRMA to act. In April 2002 it announced a new code of conduct, to be effective July 1, that paralleled Merck's new rules: From now on, everything had to be educational. Drug makers could help underwrite educational conferences, provide "modest" meals that accompanied "informational presentations," give out stethoscopes, and pay doctors as consultants if they were doing genuine consulting jobs, with a written contract, but that was about it. The rules seemed almost loophole-proof, except for the "consulting" part. And that fall, the inspector general of the U.S. Health and Human Services Department proposed new standards that could leave drug makers open to prosecution for fraud or kickbacks if they offered extravagant freebies.

Slowly, the new philosophy inched its way into the medical world. A relative who's also a pharmaceutical salesman told Dr. Robbins that he couldn't get any more free umbrellas. Another doctor says fewer reps are dropping by his office. However, other physicians say they haven't noticed any decrease in the number of visits or meals-with-speeches, and Dr. Sisson actually started getting more medically-related free gizmos—specifically, mouse-sized rubber brains. (Under the PhRMA code, brains are probably okay but umbrellas aren't.)

The change hit Dr. Delman at Southside Hospital's gala annual golf outing that September. In years past, drug companies would sponsor a tee or a hole or even an entire foursome, at prices ranging from $600 to $10,000. There would be a little sign at the tee or the putting green: "Tee sponsored by Such and Such Company." This time, he says, "I didn't see any drug company listings. And I didn't see a lot of physicians—which means the drug reps weren't buying as many foursomes."

Where does this leave the big-city internist? A few weeks into the new PhRMA rules, at least, he didn't feel particularly worried. "Hey, I can buy myself a [concert] ticket every now and then," he shrugged. The biggest impact at that point was that when his new Merck detailer called, they couldn't figure out how to get together: The rep isn't allowed to take him out for lunch just to chat, and the internist's group practice doesn't allow reps to bring food in. (Apparently, it didn't occur to them to get together without food.)

But the internist was also skeptical of just how different things will really be. He'd already noticed sales reps trying to finagle around the code, some claiming that they don't have to have an educational speaker at their meals if there are fewer than four guests. Similarly, Burr claimed that rivals—though not him and his Merck partner—"kind of push the envelope there. They're still entertaining physicians under the guise of medical education. Fabricated lunches in a super-nice restaurant." "The dust will settle," the internist predicts. "We'll still find ways of going out to dinner and socializing. Some-one will invite a friend, oh yes, this is"—pause—"*Doctor Andreotti*." (That is, pretend that the friend is a doctor.) "It won't be too flagrant, and it won't be too frequent." And as long as there are still some perks, he will still dole out his pre-scriptions accordingly.

6

Just Like Toothpaste

A grandfather helps his grandson swing a baseball bat while the grandmother applauds happily.

A couple runs on the beach.

An Olympic gold medal winner laces up her ice skates.

A grinning, if exhausted, man gestures excitedly in front of a collection of hang gliders.

A former U.S. senator discusses sex.

These are all advertisements that have run on television, in newspapers, or in magazines. In some ways, there's nothing particularly shocking about them; they could have been pitching life insurance, or breakfast cereal, or Diet Coke.

But they weren't. They were actually ads for an arthritis medicine (Celebrex, comarketed by Pfizer and Pharmacia), an allergy medicine (Schering-Plough's Clarinex), a different arthritis and pain medicine (Merck's Vioxx), a drug company (Aventis), and a medication for erectile dysfunction (Pfizer's Viagra). And that makes these ads the center of a whirlwind of controversy. In fact, until August 1997, some of these ads couldn't have been seen in the United States.

A thirty-second spot for cereal is just a commercial. Other than the occasional complaint that it encourages children to eat sugared foods or demand some tie-in toy, there's not much dispute about commercials for cereals. An ad for an allergy or arthritis drug, on the other hand, is a window into medical ethics, the role of government, the cost of health care, self-medication, and the doctor-patient relationship.

The roots of those allergy and arthritis ads lie in the consumer movement of the 1960s and 1970s. Like most strong forces, that movement exploded in unexpected directions, and it ended up a mixed blessing for consumers.

The basic idea was to give people more information so that they could exert more control over their lives—a trend that would later be labeled "empowerment." Consumers had the right to know what was in the food they were eating, so that they could make informed decisions about which groceries to buy. Neighbors should know what chemicals were being used in local factories and how much had seeped into the groundwater, so that they could determine if their water was safe to drink and go to the government to stop the pollution if it was not. Why should they just take the word of the food or chemical manufacturers? On the other hand, if consumers didn't want to bother reading the ingredient lists on their cereal boxes or protesting contaminated water, they didn't have to.

Manufacturers weren't thrilled by this trend. It was bad PR, it was potentially expensive if they had to change their practices, and they complained that they were being asked to reveal trade secrets.

Still, over the next decades, this empowerment idea grew. In fact, it spread into areas that had traditionally demanded specialized training and education. Now people were drawing up their own wills, even their own divorces, instead of hiring lawyers. They were going on the Internet to look up the illness they'd been diagnosed with and debating courses of treatment with their doctors.

Business caught on, too. Instead of seeing it as people sticking their noses into corporate secrets, executives realized that they could harness this trend. Anything that gave more responsibility to consumers could mean less responsibility—and financial liability—for companies. One of the first places this took hold, in the 1980s, was in the arena of retirement. Out went the traditional defined-benefit pension plans, in which companies promised to pay retired employees a set amount every month no matter how red or black their bottom line. In came 401(k) plans, in which companies had very little financial responsibility and it was up to the employees to save enough, and invest sagely enough, to build their own nest eggs for when they retired. In the late 1990s and early 2000s, some companies even began trying to restructure their health insurance coverage according to the same leave-it-to-the-employee principle. Republicans in Washington wanted to do likewise with Social Security. Workers and taxpayers, these businesses and politicians insisted, wanted to be in control of their own money. It was consumer empowerment.

These new manifestations were of a different order of magnitude than just reading grocery labels, however. Now ordinary laypeople were taking on tasks that seriously and directly impacted their financial well-being. Tasks, moreover, that professionals trained for years to master. In the case of 401(k) plans, health insurance, and Social Security, the consumers weren't always doing it voluntarily. What if a do-it-yourselfer wrote an invalid will? What if a would-be Warren Buffett blew his entire 401(k) in an Internet bubble? These "empowered" consumers could lose all their money. As the tasks they were being empowered for got more serious, it became more and more important for people to also educate themselves about what they were doing. Do-it-yourself books abounded; the newsstands filled with investment guides.

Mass media advertising of prescription drugs—known as direct-to-consumer (DTC) advertising—would fit right into this milieu, and also change it once again.

Historically, under the federal Food, Drug, and Cosmetic Act, consumer pharmaceutical advertising was limited though not illegal. The catch was that if a company wanted to make a claim for all the wonderful things a particular drug did, it also had to include a detailed enumeration of the side effects and other risks. While this requirement was manageable in a print ad, no one could figure out how to cram all that information into a 30-second or 60-second radio or TV spot without speaking faster than the speed of sound. So broadcast commercials tended to be what's known as reminder ads, which could mention a product by name but make no claims. A few were aired, but drug companies mainly focused their marketing on taking doctors out to dinner instead.

Then, on August 12, 1997, drug marketing entered warp drive, when the FDA issued new guidelines that relaxed the rules for broadcast ads. Now, Big Pharma could go straight to the public. Now patients could find out for themselves what drugs were available, without having to rely blindly on doctors. TV and radio commercials could give both the product name and the treatment claims without the endless list of side effects, as long as they also included other, less daunting information, generally known as "fair balance": a much shorter recitation of the major risks, limitations and warnings as to who should not take the drug (in "consumer-friendly language"); a toll-free phone number and web site address for more information; the fact that the drug was available only by prescription and that listeners should contact their doctors; and a reference to the availability of more detailed printed information, most likely through newspaper or magazine ads. Alternatively, companies could run more general "unbranded" or "help-seeking" spots that just talked about diseases and symptoms but mentioned no product names. Or they could do the old reminder ads with brand names but no symptoms. They could also put out corporate advertising about the company itself, without citing brand names. Regardless of the type, the ad couldn't be false or misleading or make claims the FDA hadn't approved.

Given the opportunity, the pharmaceutical industry poured in. Spending on DTC advertising zoomed from $1.1 billion in 1997 to at least $2.5 billion in 2001. Most big drug makers put more than twice as much money into marketing, advertising, and administration as they did into research, according to Families USA's 2000 analysis. (Merck, in that analysis, allocated 6 percent of revenue to R&D and 15 percent to the marketing/administration side.) The groundbreaker, just about everyone agrees, was Schering-Plough's no-holds-barred onslaught for the allergy drug Claritin in 1998. In fact, it's probably fair to say that Schering-Plough's ad dollars bought Claritin's market share. The company paid out a then unprecedented $136 million worldwide, and sales skyrocketed 35 percent to $3.5 billion—not a bad return on investment.

And why not? Shouldn't people be making the decisions about what drugs to put into their own bodies? Were their doctors dictators, to be issuing prescriptions without any discussion?

But the rush of drug advertising took the empowerment trend on two new big leaps. It wasn't just their diets or money that was at stake. Now consumers were taking charge of their most important health problems. And instead of getting serious advice, they were getting TV commercials. In other words, people would be making life-and-death decisions on the basis of 60 seconds of music, atmosphere, and manipulation.

The marketing starts, even before the drug is approved, with the name. This is serious business, which can take three years and cost $100,000 to $150,000 for market research, legal searches, and phonetic testing, among other things.

One school of thought holds that the brand name should have some obvious connection to the drug itself, by evoking its generic name, the ailment it's prescribed for, or the image the company wants to convey. That can make a great parlor game. What do you immediately think of when you hear "Celebrex"? Celebrating, of course. "It's all about being up, being happy"—being glad that Celebrex eases your arthritis and lets you move—points out a marketing executive who worked on that drug. Boyd Clarke, the former head of cardiovascular marketing at Merck, says the name Mevacor was chosen for the company's first cholesterol blockbuster in order to combine the prefix of its original generic name, mevinolin, with the suffix *acor*, connoting something to do with the heart. Or look at Merck's big asthma drug, Singulair. It ends, forcefully, with *air*—great news, you can breathe now!

However, marketers might also take the exact opposite approach, inventing a name with no apparent meaning at all, as Clarke and his colleagues did with Merck's second cholesterol product, Zocor. "You might use syllables. You might randomly generate them from the computer," he explains. The advantage—or disadvantage—is that buyers presumably come to the name fresh, with no preconceived connotations. That doesn't always work, though. Clarke laughs that when his group concocted Zocor, "somebody thought it sounded like a Saturday morning cartoon character."

If the drug is a new formulation of an existing blockbuster, the company may want to tie the name as much as possible to the predecessor. That's obviously what Schering-Plough was trying when it came out with Clarinex just as Claritin was about to lose its patent protection.

There's more. The name has to be different enough from those of all the other drugs out there that patients, doctors, and pharmacists will be able to tell them apart without much trouble. But it can't be too tough to pronounce or spell, and many people say short is better. One reason Clarke liked Zocor was that it was "two syllables, easy to write."

And what's with all those Z's and X's? Yes, sound matters. It depends on the target market: X, Z, T, and K are hard-hitting sounds. L, R, and S are softer, better for drugs aimed at women (Premarin for menopause, Ellence for breast cancer, Evista for osteoporosis—the last two, of course, with their hints of "elle" and "Eve" as well).

When the DTC advertising floodgates opened, it took Big Pharma a while to catch on. Unused to consumer marketing and nervous about offending doctors, the drug makers at first continued using the same health care specialty agencies that had designed their ads for professional journals. Naturally, the agencies came up with professional-style ads: wordy, boring, and (so the Madison Avenue mavens complained) with too much fair balance. Not catchy enough. Not enough like real ads.

As a general rule, marketers say, a good ad is a good ad, whether it's for denims or diuretics. Ellen Hoenig-Carlson, vice president for consumer-patient marketing at Bristol-Myers Squibb's U.S. pharmaceutical group until late 2000 and now an independent marketing consultant, promptly lists the characteristics: "breakthrough, unique, different, communicates the message clearly, it's easy to understand, and, most importantly, has an insight that is meaningful and motivating to people." Accordingly, pharmaceutical companies learned to hire the agencies used by car makers and fast-food joints. Eli Lilly turned to DraftWorldwide of Chicago (owned by The Interpublic Group of Companies), which has also handled Avis, Coke, General Motors, Burger King, and Compaq computers. Schering-Plough, Clairol, Wal-Mart, Mattel, and Kellogg have all shared Source Marketing of Westport, Connecticut.

But drug ads are not like other ads, either. Some differences are obvious. Pharmaceuticals need to accommodate the FDA requirements, which is why many TV commercials are 60 seconds instead of 30. (One ad veteran has timed the typical "fair balance" summation at nine seconds, which takes a hefty slice out of a 30-second spot.) The drug companies try to coordinate their DTC advertising with their more sober pitches to doctors, such as their professional journal ads and brochures. And they can't say anything that would bring down the FDA's hammer. Some early Celebrex spots had to be changed because the FDA objected to the tagline "Do what you want to do." That, said the feds, "overstate(d) the efficacy" of the drug—you can't do *anything* you want if you have arthritis, after all.

The differences go beyond structure, though. It's almost as though the industry has some nagging doubts about whether it should really be doing this.

There's a rough consensus, for instance, that certain types of drugs just shouldn't be advertised. The first DTC spots were for minor conditions that were more of a nuisance than a disease—toenail fungus, migraines, allergies, hair loss, herpes. Although the categories have expanded over the years, most marketing still focuses on lifestyle ailments rather than, say, cancer or AIDS. The most advertised drugs in the NIHCM 2000 survey were for arthritis, ulcers, allergies, depression, cholesterol, obesity, and sexual dysfunction. Even some of the side effects can be reasons to kill or move a commercial. Who wants to hear an announcer mention "diarrhea" following a love scene on TV?

Marketing approaches that are standard for other products give people pause when it comes to something as serious as medicine. Humor? Sex? One big company turned down a spot for an allergy drug that very gently played off the rose-petal fantasies in the R-rated Academy Award-winning movie "American Beauty" and implied that the couple in the ad just might do something R-rated of their own. In the movie, the suburban father envisions bright red rose petals whenever he fantasizes about his teenage daughter's blonde girl friend; in the rejected commercial, a woman arrives home, goes upstairs, finds her husband in bed surrounded by rose petals, and casually notes that he must have taken his allergy medicine.

For other companies, the line in the sand for a long time was celebrity endorsements. There was some haughty sniffing in July 1998 when Joan Lunden, the erstwhile anchor for "Good Morning, America," hit the airwaves talking about her itchy eyes and touting Claritin for Schering-Plough. Within a few years, though, rivals had their own big-name pitchmen. Merck brought out Olympic stars Dorothy Hamill and Bruce Jenner for Vioxx, Baltimore Orioles third baseman Cal Ripken, Jr. for hypertension drug Prinivil, and Atlanta Falcons head coach Dan Reeves for Zocor. Usually these are straightforward ads, but sometimes, and more controversially, some companies' stars have namedropped during what were sup-posed to be news interviews—without revealing that they were being paid for the endorsement.

If a drug isn't Number One or Two in its category, it may not be seen on TV at all. That's because so much of the advertising emphasizes symptoms rather than brand. Say a 55-year-old woman half-hears a commercial about an osteo-porosis drug. She doesn't catch the product's name, but she does notice the description of the disease (loss of bone mass, risk of fractures, and back pain) and the fact that it affects women around her age. She mentions osteoporosis to her doctor. If she doesn't bring up a brand name, the first one the doctor will think of will probably be the top seller. "So the market leader will benefit most," explains Margaret Crowley, a marketing director at Aventis for the osteoporosis drug Actonel, which Aventis comarkets with Procter & Gamble Pharmaceuticals. Hence, Actonel—a distant third in its cate-gory—stopped doing DTC advertising in fall 2000.

The ideal ad, for any kind of product, offers what mar-keters call "the shock of recognition," the ability for the target customer to see himself or herself in the picture. But since the targets of drug ads are customers with serious medical problems, maybe there shouldn't be too much recognition. Photos of infirm people aren't usually a great marketing tool. One way to get around that problem is to go for youthful-looking sufferers. The grandparents in the ads for Celebrex and the anemia drug Procrit seem like they're in their sixties or even fifties, not their seventies or eighties. Pfizer got a lot of positive press for a spot for its cholesterol drug Lipitor that showed two attractive women in bathing suits, sitting at a swimming pool and watching a fortysome-thing man take a belly flop, says Loretta Lurie, an executive at Lowe's Worldwide in Manhattan who has handled some pharmaceutical accounts (not that one). "If I've got high cholesterol and I'm in my forties, I'd rather see that [Lipitor ad] than see a 75-year-old sitting on the porch playing with his grandchildren."

If companies push the feel-good idea too far, however, they risk being reined in by the FDA. That happened to Merck and seven other companies in May 2001 in advertis-ing their AIDS drugs. Merck's "Going the Distance" ad, for instance, showed four men in hiking boots and shorts, prob-ably in their 20s, standing on a cliff and looking as fit as Olympic athletes—this, for a drug whose side effects can include nausea, vomiting, diarrhea, back pain and abdomi-nal pain. The FDA ordered the ads pulled. The people in the ads, it said, were just too healthy-looking.

Merck has poured on the money with the rest of the pack. Vioxx was the most advertised drug in the industry in 2000, to the tune of nearly $161 million, according to the NIHCM (the insurance industry–funded group). That's more than PepsiCo, Inc. spent on Pepsi or Anheuser-Busch, Inc. spent on Budweiser or Nike spent on its best-selling shoes. In total DTC spending, Merck ranked second in 2000 and third for the first half of 2001.

But in terms of the ads themselves, Merck is considered something of a fuddy-duddy—or, as it prefers to see itself, ethical. Certainly, it's been nowhere near as pushy as Pfizer, which *Advertising Age* lauded as "Marketer of the Year" for 2001, or Schering-Plough with its Claritin blitz. It was a little slow in joining the celebrity circuit. It doesn't usually try to test the FDA's limits. Merck got four FDA warning letters between November 1996 and October 2002, according to FDA records (which also include letters about manufacturing problems as well as misleading ads and labels). That's not the best record of the Big Pharmas but it's in the top 40 percent. Gordon Douglas, the Merck vaccine executive, actually pushed his marketing team to be more hard-hitting in its ads for the chickenpox vaccine Varivax, by including statistics on the number of children killed or hospitalized by the disease.

No one could imagine Merck doing what Pfizer did with Viagra in February 2000, when the latter declared its impotence drug "an official sponsor of Valentine's Day." (Since Viagra was supposed to be for medically diagnosed problems of erectile dysfunction, not just to enhance the user's sex life, plugging it so obviously as an aid to romance was considered too crass. Even though it didn't result in an FDA letter, Pfizer later had to back away from that one.)

"There was always tension between marketing and the research folk," recalls Charles Hyman, anti-infective drug specialist who was a director of the domestic regulatory group at Merck. "When the research folk would get uncomfortable with what the marketing folk were saying, you would hear, 'That's not the way we do it at Merck. That's how they do it at'"— he pauses, and the next words come out with the slightest tone of disdain— "'*other* companies.'"

During the marketing for Mevacor, Boyd Clarke says, it wasn't clear how the drug should be labeled for women who might become pregnant. Merck could have chosen among several categories of FDA-approved warning labels. But it went with the most conservative.

Something similar happened in the late 1990s with a package insert for Zocor. New research was showing that both Zocor and Mevacor were more prone to interactions with other drugs, even food and juice, than were rival cholesterol medications, according to Dr. Hyman. "It was dealt with in an ethical way. The approach was, if these are the data, and they are correct, then the information must be provided in the label." But if the research was being made public, did Merck have any choice? Sure, Dr. Hyman says. "You can do things kicking and screaming and dragging your feet, or you can say, 'That is the way we have to do it.'"

Another way to look at Merck's strange mix of cautious marketing and aggressive spending, though, is that it just isn't very good at getting bang for its buck. After all, while Merck certainly likes to think that its salesmanship is the best—that everything about it is the best—the truth is that it was R&D, not marketing, that had made Merck's reputation. It also lost valuable marketing traction by betting on managed care in the mid-1990s and ignoring the sales side.

The arthritis blockbuster Vioxx is a perfect example of Merck's mediocre marketing. Sure, archrival Celebrex had a slight head start, and usually, marketing experts say, the first drug out in a class dominates the category. But Celebrex's head start was less than five months. Vioxx sales just never caught up, even though its DTC spending was more than two times the amount devoted to Celebrex, according to the NIHCM.

Again, Merck spent \$91.2 million on DTC ads for Zocor in 2000, versus just \$58.2 million that Pfizer spent on Lipitor, yet Lipitor led in sales—and this time, Merck had no excuses. It was Merck that had created the whole anticholesterol category in 1987 with Mevacor. But it lost cholesterol. Lipitor blew it away with a lower price and a more potent initial dose. While the higher dose might cause worse side effects, it sure made the drug look more effective in the marketing.

"I didn't like it at all, because there are no advantages" to Lipitor, says Roy Vagelos, who, after all, had done some of the pioneering scientific work on cholesterol that led directly to Mevacor. "It was a smaller pill, good marketing."

Drug marketers have another audience: doctors. A big difference between DTC advertising and all those other "empowerment" trends is that consumers of prescription drugs can never be fully empowered. It's the doctor who has final control over the prescription pad. Therefore, DTC ads have to maneuver a delicate line between manipulating doctors and alienating them.

"In the past, the industry was very cautious. They were very nervous about offending doctors with their ads. Patients would come in and say, 'I saw this ad, maybe I need that product.' There was fear that then the doctor would say, 'I don't want to see that company again.'" recalls Bill McCutchen, the Baruch College management professor in New York City.

Some doctors are indeed annoyed that patients are coming in thinking that after watching three Vioxx commercials, they know as much about arthritis as a physician who's gone through medical school and residency. Then the doctors have to take time—unbillable time, at that—explaining why they prescribe what they prescribe. When the FDA surveyed some 950 people about DTC advertising, in 1999 and again in 2002, fewer than 5 percent said their physicians were "angry" or "upset" when asked about a particular drug; of course, that only measures the doctors who were willing to reveal their negative reaction. Among those MDs who think DTC advertising is a lousy idea, according to close associates, is Roy Vagelos himself.

One New York City pediatrician summarized—anonymously—what a lot of doctors won't admit publicly: "I don't think it's up to the consumer to say, 'I want Zocor instead of Lipitor because I saw it on the Sports Channel.'"

Dr. Donald Motzkin, a urologist in Los Angeles, is more of a realist about DTC. "In general, I don't like it. Patients that have questions about advertised drugs usually will not need an appointment, so it becomes nonbillable time for the doctor. Nevertheless," he concedes, "even though I don't like it, it probably is a good marketing tool for the drug company."

Other doctors actually like the ads (or perhaps they've just gotten used to the barrage, some experts suggest). Anything that gets patients going to their physicians and talking about their conditions is all to the good, as far as they see it. Certainly, there are millions of people out there who ought to be getting medical care, especially for depression and cholesterol, and aren't. "It makes them more participatory in their illness. It makes us work longer, but in the long run it's probably beneficial," says Ward Sisson, the Fresno, California, neurologist. "The patient shows up in the doctor's office and pulls out this little piece of paper and starts reciting symptoms and asking questions. And the doctor tears out his hair. But many of the questions are anything but silly."

That's exactly the way the drug companies like to talk about DTC. "It's clear that people want this information. They act on this information by going to see their physicians. Physicians report that they see patients that they would otherwise not see," Ray Gilmartin told ABC News in a special on the drug industry in the spring of 2002. Patrick Counihan, the vice president in Merck's osteoporosis group, points out that in his specialty area, many of the patients are Baby Boomer women in their fifties—exactly the kind of consumers who've led the empowerment movement. "This is the population who are not shy at all about talking to physicians. Boomers are the best informed about their health."

Anyway, the pharmaceutical companies are hardly ignoring the physicians. Even as they boosted their DTC budgets after 1997, they were spending roughly five times as much sending their sales reps to the doctors' offices with doughnuts, drug samples, and theater tickets. Sometimes they even tried to involve the doctors in designing the marketing. At Bristol-Myers, Hoenig-Carlson says that "we would show the doctors the [DTC] ad before we moved forward. We would make changes if we received consistent feedback that the particular ad's copy or visuals were not communicating what we intended." Later, doctors would get to see the final version of the ad "so that they would be aware of it when a patient called or asked questions."

Leaning forward over a cup of coffee one evening in a Starbucks in Manhattan, the marketer at the major drug company explained how an ad can be structured in order to carry out this whole delicate maneuver. "The doctor doesn't want the patient coming in and saying, 'I want [Drug X] because I saw it on an advertisement on TV.' They react negatively to that. On the other hand, you educate [patients] to know that when they're in with the doctor, they should say, 'Doctor, I'm always so exhausted, I can't get out of bed, I can't make dinner for my family. What can you do for me?' The doctor says, 'I know what you're talking about.' They're aware of the ads. [The drug companies] have been carpet-bombing the airwaves with this stuff.

"If you can get the patient to say, 'I'm having this problem, what can I do?'"—the marketer grinned and raised his arms straight up—"touchdown!"

If the objective of all this advertising is for patients to push their doctor to prescribe a certain drug, the effort has apparently had some success. A survey of 1,222 Americans by *Prevention* magazine in June 2000 found that 32 percent of consumers who saw a DTC ad—that's 54.2 million people—talked with their doctor about the medicine in the commercial. Some 26 percent then asked for a prescription for that medicine. And of those who asked, 71 percent walked away with a prescription. In the FDA surveys, about half said their doctor gave them a prescription that they requested after seeing an ad.

Of course, doctors have all sorts of reasons for selecting any drug, and it may be that they would have chosen the advertised one, anyway. Assuming the competing brands are pretty much the same, probably the biggest consideration is whether the product is covered by the patient's insurance plan. Another is the comfort factor of sticking with a drug they've been using for a while (one reason it's so important to be the first drug out). Doctors have to keep in mind patients' particular sensitivities to any drug's side effects. Convenience comes into play, too. In treating strep throat, the New York City pediatrician points out, "theoretically, the drug of choice is penicillin, which has to be given four times a day. For busy parents, why give penicillin when they can give amoxicillin just two times a day? But amoxicillin is ten times the cost." Some doctors have their quirks; one orthopedist in Arizona says he's more likely to prescribe Vioxx than Celebrex simply because it's shorter to write. And then there's the influence of the sales reps with their dinners and freebies; even cynics say they're not sure which form of manipulation is more influential, the dinners or DTC.

"To some extent, it's what you get comfortable with. Seeing how your patients respond. It's more important that you get comfortable with one or two products than 20 products in one class. But if there's enough of a difference in a new drug—for example, it's once a day instead of three or four times—then physicians are likely to consider such differences," explains Ira Bloomfield, the former Florida emergency room physician.

So if the doctor has always prescribed Zocor, and now a patient shows up after seeing a Lipitor commercial and wants that drug, some doctors claim they can convince the patient to listen to their advice to stay with Zocor. "You'd say, 'this is why I don't think it's right.' Most patients would be fine.

They don't really care if they have Claritin" or whatever drug, says Russell Robbins, the Connecticut urologist. If a patient asks for a medication that's inappropriate, Dr. Sisson of California says, "we have to tell them. It's a matter of, how do we work together? Usually," he chuckles, "they think we know something."

But often enough, the doctors just give in.

All else being equal—and many doctors say that all the drugs in a category usually are—patients who demand a drug they saw in an ad will often get it. They may even get it when things are not equal.

"It does make things difficult for the doctor," says Dr. Bloomfield. "You have people walking in to doctors saying, 'I want Celebrex.' For a lot of people, you could try generic ibuprofen first, it's a lot less expensive. But if doctors think it's medically reasonable, they will often bend to the patient's wishes."

Take another example. Antibiotics are so overused that bacteria are developing more and more resistance. In any case, these drugs do absolutely nothing to help a cold, which is caused by a virus, not bacteria. Nevertheless, "everybody wants an antibiotic when you have a cold, even though we know it's dangerous [because of the overuse]. Have you ever tried to talk someone out of it? They'll go to another doctor," sighs Michael Delman, the head of medical affairs at Southside Hospital in Long Island. (Dr. Delman says that he tries not to succumb to patient pressure but that plenty of others do.)

"Sometimes it's impossible" to change a patient's mind, Dr. Sisson concedes. "It doesn't cost me any more," says the

New York pediatrician, "to write a brand name rather than a generic."

Doctors are worried about losing patients. They're not getting paid extra for the time they spend arguing. They can assume the advertised drug is safe. It's probably not much different from what they would have chosen anyway. "I got a waiting room full of people, I'm supposed to see a patient every seven minutes—you want Vioxx? Here's a script [prescription] for Vioxx," sums up Jerry Avorn, the Harvard professor and specialist in pharmacoepidemiology.

Now that's empowerment: Thanks to advertising, ordinary consumers have managed to influence the decisions of some of the most highly trained, highly paid professionals in the world. But is this empowerment good—for consumers and for society?

As critics see it, DTC advertising has jacked up the nation's health bill by trying to manipulate patients into buying expensive brand-name drugs instead of generics or over-the-counter competitors, or no drug at all. Among the 10 most advertised drugs in the NIHCM study were plenty of 2000 blockbusters—Prilosec for heartburn, Zocor, Claritin, Celebrex, antidepressant Paxil, Vioxx, and Viagra—but not a single generic. The 50 most advertised drugs accounted for nearly one-third of all retail sales in the United States; the other 9,850 prescription drugs shared the remaining two-thirds of the sales dollars.

In 2000, AstraZeneca poured more than $107 million into DTC marketing for Prilosec, at that point the second-highest total for any prescription drug. A year later, with Prilosec's patent expiration looming, the company switched gears and channeled a whopping $478 million to the brand new, next-generation Nexium (while it also pursued its legal strategy to prolong the patent). Schering-Plough did the same sort of flip-flop to push Clarinex just as Claritin was going off patent. The criticism has been particularly heavy regarding the $260 million-plus that Merck, Pharmacia, and Pfizer combined spent marketing Vioxx and Celebrex, because the two drugs don't seem to be any better at relieving pain than much cheaper over-the-counter remedies like Advil or Motrin.

And sometimes there may be no need for medication. "Marketing has created two phenomenons: There is a pill for every malady, and I know what pill I want," says Tracy Lee, who has seen the impact in 31 years of handling employee benefits, working at large companies and at consulting firms. Just as Dr. Delman worries about the overuse of antibiotics, Lee points to antihistamines, which, he says, are "being consumed by people who don't have allergies. You simply have the sniffles. You go to the doctor, you want the sniffles to go away, Claritin or Allegra will solve that. Maybe what you should have done is snort salt water, which is basically free." And never underestimate the power of suggestion: There are undoubtedly viewers who watch an emotional commercial about a grandmother with joint pains, and sure enough, even though they'd never noticed it before, suddenly they're certain they're feeling that very same pain themselves. . . .

Even if every single expensive prescription were really needed—if Vioxx truly had significant advantages over Motrin, or Nexium over Prilosec—there's still the fundamental question about the empowerment trend itself: Should these decisions be made by consumers, on the basis of an advertisement?

Almost nobody (even the grouchiest of doctors) thinks it's bad that people are getting more information about their own health. "There are some conditions, like depression, incontinence, erectile dysfunction, that patients are embarrassed to talk to their doctor about. Or the doctor doesn't know there is a treatment. So there is a benefit to the patient seeing an ad on TV. Otherwise, they just stay at home," muses Dr. Avorn.

By the same token, no one pretends that commercials are thorough, sober, unbiased presentations of anything, let alone complex medical topics. None of the other empowerments—investigating a factory's pollution, or making investment decisions for a 401(k)—is based on advertisements. So how the heck did these two opposites get hooked together?

Of course, Big Pharma's argument is that people aren't making decisions based on commercials; as Ray Gilmartin said, they're supposed to talk over the commercial's message with their doctor. The doctor is still the gatekeeper. But when the talking is all done, the whole point of an ad is to persuade consumers to buy the product—or in this case, for consumers to persuade their doctors to prescribe it.

Here is where some people draw the line on empowerment. "You can make a choice about cars or insurance or a haircut, but when it comes to pharmaceuticals, the amount of information and education and danger far outstrips any other. That's why we have the FDA. In a paternalistic way, we protect people from their own poor choices," warns Paul Reitemeier, the health care ethicist. "It's arguable that the patient is not sufficiently well informed to make that choice."

Dr. Avorn says that if people are going to be taking charge of their own health, "I would rather that happen in the context of medical education or a public service announcement," not an ad. At the least, Frank Williams, the eighty-something scientific director of the American Federation for Aging Research, says the ads should be required to provide more details about their recommended uses and alternative treatments.

It cost Merck and the rest of Big Pharma some $2.5 billion to "empower" their customers in 2001. For that money, the customers got some useful knowledge about their health, some drugs they might not have gotten otherwise, some drugs they probably don't need, and, down the road, higher medical bills. Would those customers have been better off if the $2.5 billion had gone into researching new drugs? Or if the industry hadn't spent the money and had lowered drug prices instead?

7

"It Is Not for the Profits," Part One: Prices and Politics

The cost of health care became a hot public issue in the United States in the early 1990s. It swept an unknown, onetime university president named Harris Wofford into the Senate from Pennsylvania in 1991 and helped elect Bill Clinton president in 1992. Health insurance premiums were shooting up by double digits every year, some 37 million Americans didn't even have insurance, and if things kept on as they were, experts predicted, medical care would devour more than one-fourth of the gross national product by 2030. It was the rare case of an issue that seemed to unite both consumers, who couldn't afford to pay for health care, and business, which ended up being billed extra to pick up the unpaid charges of the uninsured. Some sort of national health care plan was a sure bet.

By the mid-1990s, President Clinton's health care reform plan was dead, scaring members of Congress away from even sniffing at the issue. However, now there was a new villain on the health care block: health maintenance organizations and other managed care bureaucracies. Despairing of assistance from Washington, businesses had turned to managed care, with its tough rules and close monitoring, to rein in their medical costs. Before anything except basic or emergency care would be covered, it would have to be approved by the managed care administrator: Do you really need that MRI? Do you really have to see a specialist? As for medication, the HMOs would keep prices down by covering only the discounted drugs on their formularies.

The system worked for a while: Health care expenditures dropped sharply through 1996. But HMOs, it turned out, were too tough in their requirements. Newspapers were filled with horror stories about people dying because their hard-hearted HMO refused to approve desperately needed treatment. Lousy HMO care was one of the themes of the double Oscar-winning movie "As Good As It Gets" in 1997.

The public fury forced HMOs to ease up on their rules. Moreover, in the booming economy of the 1990s, companies actually embellished their plans, rather than cutting back, in order to keep and attract prized staffers. "When they're competing for employees, our employers are very sensitive. No one really wants to be the outlier," notes Barbara Hawes, a consultant at the consulting firm Towers Perrin.

On the drug front, formularies swelled up with expensive brands as doctors lobbied to add their favorite medications. It wasn't that hard to do: A doctor could just go to the monthly meeting of the HMO's formulary committee, or ask a friend who might be on the committee, since the groups consist mainly of pharmacists and physicians. Even drug company sales reps lobbied the supposedly secret committees. The New York Health Plan Association (the trade group for managed care plans in New York State) estimates that the number of choices on a typical formulary grew 20 percent from 1997 to 2002, although part of that was because the industry was bringing out more drugs.

The problem was that now things were coming back full circle. All these changes made the HMOs more humane and flexible, but at the cost of cost controls. Starting around 1997, spending began picking up again just about as fast as it had dropped, creating a perfect V curve. A decade after President Clinton's election, medical care was a headline political issue again.

This time, the issue was the price of prescription drugs. While all health care costs were growing, drugs were the fastest-rising component. Spending on drugs had been increasing at double-digit rates for four years. By 2003, Americans were shelling out some $170 billion per year on over 3 billion prescriptions.

The good news for patients was that more and more employers had added drug coverage to their medical plans since the last attempt at health care reform. But more than 40 million Americans still had no medical insurance through work or any other way, a number that got worse as people lost jobs in the 2001 recession and some small companies eliminated coverage. And—what really pushed the topic onto the political agenda—about one-third of the elderly lacked coverage for drugs. Medicare, the government health insurance program for the elderly, doesn't usually pay for drugs outside of hospitals, so the only way to get any financial help was from Medicaid (the joint federal-state program for the poor and disabled), postretirement coverage from the companies where they used to work, or expensive private policies. To make matters worse, people over age 65 use more medications than younger people.

President Clinton had failed to bring down health care costs. HMOs had failed. Now it was the drug companies' turn.

Beyond the bloating of managed care, there are other reasons why America spends so much on prescriptions.

Insurance companies and employers blame the structure—even the very existence—of company-sponsored health insurance. It's a classic case, they say, of the free ride: The typical prescription costs around $40 or $45, but people with insurance pay only $5 to $15 for a drug that's on the formulary. Their insurance pays the rest. Therefore, this argument goes, they don't appreciate how much their prescriptions are contributing to the overall rise in medical spending and keep going back to the drugstore without a second thought.

Employers "recognize that we sort of created this by historically allowing employees to have whatever prescriptions they want," Hawes, the Towers Perrin consultant, says. Unlike the case with other medical treatment, "prescriptions are written with no diagnosis required. Physicians are not monitored so much on their prescription use. It's not as though doctors don't get paid" if they write too many prescriptions.

Insurance companies also are at fault for tilting their coverage in favor of drugs over prevention, nutrition, exercise, and other, less expensive alternatives. Under typical guidelines for how long a doctor should spend with a patient, there's enough time to do a quick exam and scribble a prescription, but not enough for a detailed discussion of lifestyle and diet. Insurance policies will generally pay for prescriptions but not for vitamins or health club memberships.

The drug companies happily do their share, too, by drowning the airwaves in ads. The aim, of course, is to persuade consumers to demand the newest brand-name drug for every little ache, when they might get just as much relief from a generic, or even aspirin.

True, part of the rise in spending is actually good news. People are living longer—average longevity increased from 70 years to 78, from 1960 to 2000, according to Columbia University economics professor Frank Lichtenberg—which means more years of drug buying. In addition, there are more medicines to spend money on. Drugs have been developed for diseases that used to have no treatments or very ineffective ones—cholesterol, depression, AIDS, and some forms of cancer. What wouldn't people be willing to pay for a cure for cancer or obesity?

Somewhat compensating for the increase in spending, drugs can actually reduce other health care costs: A $40 prescription is probably a lot cheaper than the alternatives of spending days in the hospital, missing work, and undergoing surgery. PhRMA, the industry's trade group, has pulled together dozens of reports showing, for instance, that antidepressants saved $822 in annual medical costs per person, and that ACE inhibitor drugs for congestive heart failure trimmed hospital costs by $9,000 per person over three years.

More controversially, Professor Lichtenberg argues that newer drugs save more money than older ones, although they also cost more, presumably because they're more effective. Among his studies, he looked at the federal Agency for Healthcare Research and Quality's 1996 medical expenditure panel survey. Using its data on 171,587 prescriptions bought by a nationwide sample of 23,230 people, he broke the numbers down by the patient's medical condition, age and cost of the drug, missed days of work, non-drug medical spending, and other variables. Result: "[P]ersons consuming newer drugs had significantly fewer hospital stays than persons consuming older drugs had." A newer drug costing $18 more than a 15-year-old version would save a patient $56 in hospital costs, Lichtenberg said, and a little less in lost work time.

The drugs-equal-savings equation doesn't always work, however. It's a cynical calculation, but if these not-cheap wonder drugs are keeping people alive longer, the ongoing cost of using them could eventually outweigh the savings from not having surgery or hospital care. And the spanking-new drugs that Professor Lichtenberg touts are more likely than older ones to produce undiscovered side effects or be withdrawn precisely because they haven't been tried by as many people.

Consider drugs like ACE inhibitors or beta-blockers, which can reduce the risk of heart attacks. As Daniel Callahan, cofounder of the Hastings Center—a think tank in the exurbs of New York City, specializing in health care ethics—writes in his new book, *The Research Imperative: What Price Better Health?*[1]

For one thing, those saved from heart attacks will ordinarily remain under medical treatment, at high cost, for the rest of their lives; treatment in the aftermath of heart attacks is expensive and life-long. For another, many of those who have suffered heart attacks will not return to the work force, brought down by chronic heart disease. For still another, by an aggregate mode of accounting . . . the true cost of saving the life of someone from a heart attack must also calculate the costs of whatever other illnesses they [sic] incur over the remainder of their lifetime, which would not have happened if they had died from the attack . . .

And that's the *good* news about rising drug costs.

The American public, for its part, blamed the rising drug bill on drug company greed. Which certainly is a factor. The problem is that people don't really understand how drug pricing works, and thus they focus their fury on the wrong issues—the cost of research, price increases, and Big Pharma's profits.

After the Tufts Center's disputed study on the cost of pharmaceutical research came out in the fall of 2001, for instance, the health care world got all caught up in a debate over how much the industry really spends to develop its drugs. Is it $800 million per drug, as Tufts and the manufacturers claimed, or far less, as consumer groups argued? To some degree, the drug makers encourage the connection between prices and R&D spending by screaming that they won't be able to afford all that wonderful research if generic competitors are allowed to undercut them or if prices are restricted in any way by government regulation.

But in fact, as Princeton economics professor Uwe Reinhardt notes, the price of drugs "has nothing to do with cost of research. It's whatever the drug companies can get. If they have a drug for which there is really no good alternative, that is what they will hit [with high prices]." In other words, just as in any industry, drug makers will charge whatever the market will let them get away with.

Okay then, how about the role of price increases? When drugs are popular enough, of course, the manufacturers boost their prices, just as any company in any industry does. Studies by Families USA show, year after year, prices of the prescription medication most commonly used by the elderly going up faster than the rate of general inflation. One of the drugs with the biggest jumps in the group's 2001 study "Enough To Make You Sick" was Premarin, the hormone replacement therapy sold by Wyeth. Why? It dominated its market and had no generic competition. (That was a year before well-publicized studies raised questions about the therapy's risks.) For that matter, a common ploy by Big Pharma is to get wholesalers to stock up—thus temporarily inflating the drug makers' revenues—by warning of upcoming price hikes. Wholesalers, did exactly that in the summer of 2002, right before Merck kicked Vioxx's price up by 4.5%. Drug makers also tend to spike the prices of blockbusters that are about to go off patent, to take advantage of the last chance they have at monopoly-style control.

Still, price increases (as opposed to the originally high cost with or without any increase) are not the major contributor to the growing tab to fill the American medicine chest. Managed care, for all its disappointments, has managed to keep somewhat of a lid on prices because drug companies have to negotiate discounts if they want to get on government and HMO formularies. According to the NIHCM, actual increases in price accounted for only 22 percent of the total rise in drug spending in 2000 and 37 percent in 2001; the biggest single factor both years was simply a jump in the number of prescriptions. Sean Maguire, director of client development at the consulting firm Watson Wyatt Worldwide, estimates that prices typically go up 5 percent when they do rise, a figure in line with the NIHCM's findings. Sure, that's significantly above the inflation rate of the late 1990s and early 2000s. But annual spending on prescription drugs was shooting up far faster, by 17 to 19 percent over the same period, which means that something else, not price hikes, must have been pulling up the drug spending rate.

To the public, the next step in the chain of greed was obvious: The high prices are the reason Big Pharma is raking in obscene profits. Every year, the drug industry led the rankings among the Fortune 500 in most if not all the categories (return on revenues, return on assets, and return on shareholder's equity). Its double-digit return on revenues—over 18 percent in the 2001 and 2002 charts—was way above the average for all industries. "The industry is by every indicator far higher in profit than any industry in the United States," declares consumer activist Ron Pollack, Families USA's executive director. Or, to put it in Wall Street's more positive terms, pharmaceuticals are a reliable play even in poor economic times. People will always need medicine, and the demographic tilt of the population promises even faster growth as more and more Americans reach the age of arthritis, osteoporosis, Alzheimer's, and other ailments.

If the cause of soaring drug expenditures was so obvious to the public, so was the solution: Big Pharma could well afford to lower its prices. It could take a little cut in profits—how about down to 17 percent? Maybe spend less on advertising those expensive drugs. There are plenty of places where the drug makers could find savings that could be used to keep prices down without having to slice into R&D, as the companies so often threaten. "What the industry would have us believe," Pollack scoffs, "is that if any steps are taken to moderate prices, R&D would go out the window. That the only discretionary resources are R&D resources. That's poppycock." "All we ask is that their profit bear some relation to their actual research, development and manufacturing costs," adds Mark Milano of ACT UP (an acronym for the AIDS Coalition to Unleash Power, perhaps the most militant of the AIDS activist groups.)

Again, the public perception has some basis in truth. No doubt Big Pharma could haul back on its advertising overkill—which is ethically questionable anyway—and trim some administrative fat. After all, Merck managed to shrink its marketing and administration budget by 4 percent in the first nine months of 2002, albeit under tremendous bottom-line pressure, as part of a multiyear efficiency review and work redesign. And certainly some drug companies still show strong numbers. But for the industry as a whole, even as *Fortune*'s 2002 rankings were hitting the stands, 18 percent returns were becoming only a fond memory. Their bottom lines were being eaten away by the loss of patent protection on a number of blockbusters, difficulty in coming up with new drugs, the prospect of a government crackdown on generic game-playing and prices, and, in some cases, regulatory problems. Merck had warned investors to expect flat earnings for 2002 as generics took over the markets for some of its best-sellers and it plowed more resources into R&D; its first- and second-quarter numbers were both down by single digits. Lilly saw earnings drop 20 percent in the second quarter, mainly because of generic competition for Prozac and manufacturing problems. Schering-Plough's second-quarter earnings were flat. Bristol-Myers Squibb was probably the hardest hit: Its second-quarter profit plunged a whopping 63 percent, as three big moneymakers went off patent, its hoped-for deal with ImClone fell through when the FDA turned down the cancer drug Erbitux, and regulators launched an investigation into the incentives it gave wholesalers to overstock its products.

For that matter, some experts argue that the industry's profits have been overstated anyway. Joe DiMasi, the economist who wrote the Tufts Center study on R&D costs, outlines the argument: Say one company makes a $2 profit on $4 of assets, and another makes the same profit on $8 of assets. The first company is going to have a much better rate of return. Well, that $802 million per drug that the industry spends on R&D shouldn't be viewed as spending. It should be treated as an asset, just like plant and equipment, since that's what it really is—brainpower, libraries of compounds, and an investment in the future. It should be part of the $8 denominator. However, "accounting doesn't know how to treat it," so R&D is handled as an expense. Instead of being in the denominator of the profit equation, it's in the numerator—artificially cutting that denominator to $4 from $8 and, therefore, artificially hiking the supposed rate of return. DiMasi says this isn't a common problem for other companies because this kind of issue occurs only in R&D-intensive businesses, and "there probably isn't another large industry that is as R&D-intensive as pharmaceuticals." "As a whole," he claims, "the industry is earning a rate of return pretty close to the normal rate of return [for all industries]. There were not significant excess returns."

To that, Big Pharma—and many sympathizers among doctors, academics and even the public—adds that it deserves something of a premium for the tremendous risks it takes. The millions of dollars down the drain, the 9,999 molecules that are investigated and 4,999 that are tested that never turn into feasible drugs. It's Lesson One in Basics of Investment, risk versus return. "One also wants to do a kind of risk adjustment. The average returns have to be higher, or no one would want to invest," points out Lichtenberg, the Columbia professor.

Still, if the public was focusing on the wrong issues, it had the right villain. Big Pharma did help pump up drug spending by pushing the edges of the profit envelope. It used every trick in the law to delay generic alternatives. It poured on DTC advertising to encourage patients to demand expensive new medicines rather than generics and over-the-counter products, and then buttressed that effort by courting doctors with fancy meals. It harnessed its clout in Congress and state legislatures to try to block measures that would restrain the cost of drugs, give a leg up to cheaper competition, or—most notably—add a prescription drug benefit to Medicare.

"This is an industry with a lot of money to spend. In the past they have used pretty hard-knuckle tactics to get their point across," says David Certner, director of federal affairs for AARP (formerly the American Association of Retired Persons). By most accounts, the industry spends around $75 million a year on lobbying. The consumer group Public Citizen says that the drug industry (which it defines to include generic drug makers, some large biotechs and their trade organizations, as well as big pharmaceutical manufacturers and their trade group PhRMA) spent more in lobbying than any other sector from 1999 to 2001 and had nearly a hundred more registered lobbyists than there are members of Congress. PhRMA was one of *Fortune* magazine's Washington "Power 25" trade lobbyists in May 2001. Nor did it exactly hurt that both the Secretary of Defense and the budget director in the George W. Bush White House were former pharmaceutical executives (Donald Rumsfeld from G.D. Searle and Mitchell E. Daniels, Jr., from Lilly). To be bipartisan, Linda Daschle, wife of Senate Democratic leader Tom Daschle of South Dakota, in 1999 lobbied for a bill to extend Schering-Plough's patent on its blockbuster Claritin.

PhRMA President Holmer bragged at the 2002 annual meeting that the organization had boosted its full-time lobbying staff from 1 to 17, set up 8 regional offices, made common cause with a range of interest groups, influenced the

U.S. free trade agreement with Jordan, and pushed back a measure in Japan that would have lowered prices for popular drugs. (He might have added, as Public Citizen did, that PhRMA also defeated an effort in the United States to reduce the financial incentives drug makers get for testing products on children.) Moreover, individual companies field teams of their own lobbyists, many of them former congressional staffers, and especially influence the delegations from states where they have headquarters or plants.

Within the political realm, Merck is viewed as one of the less aggressive, by and large. It was not among Public Citizen's list of the five biggest contributors of unregulated "soft" dollars and political action committee money from 1997 to 2002. It gained some goodwill by breaking with PhRMA early on two key issues, a Medicare drug benefit and reform of the generics law. In 2000, when Bill Thomas of California, the chairman of the House Ways and Means Committee, first tried to pass a Medicare bill, Merck gave him crucial industry cover. (The effort failed in the Senate, and one lobbyist for the elderly says Merck subsequently cooled down on its support for a while.) If Bristol-Myers has a reputation as the drug company that fights generics most ferociously, and Lilly is known for its strong contacts with the White House, this lobbyist says, Merck's image is fairly benign: It's the one that makes childhood vaccines.

During the heyday of managed care, when it looked as if HMOs would succeed in squeezing drug prices, several big pharmaceutical manufacturers thought they'd found the route to success: buy a pharmacy benefits manager. PBMs are essentially middlemen that administer prescription plans for employers and insurers. As part of their role, they use the combined buying clout of all their clients' workforces to negotiate discounts with drug companies and pharmacies, which means they can influence which drugs get on their clients' formularies. They can even call up a physician who wrote a prescription for an employee and suggest switching to a different brand. (The amount of the discount is one of the big secrets of health care—employers and trade groups representing HMOs both claim they don't know—but one benefits consultant says it usually comes to about 10 percent.) The PBMs are supposed to use this power to get their clients the best deals possible. But a drug company that owned a PBM could negotiate with itself. It could control both the demand side and the supply side.

In 1993 and 1994 Merck, Lilly, and the then SmithKline Beecham all bought PBMs. In addition, Bristol-Myers Squibb had bid against Merck, and Pfizer and Johnson & Johnson at one point considered purchasing benefits managers, too. Yet by 1999, Lilly and SmithKline had sold theirs at a loss, and Bristol-Myers, Johnson & Johnson and Pfizer never got in. Merck alone seemed to be able to make its PBM, Merck-Medco Managed Care, work. By 2001, its market share was nearly 29 percent; by 2002, it handled the prescriptions for 65 million people, or almost one-fourth of all Americans.

Outsiders came up with several theories as to why the Merck-Medco combination survived. Having a mail order capacity—which not all PBMs do—certainly helped, because of the efficiency in handling ongoing orders. Mainly, though, everyone assumed that Medco favored Merck drugs on its formularies. "[Merck] bought a distribution arm for their products," Sean Maguire of Watson Wyatt said admiringly.

As it turned out, there were several cracks in that strategy—legal, ethical, and financial. Buying Medco would ultimately prove to be probably Roy Vagelos's biggest misjudgment as CEO, and not selling it sooner would be one of Ray Gilmartin's.

For starters, the Federal Trade Commission quickly put a stopper to the idea of a drug maker's using a PBM to encourage sales of its own products. Merck insisted that it was complying, and it even set up a highly praised program that encouraged Medco members to use generics. Richard T. Clark, president of the subsidiary, told the Associated Press in 2001 that only 6 percent of the claims Medco handled were for Merck products (though he didn't indicate what percentage of the PBM's total orders Merck didn't make products for). "I don't think Medco aggressively pushed or recommended any Merck products. Half the job was trying to battle clients that were concerned with just that issue," says Sean Brandle, the Segal Company vice president and finance director at Medco from 1997 through 2000—although, he notes, he wasn't directly involved in formulary decisions. Another former Medco manager, who was in a better position to know what was going on, says that "while they were sensitive to Merck products, I don't think the Medco people were shills for Merck products."

The self-justifications weren't very persuasive. By 2002 more than half a dozen PBM clients had filed lawsuits against Merck, alleging that it had entered into prohibited self-dealing transactions under the federal Employee Retirement Income Security Act, and the U.S. attorney for the Eastern District of Pennsylvania was investigating the PBM industry. (In December of that year, Medco agreed to pay a modest $42.5 million to settle five of the ERISA suits without admitting to liability. However, some plaintiffs' lawyers said that wasn't enough.) The attorney general of West Virginia filed suit in November 2002. Moreover, small pharmacies unleashed on Merck and Medco all their fury at the clout of HMOs and mail-order houses. "Their purchase of Medco did a lot of damage. It was obvious they wanted to push their drugs," says Abbey Meyers, president of the National Organization for Rare Disorders, Inc. (a federation of non-profit health groups that tries to get pharmaceutical companies to manufacture medications for limited markets) and normally a fan of Merck's. Suddenly, Merck was no longer the industry's paragon of ethics.

Yet if Medco truly wasn't favoring Merck drugs, what was the advantage in owning it? "The more restrictions that are put on the relationship, that means Medco is no longer as valuable to Merck as it was," points out industry analyst Hemant Shah. Certainly there was little financial gain, since PBM margins—around 3 percent usually—were far thinner than the double digits that Merck was accustomed to on the pharmaceutical side. And within a year of the purchase, the Clinton health care plan had gone under, taking with it the vision of government regulation and a world dominated by managed care that had been the original motivation for purchasing Medco.

"How much more innovation"—say, by buying a biotech or investing in R&D—"could they have gotten for the same amount of money [$6.6 billion] they paid for Medco?" asks analyst Richard Evans.

In the winter of 2002, Merck implicitly confessed that Medco had turned into a liability by announcing that it would spin off the PBM in stages within the year, starting with an initial public offering (IPO) in the summer.

Even then, Roy Vagelos didn't express any regrets (at least publicly) about acquiring Medco. "It was a great move," he said tersely.

Why? "The obvious impact on the marketing of Merck products."

But didn't that marketing tie-in hurt Merck's reputation? "That could be an opinion. It wouldn't be mine."

Other executives who'd been at Merck at the time of the acquisition admitted to some doubts. "We paid a lot of money for it. The question was whether it was worth the price, not just in economic terms, but in everything that went along with Medco—the significant differences in cultures, business time horizons, profit margins, the lawsuits, whether the combination could be effectively managed, etc.," says Simon Benito, who, in addition to his other titles at Merck, also spent three years as executive vice president of the subsidiary. Gilmartin, in his speech at the Merck annual meeting in 2002, said by way of explanation that "it is clear that Merck-Medco is a much different company than it was nine years ago. The environments in which both businesses operate have changed dramatically as well."

However, the bad news wasn't over. The IPO forced Merck to put into the public record some of the hidden workings of the subsidiary. First came the revelation in the official registration statement that, well, yes, Medco did favor Merck drugs and would be obligated to do so for the next five years. "In the past," the filing said, "the market share of Merck products under plans we manage or administer has in the aggregate exceeded the market share of Merck products from sales by Merck to other customers"—that is, Merck's market share had generally been higher among Medco plans than among plans run by other PBMs. Even after the spinoff, "the agreement also requires us to use our best efforts to avoid any practices that restrict or discourage use of Merck products and not take any action to prefer other products, in each case except for clear and objective safety reasons or where those actions would have a clear and objective material adverse economic impact on a plan sponsor." The filing went on to admit: "These provisions, in some respects, impose greater obligations on us than similar agreements we have with other pharmaceutical manufacturers."

Investors had barely digested that distasteful nugget when even more was revealed. *The Wall Street Journal*, analyzing an amended SEC filing, reported in early July that Merck had booked as revenue some $12.4 billion that Medco never actually received. The revenue was the $5 or $10 or $15 copayments that pharmacies collect from patients but don't pass on to Medco.

Merck pointed out that booking the revenue didn't affect its bottom line, because it deducted the same amount as an expense. The company also noted that this tactic was allowed under generally accepted accounting principles (GAAP). And one of its three main rival PBMs used the same system. Even many outsiders didn't see securities fraud, but simply a way to attract clients: The overbooking would make it look as though the PBM handled a larger volume and passed on more of its profits than it really did. Benito, the former Medco executive vice president, explains that the accounting method was used even before Merck bought the PBM; it was consistent with GAAP, and other PBMs did the same thing, "and therefore Merck saw no reason to change it." He also notes that it was only after Medco was acquired and HMOs started demanding higher payments from patients that "the copays were getting so big that it got to be a significant amount."

However, none of those explanations seemed to matter to a public that had been hammered for more than half a year by truly egregious accounting scams at companies like Enron Corp. and WorldCom, Inc. Merck's stock sank over the next couple of weeks; of course, so did the stock of almost every other company, as the markets plunged to lows not seen in four or five years under the combined effects of what seemed like nonstop corporate bad news. Starting even before the accounting revelations, the Medco IPO was put off a week, then another; its asking price range was lowered; then it was postponed with no date set—"solely due to market conditions," Gilmartin claimed in an open letter to shareholders. Finally, the offering was withdrawn. (Merck still promised it would happen by July 2003—"subject to market conditions.") More than a dozen class-action lawsuits were filed within days.

Things calmed down as other companies moved in to take up the bad headlines—questions about manufacturing safety at a Johnson & Johnson plant in Puerto Rico, a bankruptcy filing by WorldCom, the arrest of the former chairman of Adelphia Communications. And an announcement by Merck that it would buy back $10 billion worth of shares helped revive the overall markets. But now the ethical paragon had two stains on its image.

If managed care wasn't keeping prices down—and if some pharmaceutical makers just didn't have much in the way of profits any more to cut into—and if people were not going to stop taking medicines that could save their lives—then some other way would have to be found to rein in the cost of drugs. By the early 2000s, Congress, state officials, consumer groups, and private employers were overflowing with tactics—some carrots, some sticks; some solid, some desperate; and most of them ideas that the drug industry had long fought. The main areas of focus were to provide insurance for the elderly, spur more use of generics, and make employees pay more.

At the same time, Big Pharma had lost some of its ability to block measures it didn't like. Even its 600-plus lobbyists and the Republican takeover of the White House and Congress in the 2000 and 2002 elections couldn't totally overcome the rising public fury at the industry and its high prices. Democrats and unions targeted drug costs as one of their top issues for the 2002 elections—with mixed success. The topic was raised in races as disparate as those for governor in Michigan and New York; the U.S. Senate in Arkansas, Maine, Missouri, New Jersey, North Carolina, and South Dakota; and Congress in Florida, Illinois, Iowa, Maine and Pennsylvania, among others. Andrew Cuomo, running for the Democratic nomination for governor in New York, promised to "fight the drug companies' price-gouging." In Pennsylvania, TV spots urged viewers to "call [Republican Congressman Patrick J.] Toomey. Tell him to stop siding with the drug companies."

That summer, the Senate's lopsided 78-to-21 vote to tighten some of the loopholes in the Hatch-Waxman Act regulating generics was billed as the first major legislative thumb in the industry's eye. The measure, long pushed by Senator Charles Schumer of New York and opposed by most big drug makers—though not Merck—would prevent brand-name companies from trying to extend their monopolies by filing lawsuit after lawsuit against generic drug makers. Instead, the branded companies would be limited to one lawsuit, worth one 30-month extension. So strong was the public pressure that even the Republican White House was forced to announce in October that it would propose similar changes in the FDA's rules.

Not only would the Senate bill give a boost to generics, but it also included another provision hated by the industry, something known as reimportation. That would allow pharmacists and wholesalers to import prescription medicine from Canada, where prices are often far lower because they are regulated. PhRMA claimed that the safety of the Canadian drugs couldn't be guaranteed if they didn't go through the U.S. regulatory process.

Still, faced with this political monsoon, PhRMA smoothly changed course on the most important issue, Medicare drug coverage. Originally, it had opposed the concept for fear that any government drug program would mean government price controls. Now—discovering the wisdom of legislation that might encourage more people to buy more prescription drugs—the lobbying group declared itself in favor of Medicare coverage if private insurance companies ran the show. Proving that the industry hadn't completely lost its political touch, House Republicans in the summer of 2002 passed a Medicare drug bill pretty much along the lines PhRMA had prescribed. In their version, private insurance companies would provide the drug coverage, with government subsidies. Democrats backed a more generous and less radical change that would simply add drugs to Medicare's existing coverage, but with the Republicans grabbing control of Congress in the 2002 elections, odds were that PhRMA would get the version it preferred.

Meanwhile, state legislatures focused on the formulary angle. There were several variations, but the basic idea was to use the government's purchasing clout, through Medicaid, to force drug companies to cut their prices. (The Senate's generics bill would give them added authority to do this.) Among the strongest moves was a Maine law that said that if drug companies refused to negotiate big discounts—which would apply to all residents, not just Medicaid recipients—then their drugs could not be dispensed to Medicaid patients unless they got special approval from the state. In Florida, Michigan, and about a dozen other states, drug manufacturers had to agree to deep discounts in order to get their products on preferred Medicaid lists; Michigan's law applies to other state assistance programs as well as Medicaid. Big Pharma sued to stop most of the legislation, generally on the grounds that it blocked interstate commerce or limited patient choices.

As well, a slew of states took to court and Congress to get generics onto the market faster. Twenty-nine states, for instance, sued Bristol-Myers for delaying the generic version of the cancer drug Taxol. And the National Governors Conference called for congressional hearings on generics. Other state-sponsored lawsuits and investigations looked into the drug makers' wholesale prices and marketing tactics. What was the states' stake? The tens of millions of dollars extra that Medicaid had to pay for brand-name drugs instead of generics or for inflated prices.

In the private sector, employers were also aiming to curtail what they spent on drugs (as well as health care of all sorts). Inevitably, that meant pushing more of the cost onto their workforce. Various surveys showed plan premiums, deductibles, and copayments going up by double digits. For prescriptions, an approach that quickly took fire was a three-tiered payment system, in which workers pay the smallest amount for generic drugs, a middle amount for brand-name drugs that have negotiated a discount to get on their plan's formulary, and the highest amount for brand-name drugs that aren't on the formulary—on the theory that people weren't being hit hard enough in the wallet to change their behavior. Lifestyle drugs like Viagra and second-generation me-too drugs like Nexium might also be in the top tier—if they were allowed at all. "You can get a limited prescription, but if you want a refill you have to produce evidence that you do have the illness," is how Edward A. Kaplan, a vice president at the Segal Company consulting firm, explains some plans' thinking. A few insurers even refused to cover Vioxx and Celebrex, or required doctors to get authorization in order to prescribe them, arguing that over-the-counter pain relievers worked just as well for most people.

Some companies tried what were known as disease management programs, in which a nurse or other professional is supposed to monitor employees' medical treatment, especially preventive care. The idea is that, under an expert's watchful eye, people will remember their medication, go for checkups and tests, keep up with the newest advice, and maybe even exercise and eat right, thus saving money on hospitalization and other expensive treatment down the road. The approach has plenty of critics, however. Some programs are hardly more than a brochure. On the other hand, some are administered by the drug companies themselves and are therefore suspect. ("If you don't have a drug for depression, you're not going to be filled with a passion for creating a disease management program for depression," Maguire, the consultant from Watson Wyatt, noted dryly.) It's also hard to prove whether or not the programs work, or at least, work well enough to justify the cost, which can come to several hundred dollars per employee per year. People switch jobs or don't keep track of their medical care, so companies can't collect reliable year-to-year data. If a company's costs went down one year, was that because of its disease management programs, or because that year their employees just had fewer babies, car accidents, and broken bones?

Employers and their consultants wracked their brains for yet other ways to control drug prices. More than a dozen large companies—including General Motors, Weyerhaeuser, United Parcel Service, and Wal-Mart Stores—joined several labor unions and governors from both parties in a lobbying effort to push Congress to pass the generics reform bill. There was talk of pooling the financial power of big employers, maybe through purchasing cooperatives, or directly negotiating with the drug makers and bypassing the PBMs. As a minimum, many companies set up web sites on which employees could compare various drug and nondrug treatments and costs. One of Tracy Lee's previous employers got so fed up—even its three-tiered approach wasn't doing enough—that it considered simply setting a fee schedule: This is what we'll pay for this or that drug, maybe the median price for each category of drugs—and that's it. In the most extreme case of passing the buck to workers, some companies seriously toyed with the idea of 401(k)-style health coverage: Rather than set up an insurance plan, they would just give employees a specific amount of money to cover medical costs, after which the employee would be entirely on the hook for the next several hundred or thousand dollars' worth.

And consumers took matters into their own hands. If it still wasn't legal for pharmacists to reimport drugs from other countries, reimportation for personal use was allowed. So Americans headed to Canada and Mexico by the busload or bought their drugs from Canadian pharmacies over the Internet. When Long Island computer engineer Paul Kaplan went to San Diego on business, he'd walk across the border to a drugstore in Tijuana, pick up some antibiotics like amoxicillin and Pfizer's Zithromax, get the generic version of Prilosec for his mother-in-law at less than one-fourth the U.S. price, and then walk back across the border with a few packets in his pockets—no prescription needed.

For their part, hoping to head off regulation, drug makers hurriedly trotted out discount programs for the poor, elderly, and disabled. Within months of each other, GlaxoSmithKline, Lilly, Novartis, and Pfizer all produced plans that would let people who met certain income, age or disability criteria—and who weren't covered by insurance—buy some their drugs at a reduced price. Then seven companies announced a joint discount-card program, covering more than a hundred of their various medications. The Bush White House proposed a similar multicompany discount card. Merck said it didn't need to put out any new card, because it had had a program of giving free medicine to low-income people since 1952. But it would try to publicize the program better and make it easier for people to get the medications without going through a doctor. Consumer activists countered that discounts or even free drugs were hardly a complete solution. They were limited to only the very poorest, some of the discount cards charged a fee, and the discounts still could leave the drugs with high price tags.

A handful of manufacturers, faced with the loss of patent exclusivity, moved to sell their once-prized blockbusters—including Claritin and Prilosec—over-the-counter, without a prescription. Partly these were complex marketing ploys having to do with fending off generics or outmaneuvering rival brand names that had already gone OTC. But the manufacturers also figured that if they couldn't get a full dollar for a drug as a brand-name prescription, it was better to pick up a nickel on an OTC sale than lose everything to a generic. This, too, could help lower public spending to some degree, since OTC drugs are less expensive than generics or brand names. However, there weren't enough drugs at the blockbuster-to-OTC status to make much of a dent overall.

Ultimately, the drug makers' tried-and-true defense is to change the topic. They take the high moral ground. When critics talk about profits, they talk about the risks entailed in coming up with a breakthrough drug. When critics talk about prices, they talk about saving lives. When critics talk about generics and patents, they talk about protecting the fruits of their labor while they seek a cure for cancer.

Many consumer advocates and politicians, after years of fighting hardball against Big Pharma's high prices and political clout, scoff at the highfalutin terms. "Do the drug companies do anything valuable? Of course they do," shrugs Jim Love, the ardent consumer activist who heads the Naderite Consumer Project on Technology. "But at the end of the day, it's an argument about price."

"It Is Not for the Profits," Part Two: The AIDS Debacle

If you wanted to write a melodrama with a scowling, mustache-twirling villain, you couldn't come up with a better plot than the drug companies and the AIDS epidemic in the developing world in the 1990s. First the companies priced their drugs for AIDS and HIV (the human immuno-deficiency virus that causes AIDS) in the poorest parts of Africa as if they were in suburban Connecticut. They sued South Africa when it wanted to let in cheaper generic copies from India. They went to the U.S. government to block countries like Thailand and Brazil from manufacturing generics. When they finally announced discounts, the prices were still way above what the locals could afford. It was even worse than the controversy over drug prices in the United States. The melodrama wrote itself—and Merck was right in there with the rest: Millions of poor people die because they can't afford medicine.

"The HIV story is not a pleasant one," Roy Vagelos says in a clipped voice that leaves the distinct impression that he's holding in an even harsher rebuke. "Not coming up with a [discount or donation] program earlier was very damaging to their reputation."

What's so sadly ironic is that the AIDS saga didn't start that way. In fact, in the first chapters, during Vagelos's era as CEO and for a few years beyond that, Merck was a true hero.

AIDS is a particularly complex target for scientists who work on drug development. HIV stays latent for years, and then mutates readily. It causes not just one infection or one type of cancer in one organ, but multiple illnesses and infections in multiple organs. And it attacks the body's main natural weapon against disease, its own immune system.

As of the late 1980s, less than a decade after the initial AIDS cases were diagnosed in the United States, there were several drugs on the market. However, they usually had serious side effects, like nausea and abdominal pain, and resistance to any single treatment developed quickly. The number of victims kept climbing. At the turn of the twenty-first century, nearly a million people in the United States and 36 million worldwide were infected.

At least a dozen pharmaceutical companies, including Merck, were plugging away looking for better approaches to the disease in the 1980s and 1990s. Many of them had homed in on the protease enzyme, which plays a key role in

allowing HIV to replicate. If they could block (or, in pharmaceutical jargon, inhibit) the enzyme, they might be able
to slow down the rate at which the virus tore through the
body. Although Ed Scolnick, then Merck's head of research,
wasn't all that keen about the effort, according to some
well-placed sources, Vagelos pushed hard. "There was an
absolute need for it," says Al Alberts, Vagelos's longtime
research colleague. "There was also," he admits, "definitely
public pressure." By December 1988, Merck was on the
verge of publishing the secret of the protease structure.

Then the leader of that project, Irving Sigal, was killed on
the Pan Am flight that exploded over Lockerbie, Scotland.
Another clutch of scientists bolted to form their own
biotech, which they named Vertex Pharmaceuticals.

Merck still managed to publish the protease structure
ahead of any rival, but more problems piled up. Its first
attempt at a protease inhibitor proved toxic in animal tests.
It switched to a different approach for blocking HIV repli-
cation, and that fell through, too. Finally, it went back to the
protease inhibitor approach, making changes to eliminate
the toxicity, and this time things seemed to go better. However, the new compound (which would later be named
Crixivan) was so complex, involving a 16-step production
process, that Merck was constantly scrambling to come up
with enough samples for research. Even worse, during Phase
II trials in 1994, every single patient showed signs of developing resistance. Every patient except Number 142.

If a drug works for only one person, maybe it's mistake in
the data or some unusual immune response in the patient.

For Merck, though, it was a reason to keep trying. "There was no way that patient could have been a fluke," Dr. Scolnick (whose enthusiasm for the project had grown) later told *The Wall Street Journal.*[1]

"Because of that one person, they did not drop Crixivan. That made all the difference, because they didn't drop the drug," says Mark Milano, the ACT UP activist—and not one usually given to praising Big Pharma.

Boring into the trial data, Merck's researchers decided to try raising the dose and using the drug in combination with other AIDS drugs already available. As it turned out, that was the secret, to have a three-part mix of Crixivan and the drugs AZT and 3TC, what would become known as an AIDS "cocktail." The virus level in the blood of patients on a cocktail regime was reduced by 98 percent. "The paradigm changed as a result of this approach," says Charles Hyman, the anti-infective drug specialist. "It changed HIV from being a rapidly fatal disease to one that's chronic and manageable."

Others were hot on the trail, too. By early 1995, Abbott Laboratories and Roche were close to seeking FDA approval for their own protease inhibitors. Sold as Norvir and Invirase, respectively, they would ultimately beat Crixivan to market by a few weeks (Norvir) and months (Invirase) in 1995 and 1996. But with people dying, AIDS activists didn't want to wait for the FDA to rule. They wanted Abbott and Merck to make their drugs available early, even while clinical trials were still going on, under what's called an expanded access or compassionate use program. That means giving it to patients who've already tried everything else—who have nothing to lose. And the activists knew how to get attention. From meetings with government officials to newspaper headlines, the pressure built on the drug companies.

Merck had plenty of reasons to balk. Not only was it still testing Crixivan, but it didn't think it even had the capacity to make enough for all the extra users in an expanded access program. It was already rushing like mad to build factories in Virginia and Georgia. Production was so squeezed that the company talked about operating on Crixivan—that is, speeded-up—time. Famously, when a storm buried the unfinished Virginia plant under four feet of snow, staffers showed up with shovels to dig it out.

But the pressure succeeded. As the company's official history of Crixivan describes those days, "It was difficult, indeed, not to be affected by demands that Merck assist patients in the United States and other countries who . . . faced imminent death."[2] In the summer of 1995, nine months before getting final FDA approval, Merck agreed to provide Crixivan on an expanded access basis to 1,400 people in the United States and 750 in other countries.

"Merck was more responsive [than Abbott]. Merck agreed to do a program, and it wasn't at the last minute, it was enough in advance so there was some advantage," recalls Jules Levin, a leader of the expanded access effort; and the founder and executive director of a New York City group called the National AIDS Treatment Advocacy Project, which aims to educate people about AIDS and hepatitis.

Skeleton-thin, with hollow cheeks, close-cropped silver hair, and incongruously broad shoulders, Levin contracted HIV and hepatitis in the mid-1980s. Crixivan didn't work for him. But the expanded access program did help three friends of his. "It saved their lives," he says matter-of-factly.

"Every now and then," he adds, even six years after the program ended, "I run into people who don't know about my role, who say, 'I wouldn't be alive today if it weren't for that Crixivan expanded access project.'"

The expanded access program wasn't the only reason Merck earned so much good will in the AIDS community. Its pricing was also key. With three protease inhibitors finally on the market by spring of 1996, Crixivan was considered the best, more powerful than Invirase and with fewer side effects than Norvir. By rights, the best drug might be expected to carry a higher markup. But Merck priced Crixivan some $2,000 a year *lower* than the less effective competitors.

Merck was also viewed as more respectful of AIDS activists than other companies. During the long years of research, Merck had taken some unusual moves to open its laboratory doors—moves that were particularly startling for a company usually so secretive about its R&D. Vagelos and Dr. Scolnick set up a forum where scientists from competing firms could share ongoing results. Company officials met regularly, too, with a select group of AIDS activists—"people who cared about Merck, people who cared about our research, who cared about our drugs," as spokesman John Doorley put it in the official history[3]—and told them more about its research and trials than it had ever released to the public. Jules Levin gives Merck credit for agreeing to his request in 1995 to let outside consultants evaluate whether it really was churning out Crixivan as fast as it could. (He doesn't, however, actually accept the consultants' findings, which sided with the company.) All those factors outweighed the complaints Merck generated in the early days of Crixivan, when it said it would limit the drug's distribution temporarily until it could get production cranked up.

In large part, the drug maker admits that it cooperated so much because it was worried about how people would view it if it didn't. The AIDS activists—educated, angry, often deathly ill—were a far cry from the professional lobbyists the industry was used to. "They had already made life miserable for Burroughs Wellcome over the design of its clinical trials and the price it charged for AZT," the history of Crixivan notes,[4] with unusual candor. In turn, the activists targeted Merck partly because they knew it cared about its image.

Of course, when talking about AIDS activism, things like goodwill and image have to be measured by a special set of yardsticks. For instance, Mark Milano says that part of ACT UP's routine at major AIDS conferences is to march through the display area, stop at drug company booths, chant "Shame" for their high prices, throw their promotional material on the floor, and paste stickers all around. That takes half an hour per booth. Then the protestors leave, and the drug companies spend another half-hour cleaning up. Naturally, at the 1996 International AIDS Conference, held in Vancouver, "we stopped at Merck's booth and accused them of price-gouging. But we didn't trash their booth," Milano points out.

Over the next two years, second-generation protease inhibitors started to hit the market, and Crixivan lost its allure. Where Crixivan needed to be taken three times a day and with two other drugs to make an effective cocktail, the newer products could be taken only once or twice a day, or with just one other drug. Merck itself, in its joint venture with DuPont, came out with a once-a-day drug that DuPont (and later Bristol-Myers Squibb, which bought out DuPont Pharmaceuticals) would ultimately sell in the major markets as Sustiva and Merck would sell elsewhere as Stocrin. On top of the tougher competition, Crixivan faced a problem that can hit any drug that's been around for a while: People started to develop resistance to it.

But Merck had some other products brewing. It was working on a new variety of drug, an integrase inhibitor, which was supposed to attack an enzyme called integrase that HIV needs to replicate itself. A handful of pharmaceutical companies, including Bristol-Myers Squibb, Pfizer, Roche in collaberation with North Carlina biotech Trimeris, Schering-Plough, and GlaxoSmithKline in a joint venture with the Japanese company Shionogi & Co., were also researching integrase inhibitors or other approaches that they hoped would stop HIV earlier in its tracks than the protease inhibitor class. About half were further ahead than Merck, and half not quite as far; Roche and Trimeris looked to be the first out the gate.

Merck was also trying something else: a vaccine. "From the beginning, people realized that an AIDS vaccine was going to be different" from other vaccines, recalls Gordon Douglas, who was in charge of Merck's vaccine division during part of the AIDS work. In theory, a standard vaccine is better than drugs because it prevents a person from being infected to begin with. That wouldn't work with AIDS, however. "What a vaccine does is mimic natural immunity," Dr. Douglas explains. "There's no evidence of natural immunity [with AIDS]. If you get measles, you don't get it again. If you get AIDS, you die." Similarly, the standard method of vaccination—injecting a person with a weakened or killed form of the virus, in order to stimulate the body to produce antibodies—wouldn't work for something as lethal as AIDS. Who would volunteer to be injected with HIV, no matter how weakened?

There was an alternative: recombinant DNA technology. Instead of being injected with a form of the virus, a person could be injected with the DNA that codes for the virus. For its first attempt at a recombinant DNA vaccine, Merck had been considering using influenza. But Dr. Douglas says he argued that HIV was a better target—and the need more critical.

Merck had initially launched its vaccine work at around the same time it was unraveling the secrets of the protease enzyme, setting up a consortium with researchers at Duke and Harvard plus two biotech companies. On Merck's side, the vaccine work was run by Dr. Emilio A. Emini, the head of vaccine research. For a while, a vaccine had even looked like the more promising strategy. However, it foundered against the complexity of the virus; Merck was trying to target a surface area of the virus, but there were too many varieties to protect against. So Merck shut down the vaccine research, while the protease inhibitor roared ahead. Dr. Emini switched to protease.

Then in 1997, once Crixivan was on the market, Dr. Emini switched back to the vaccine side, to try again. By 2000, his vaccine team had concluded that a disease as powerful and complex as AIDS needs a double-barreled approach. Patients would first be inoculated with AIDS DNA to stimulate the release of a kind of white blood cell known as killer T-cells, which seek out and destroy cells already infected by HIV. Then they'd get a second shot, this one of an HIV gene attached to a genetically modified cold virus.

Plenty of other researchers were also looking into vaccines, including Aventis, Wyeth, Glaxo, and a small company in Brisbane, California, called VaxGen. So were scientists at Harvard, Yale, Emory, the National Institutes of Health, the National Institute of Allergy and Infectious Diseases, the Institute of Human Virology, and the Aaron Diamond AIDS Research Center in New York.

Merck was the first to get to human trials, however. A wave of hope greeted Dr. Emini's report early in 2001 that monkeys inoculated with the virus and then infected with a particularly virulent strain of HIV had not gotten sick. A year later came the preliminary results from human trials and more good news: The trial subjects were showing a strong immune response.

Even the two-inoculation strategy still would not prevent a patient from being infected. What Merck was aiming for was what is known as a partial protection vaccine that keeps the virus in check once it's inside the body. This is somewhat controversial; there's the risk that people, thinking that vaccination means they're immune, will let down their guard and have unsafe sex. It's also not clear whether a vaccine could work against more than one strain of HIV if a person should get a multiple infection. So AIDS activists greeted the effort with mixed responses. But it was the best anyone could do at the moment.

In light of all their experience fending off critics of their access and prices in the United States, the mystery is why Merck and the other companies stumbled so badly in Africa and Brazil.

More than 25 million people in sub-Saharan Africa were infected with HIV by the early 2000s, with the worst impact hitting South Africa, Botswana, Swaziland and Zimbabwe. Some 5 million people developed new cases every year and 2.3 million died. For a long time, the pharmaceutical makers just didn't pay attention. They were focused on the home market, which was more lucrative and in which AIDS had been diagnosed earlier. Still, by 1998, if not before, the problem was clear, and the United Nations had even announced a pilot program, at that year's International AIDS Conference in Geneva, to provide HIV drugs to developing nations at a discount. Here was the manufacturers' perfect chance.

And they blew it.

In a region where the average annual income per person might not even hit $400, and with a year's supply of AIDS drugs selling for $10,000, Merck and other companies insisted that price wasn't the problem. Rather, they said, the focus should be on infrastructure and prevention. People needed trained medical personnel to administer the complex cocktails, and public health education to make sure they understood how to take their drugs. Merck then gave a stingy $3 million to Harvard to come up with ways of providing this infrastructure, starting by sending teams of experts to study AIDS care in Senegal and Brazil. Beyond that, the official line at Merck was that "Merck's most important contribution in the battle against HIV/AIDS worldwide is continued research toward the discovery and development of innovative HIV antiviral drugs and a safe and effective HIV vaccine." This time, at the 1998 AIDS conference, activists did trash Merck's booths.

Merck and the others did have a valid point: Without a solid health care system behind them, patients might not follow through on medication they started, which could lead to more resistant forms of the virus. Certainly, too, there needed to be more effort on the prevention side, at least to educate people about how AIDS spreads. It would be hard to ensure any of this while too many governments, particularly South Africa's, were pretending the problem didn't exist or denouncing standard HIV treatments as a Western trick. However, the countries still needed drugs they could afford.

Some companies caught on faster, but amazingly, it took Merck and others nearly two years to officially change their approach—while their public image (along with the population of sub-Saharan Africa) was being devastated. By May 2000, the new United Nations program, known as UNAIDS, had finally persuaded five big pharmaceutical makers—Merck, Glaxo, Bristol-Myers, Roche, and a German company, Boehringer Ingelheim, later joined by Abbott Labs—to cooperate in its Accelerating Access initiative to make HIV and AIDS medications available to low- and middle-income countries. The governments would buy the drugs at a discount and then distribute them for free to patients. One key factor in persuading the companies, Merck officials said, was a statement by Gro Harlem Brundtland, director-general of the World Health Organization, that the program must include agreements honoring the drugs' patents. The *Asian Wall Street Journal* quoted Per Wold-Olsen, head of Merck's Europe, Middle East, and Africa operations, as saying, "She [Brundtland] deserves tremendous credit. She's been severely criticized by her own people and governments in the developing world for her willingness to partner with industry."[5] So prices were slashed 80 to 90 percent, to around $1,000 a year. At last, something was getting done.

It was still not enough. The discounts had to be negotiated in private, company by company and country by country. Moreover, the pharmaceutical makers loaded the deals up with conditions. Some wanted assurances from the purchaser governments that they had the infrastructure to get the medicine to the patients. Some wanted the U.N. to be in charge. Some wanted reports on the training of staffers who administered the drugs. Some restricted the deals to Africa.

With all the red tape, only a handful of countries had managed to reach pricing agreements after nearly a year. Activists continued to barrage the industry with criticism. Brazil threatened to make its own generic copies. The 2000 meeting of the International AIDS Conference, held in Durban, South Africa, that summer, brought the suffering right to the noses of the industry (and, even more important, the press). Pharmaceutical executives could hardly move without hitting a rally at city hall, a protest march, a display of quilts commemorating people who'd died of AIDS, a speech by an HIV-infected South Africa High Court judge.

Merck succumbed fastest. In March of 2001, it announced even deeper price cuts, to a level where it said it wouldn't make a profit—$600 a year for Crixivan and $500 for Stocrin. The discounts were available to any country that the U.N. rated "low" in human development as long as the drugs would not be reexported. ("Medium"-rated countries might be granted smaller discounts.) And Merck made the deals public. Within three months, Abbott, Bristol-Myers, and Glaxo had followed with similar price cuts. Finally, it seemed, Big Pharma had gotten the message.

There were other signs of cooperation, too. The previous summer, acting on the industry's argument that infrastructure had to be fixed first, Merck had launched a sweeping five-year AIDS program in Botswana with the Bill & Melinda Gates Foundation (the eponymous charitable organization of the Microsoft Corporation founder and his wife; Merck CEO Gilmartin is on the Microsoft board). Merck and the Gates Foundation each contributed $50 million, and Merck also donated AIDS drugs, to help train health care workers, keep track of medicines, establish counseling programs and community-based support networks, improve testing labs, set up information and referral centers, and distribute condoms. Botswana was chosen for a combination of reasons, including a serious AIDS epidemic, relatively high per capita income, and political stability. The ambitious aim was to offer treatment to all of the country's 300,000 infected citizens—the first sub-Saharan nation to do so.

Yet somehow, the industry still couldn't keep its foot out of its mouth. Even as it was announcing its second round of price cuts, Merck was joining 38 other pharmaceutical companies in a courtroom in Cape Town for a trial aimed at blocking South Africa from importing or manufacturing generic copies of their AIDS drugs. The companies were challenging a 1997 law that allowed the government to waive patent protection in matters of public health. It wasn't just theoretical: At least two companies in India were offering generics at prices even lower than Big Pharma's new discounts.

The public anger at this court case threatened to wipe out any goodwill the drug companies had earned from their discounts. Even the U.S. government had dropped its objection to South Africa's law. AIDS activists mounted protests, and shareholder groups filed resolutions against the lawsuit. In a painful reversal of George W. Merck's old maxim about medicine being for the people and not the profits, the revered antiapartheid leader Nelson Mandela accused the drug makers of putting profits before people's lives. Six weeks later, they finally dropped the suit.

Seven months after that, the industry lost again, this time in a fight over World Trade Organization rules allowing poor countries to make and acquire generic versions of expensive brand-name drugs if they determine there's a public health emergency.

How could an industry known for its political prowess in the United States be so politically tone-deaf on AIDS?

It wasn't simple greed. In terms of profits, the countries in question were washouts. There was never going to be any money to be made, whether the drugs were priced at $600 or $6,000. At $600, maybe the manufacturers broke even; at $6,000, they had no customers. And producing an extra batch of pills, when they were already making them for the United States market, cost just pennies.

For the drug companies, however, there were broader issues at stake, issues of precedents and intellectual property. They worried about cheap drugs slipping out of government control in Africa and snaking their way back to the West via the unofficial gray market, undercutting the prices in higher-income nations. Considering the weak governments in some of the hardest-hit countries, that was hardly a silly concern. In fact, in October 2002 European officials announced that they'd intercepted a bootleg shipment of Glaxo's AIDS drugs from Africa. The drug makers also worried that Americans with AIDS would demand the same deep discounts as those in the developing world, which, in fact, some activists did (but others didn't). Most important, they were terrified of any crack in the fortress of patent protection. If they let Brazil or South Africa ignore a patent and sell copycats, would the United States be next? Their fears were only intensified during the anthrax scare in the autumn of 2001, when Canada declared that it was overriding Bayer's patent on the antibiotic Cipro and buying 1 million tablets of the generic version from another manufacturer. Sure, this was an emergency, what with all those letters containing anthrax or threats of anthrax, and Cipro was considered the most effective antianthrax treatment. But what was AIDS, if not an emergency, too?

In this sorry story, Merck comes out marginally better than most.

Although it was slow in joining the United Nation's AIDS initiative, it was the first to announce a second round of discounts, in the spring of 2001, and it reportedly was ready to drop the lawsuit against South Africa before most of its fellow drug makers. Furthermore, in October 2002 it announced another price cut, for a reformulated version of Stocrin. It also gets credit for the Botswana arrangement. According to Julian Fleet, a senior policy advisor in Geneva for UNAIDS, Merck gives its discounts to a slightly wider list of eligible countries than do most other companies. "They even had a [middle-class] country like Romania in there," Fleet notes. He likes to include middle-class countries because they have the infrastructure in place to efficiently get drugs to those who need them.

"The good thing about Merck's program is that it's very transparent. It's clear what discounts they're offering and in what areas," adds Daniel Berman, a coordinator of Doctors Without Borders' special campaign to give developing countries access to essential medicines. Transparency in discounts is significant, because it can be a step toward a public database that would list all drug prices and discounts—a priority of many humanitarian groups, but opposed in general by Big Pharma. Fleet, too, calls Merck unusually "flexible" about harmonizing its list with those of other companies, another small step toward transparency. Berman also says his organization runs into comparatively little hassle when it wants to buy a batch of Merck drugs. In general, he considers Merck's program to be more solid and less of a PR play than those of companies like Bristol-Myers and Pfizer.

On the other hand, Merck's discount is stingier than others', including Bristol-Myers. And when it comes to lobbying Washington or pressuring Brazil and South Africa to keep out generics, Merck doesn't exactly turn into Robin Hood. "Merck pulls its weight" in the Big Pharma versus consumer battles, insists Jim Love of the Consumer Project on Technology. "You may think they're good guys because they price something for 50 dollars [a month]. But India could have made a *triple* therapy for 30."

However much Merck and the others have or haven't done for AIDS, they are still not off the hook. And if they do manage to wiggle off, there are a half-dozen other hooks ready to catch them.

Some activists, such as Doctors Without Borders, are convinced that more discounts can be squeezed out of the drug makers. After all, they already lowered their prices twice under pressure. If one Indian company was claiming it could sell generic versions for $350 or $400, what was so great about a supposedly discounted price of $600?

Many groups don't like discounts, however, because that puts prices too much at the mercy of the pharmaceutical companies and often involves a heavy load of bureaucracy. A better solution, they say, would be for Big Pharma to stop fighting the generic drug makers. Give them free rein to come in with their lower-cost versions, and let the market duke it out. Yet another approach, favored by some Europeans, is a bidding process similar to the one often used for vaccines and contraceptives.

No matter how low the price, it will still probably be above the means of most of the target countries. So then the drug makers, along with Western governments, international organizations, and charities, are expected to pony up for a new U.N.-backed fund that would issue grants to middle- and low-income countries to buy drugs to treat AIDS and other epidemics. U.N. Secretary General Kofi Annan has said he hopes to raise $10 billion every year.

Once the discounting started overseas, there was pressure, as well, to cut prices in the United States. Not to the levels of Africa, of course. But the same issues that advocacy groups were using in trying to get Medicare drug coverage for the elderly—how the industry stymies generics, its fat profits—could also work for AIDS. This time, it was Pfizer and GlaxoSmithKline that cracked first, in the spring of 2002, temporarily freezing the prices of their AIDS drugs in the United States for two and four years, respectively.

If a low price is good, shouldn't a zero price be even better? Several companies offered outright donations. Pfizer announced in April 2000 that it would donate its antifungal medication Diflucan to South Africa for two years. Fourteen months later, it one-upped itself and promised to provide 50 of the poorest nations in the world an unlimited, free supply. (Diflucan treats two ailments that commonly afflict AIDS patients, a deadly form of meningitis and the severe fungal inflammation called thrush.) But activists actually don't want donations. They argue that there's no such thing as a free drug—that freebies tend to involve extra red tape or restrictions, such as being available only at government clinics. Because they're special deals, moreover, they can't be used to establish a pricing trend. And activists question how long a company will keep up such an expensive commitment. One exception is Boehringer's five-year program, launched in July 2000, to donate Nevirapine, which is used to block HIV transmission from an infected mother to her child. This arrangement works, activists say, because it's time-limited and the drug requires only a couple of treatments.

Beyond prices, the old problem of infrastructure remains, as the drug makers had always pointed out. "We haven't scratched the surface yet," Fleet of UNAIDS says. "We need to find a new way of doing business to scale up the access. A comprehensive approach requiring expansion of voluntary testing and counseling, and psychological support."

For that matter, AIDS is hardly the only epidemic rampaging through the developing world. Over a million people die each year from malaria. Half a million people are afflicted with sleeping sickness, and tens of millions more are threatened. Tuberculosis kills 2 million people each year throughout the world. Yet little effort goes into finding cures for these so-called neglected diseases. Of 1,233 new drugs marketed from 1975 to 1999, only 13 were specifically for tropical diseases, which primarily affect the poor, according to a report by the World Health Organization—and six of those came from WHO's own research, not from pharmaceutical companies. By comparison, in that same 25-year period, there were 179 new products for cardiovascular diseases. There hasn't been a new drug for TB since the 1960s.

It's no secret why AIDS gets attention and the neglected diseases don't: It's the only one that also affects a large number of people in the United States with the money and health insurance to pay for prescriptions and the political clout to influence government and pharmaceutical officials. Now, is Big Pharma supposed to be working on those other diseases when it is unlikely to make any money?

Groups with a broad interest in health care, like Doctors Without Borders, want to push the drug makers on all fronts. They suggest that governments could make patent extensions for other, more profitable drugs dependent on companies' doing research on medications for neglected diseases, or the governments could just mandate that a certain percentage of pharmaceutical sales be invested in R&D. If it wasn't financially worthwhile to develop a drug for these epidemics, the companies could pass on to a nonprofit group any promising compounds they discovered. Big Pharma might even find that the PR value was worth any lost revenue. "Can you imagine the mileage they could get out of a new malaria drug?" muses Berman of Doctors Without Borders.

There has been, in fact, some movement beyond AIDS, though it mostly involves providing free or discounted medication and treatment, rather than researching new cures. Periodically, Merck and other pharmaceutical makers donate vaccines for children in developing countries. Roy Vagelos is particularly proud of how Merck in 1993 built two plants in China to make vaccines for Hepatitis B, in what is probably the largest vaccine program in the world. The $10 billion-a-year U.N.-backed fund that's supposed to give impoverished countries grants to buy AIDS drugs is actually called the Global Fund to Fight AIDS, Tuberculosis and Malaria. The World Economic Forum, similarly, has a Global Health Initiative that hopes to encourage private-sector investment in the developing world in order to combat malaria and TB, as well as AIDS. And the World Health Organization in July 2002 announced a joint HIV-TB campaign.

On the research side, Gilmartin and two other Merck executives met with Doctors Without Borders experts in September 2001 to discuss the question of neglected diseases and whether Merck might have interesting scientific leads to pass on. A smaller group met for a follow-up talk a year later. Deep within Merck's vaccine division, moreover, "we always had a small action going in TB," maybe two or three researchers, Gordon Douglas says. There is, after all, somewhat of a U.S. market for a vaccine. A sizable outbreak hit New York City in the early 1990s, and a decade later the disease seemed to be stirring again among some of the city's immigrants. Health care workers, police officers, and other types of emergency workers would be susceptible. But that's maybe a million-person market, Dr. Douglas estimates. Merck's work is mostly, he says, a humanitarian obligation.

Meanwhile, other AIDS activists strongly oppose anything that would dilute the drug makers' interest in their own disease. For once, they offer some sympathy (relatively speaking) for the companies. "I highly doubt that they'll use their profits to research treatments for diseases that are prevalent only in poor countries. If a new treatment will not make money, I don't know if you can expect private industry to develop it—that may be more appropriate for public research institutions," says Milano of ACT UP.

The idea of profit-making companies working on unprofitable causes gets really problematic when it came to vaccines. Even in the Western market, vaccines have traditionally been low-profit and high-hassle. Unlike drugs for chronic conditions, which patients will probably need for their entire life, vaccines are taken only temporarily. And because they are often used to fight highly publicized epidemics, there is tremendous public pressure to keep the price low and tremendous public attention to every reported side effect. In developing countries, the price pressures are even worse, and the profits even skimpier. More than half of the big manufacturers in the vaccine business dropped out by the 1990s. Merck simply stopped making some vaccines, including ones for meningitis and flu, and periodically went through soul-searching as to whether to continue at all.

By the late 1990s and early 2000s, Big Pharma's interest in vaccines had picked up, in large part because the drug companies had discovered they could charge high prices for ones that affect Western patients, and also thanks to improved technology. Merck, for instance, was working on vaccines for such ailments as the sexually transmitted disease human papillomavirus and rotavirus (an intestinal infection that causes infant diarrhea). But infectious disease researchers aren't counting on much from the drug makers. Lee

Reichman, the TB expert from New Jersey, says he doesn't expect Big Pharma to jump in to find a cure for the disease he specializes in. "People forget that drug companies are responsible to their shareholders. They're not responsible to mankind," he says. He puts his hopes in public-private partnerships that could bankroll small companies willing to develop new drugs. Others say the government will have to end up funding the research.

If the drug companies have no moral obligation when masses of people are at risk, what should they do about "orphan diseases," the serious illnesses that affect only a few? Congress passed the Orphan Drug Act in 1983 specifically to encourage pharmaceutical companies to manufacture drugs for these rare diseases by granting tax credits and exclusive marketing rights for seven years. At least at the beginning, Merck seemed to feel that it did, in fact, have some obligation. "Merck volunteered to be the first one" to produce an orphan disease drug under the new law, says Abbey Meyers of the National Organization for Rare Disorders. "I think that Vagelos realized, hey, we were right, these drugs are needed." And Merck had a history, going back to the 1920s, of making orphan drugs like antivenoms for black widow spider bites, Meyers says. For that matter, river blindness—target of the famous Mectizan—is a typical orphan disease. As the orphan drug law's first volunteer, Merck manufactured a compound that had already been developed and tested for the genetic disorder Wilson's disease—for a target population of barely 200 people.

Merck's kind of volunteerism is more the exception than the rule for Big Pharma, however. The law's incentives really aren't much good to these companies. Who cares about market exclusivity, when no one else is making these drugs anyway? And a tax break for research doesn't help a company that's merely selling a drug some other organization has already researched, as Merck did with Wilson's disease. In a few lucky cases, the orphan disease drug might be found to work on a more widespread disease. Or the companies would charge a steep price for the captive market. But by the 1990s, according to Meyer, the orphan drug work was being done mainly by small companies and biotechs that could make a profit on just a $200 million product. Some patients' families have set up foundations to finance research by these companies; one ex-Bristol-Myers executive even became the CEO of a biotech seeking to develop a treatment for his children's rare illness.

If Merck and its fellow drug makers want to be the good guys in the AIDS story, in short, there are plenty of worthwhile causes they could volunteer for. And after the way they botched the AIDS epidemic, they need all the Brownie points they can get.

Living with Mother Merck

Charles Hyman had always turned down headhunters who dangled job openings at drug companies. He enjoyed the clinical experience he got as the director of clinical affairs for the department of medicine at Kings County Hospital Center, a public hospital in Brooklyn. Besides, "I was very hesitant to go into the pharmaceutical industry. I felt like it world be going over to the dark side"—he would go from being Anakin Skywalker to Darth Vader—Dr. Hyman laughs, in an accent that combines a childhood in London with teenage and adult years in the United States.

By 1996, with New York City squeezing its public hospitals' budgets for several years in a row, his work at Kings County wasn't so enjoyable any more. He still might not have listened to just any headhunter. But this time, the job offer was at Merck, as the liaison between the researchers working on two antiinfective drugs and the FDA. "The fact that it was

Merck," says Dr. Hyman, "made me confident that it was a top-notch company with high ethical standards."

There is something about Merck that makes people talk that way.

In an era of temps and contract workers, of 401(k)s instead of pensions, Merck is the classic paternalistic company. "Mother Merck" works her employees ragged, expects long hours and utter loyalty, checks everything to the tiniest molecule, grants a large degree of freedom, pours on the perks—and as a result, has always attracted some of the most brilliant and egotistical people in the business.

To put things in perspective, Big Pharma in general is known for good benefits and high production standards. In *Working Mother* magazine's annual ranking of "One Hundred Best Companies for Working Mothers," the largest pools of contenders always come from pharmaceuticals and financial services, according to former articles editor Sharman Stein. "These are profitable companies with a workforce that has a lot of women," Stein points out. "They can afford to provide onsite child care and family leave." Steven Darien, Merck's longtime head of human resources, notes that during his tenure from 1964 to 1994, "there was a tremendous competition for talent. [Drug] companies were trying to stay ahead of each other in terms of what benefits they were providing to employees." As for being careful and thorough in research, well, the FDA is supposed to make sure everyone does that.

Even within that context, however, Merck constantly stands out. When people from other pharmaceutical companies gathered around the water cooler or met at industry conferences, says Pat Terry, who worked in finance at Pfizer for nearly a quarter-century until 2000, they compared notes: "You know, Merck has a day care facility. You know, Merck has a gym. You can go jogging on your lunch hour." And if an industry group needed to schedule a big meeting, "let's have it at Merck." "'We're Merck, this is the way we do it'— it was part of the esprit de corps," Dr. Hyman says.

Rahway—the old red-brick plant on the swampland that George Merck bought—holds the essence of the Merck image. It was the great leveler. It's hard to be too stuck up, after all, when headquarters is in a blue-collar town known mainly for its state prison.

Except for the ID check at the security gate, a visitor can almost stumble onto the property without realizing: The Merck facility sits right on Highway 1–9, across from World Wide Auto, Dinettes Beautiful, and Murphy's Towing on one side and a row of vinyl-sided houses on another, anchored by a McDonald's on the corner. Inside, it's like a small city— Merck folk tend to compare it more to a college campus— with a population of 4,700 on 250 acres of one-to-three-story office buildings, research labs, manufacturing plants, parking garages, a power plant, a health club, a fire station, and lawns with picnic tables. The thoroughfares are named (Seventh Street, Avenue A, Gadsden Avenue—in honor of a former CEO). No one wears a jacket and tie, not even plant manager Larry Naldi.

Along with the hominess comes an inevitable sense of history. George W. Merck had his headquarters in the brick building at the end of the entrance drive, with the three faux-Greek columns and "Merck" carved above the doorway. Mevacor was discovered in Rahway's labs; streptomycin was manufactured there.

To researchers, one of the glories of Rahway is the collection of brainpower and facilities all in one place—from production lines to chemistry labs to animal testing. "You can tell from the campus that there's a large commitment to research." says David Perlin, scientific director of the Public Health Research Institute in Newark, who has worked on a couple of antifungal projects for Merck.

Not only does Rahway house all that research, but for many years global marketing, the executive offices, and some manufacturing were also jammed in with the scientists and lab rats, and there was, inevitably, the kind of socioeconomic mingling that occurs in a pedestrian city. Because car and truck traffic are strictly limited, vice presidents as well as factory workers had to hoof it between buildings. "You'd see the CEO walking down the hall, you'd say hi," recalls Guy Fleming, president of Local 2-575 of PACE—that's the Paper, Allied-Industrial, Chemical and Energy Workers International Union, the largest of Merck's labor groups. (The union represents mechanics, factory workers, janitors, animal attendants and other hourly workers at three plants.) Keith Elliston, who headed Merck's bioinformatics research in the 1990s, says that with all the stopping and chatting, it could take two hours to walk across the plant. Most famously, everyone, including CEO Vagelos, ate together at long tables in the cafeteria. Sure, the VP of sales wouldn't make a lunch date with the office janitor, but on the other hand, since there wasn't all that much dining space, that VP just might have to sit down at a table full of janitors.

Then, in 1992, global marketing and the executive headquarters moved 20 miles west to Whitehouse Station, in New Jersey's upper crust horse country. And while the casual dress code and the research brainpower remain at Rahway, some of the site's egalitarian spirit and camaraderie were inevitably lost when there were fewer top managers for ordinary workers to be equal to, and fewer departments to mingle among.

Whitehouse Station, meanwhile, is a world and nearly a century away from Rahway. As late as the mid-1980s, while Rahway had been churning out drugs for more than 80 years, the Whitehouse Station area was largely farmland, with a few homes and one-lane roads. Until the end of 1999, Main Street had no traffic lights. Down the road from the Merck headquarters, there are still huge stands of trees, a pick-your-own orchard, and a tack shop.

Instead of vice presidents and janitors, wild turkeys and deer wander through Merck's 1,000 acres of trees, lawns, ponds, and rolling hills. The access road takes its time winding up the hill from Route 523 to the security gate. Inside the main building—the site also includes a smaller outpost, called "the cup"—Whitehouse has the serenity of a monastery and the luxury of a presidential suite. It is built around a five-story central atrium, with hand-woven tapestries mounted on the walls from countries where Merck has had some presence. The dark wood of the banisters and furniture is smooth and thick. No expense was apparently spared: Fleming says that the trees that had to be removed to build the headquarters were saved and replanted. Frank Lichtenberg, the Columbia Business School finance professor, remembers going out to the new headquarters on its second day in operation, and "they hadn't figured out how to open the doors, it was so high-tech."

It's as quiet as an empty cornfield. Somewhere, 2,000 people are working in offices, of course, but you might never run into them.

Outsiders generally describe the Merck spread as beautiful. Compared with Pfizer's Manhattan high-rise headquarters, crammed up right against a brown-brick skyscraper two blocks from Grand Central Terminal, or Bristol-Myers Squibb's offices on more elegant Park Avenue, where the only outdoor space is a plaza running along two sides, Whitehouse Station is like a country retreat.

People at Merck hate it. They call it "the mountaintop," and they see it as the stuffy antithesis of Rahway, a place where everyone wears suits and ties and no one meets in the halls. "Whitehouse reminds me of going to a wake sometimes," Guy Fleming grins. Some say the move also has had repercussions—bad ones—for Merck's new products pipeline. With top management no longer bumping into scientists as a matter of routine, there's a lot less batting around of ideas. The troops don't get to eat with Gilmartin in the cafeteria.

Roy Vagelos defends his decision to move there—somewhat. Merck was running out of space at Rahway, even as it kept putting up more buildings, he explains, and "we wanted to have enough land that it was sufficient for generations of Merck people." Then he adds, "I certainly did not relish leaving Rahway, because Rahway is the microcosm of the Merck that I loved." His voice is not arrogant now.

In May 2001, reporter Annie Finnigan spent a week at Rahway and Whitehouse Station to profile the company for *Working Mother.* Asked to sum up the atmosphere in a phrase, she promptly replies: hard-working. "Merck is a place where people work really hard, they expect a lot of themselves, and the company expects a lot, too," she explains. Not that the atmosphere is frenzied. "It looks very orderly and calm. A well-oiled machine. But there's a sense that there's a lot of work that has to be done." More than half the employees in a recent company survey, she reported, called their workload excessive.

It's not just a case of working long hours; professionals everywhere do that. It's something about the attitude toward the work at Merck, an intensity, down to the smallest detail. The attitude can produce a bureaucratic drag, if managers all the way up to research chief Ed Scolnick or Peter Kim have to sign off on a new hire or a change in a particular study. On the other hand, almost everyone says the intensity and thoroughness help explain the company's reputation for quality and the fact that it has never had a drug recalled in the United States.

More than that, Merck applies the same intensity and thoroughness to issues that have nothing to do with drug research—its retirement plan, for instance. In 1998, Merck was one of the first companies to consider supplementing its 401(k) with an online investment advice program from a new,

California-based firm called Financial Engines, Inc. Other clients had signed on after testing just a dummy account or two, says Jeff N. Maggioncalda, Financial Engines' president and CEO. After all, the program had been devised by a Nobel Prize winner in economics, William Sharpe of Stanford University. But that wasn't good enough for Merck. "They ran us through what felt like clinical trials," Maggioncalda says. In the program's Phase I, 10 "power users," including Gilmartin, tried the software. Phase II involved 500 people for six months. That was followed by "really intense surveys" of the Phase II users, plus a series of tests of the system's tech backup, security, and service. Says Maggioncalda, "Their basic attitude was, we believe our participants need this, so we're going to do our own test to make sure this works."

When the corporate headquarters was still in Rahway, top brass could follow exactly what was happening on the site's manufacturing lines. Vice presidents "looked to see if steam was coming out of the columns, to see if things were running." And if they didn't see any steam, "they'd call to the factory to see why things were shut down," Guy Fleming, the union chief, says. In fact, Fleming wishes that management maybe wasn't quite so thorough. In contract negotiations, "they bring up exactly what was said, when you think it was said a little differently—things you wish you hadn't said sometimes."

The hard work is tempered by an extraordinary amount of independence in how and when the job is done. In the labs, the freedom to pursue pet projects on company time, dating back to the Vagelos era, is part of that philosophy. Beyond that, many employees can negotiate alternative work arrangements, including flextime (flexible starting and closing hours), compressed work weeks, working at home, job-sharing, and part-time work; for the last two, the company prorates the benefits, and it will provide equipment such as high-speed Internet connections for those telecommuting from home. At Rahway, the most popular arrangements are probably flextime and job-sharing. "People really do feel they can come and go as they like," Annie Finnigan says. "If they needed to take a break to go take cupcakes to school, they could do that. They didn't need to do any explaining."

Line workers don't have that flexibility, but on the other hand, they don't punch a time clock. Guy Fleming brags that, within the limits of safety and practicality, his union members have a lot of control over how their jobs are done. If batches of drugs have to be transferred from one vessel to another, the workers determine how to do it. If Fleming himself—a Merck chauffeur since 1955—has to drive to Pennsylvania, he decides the route.

Merck also prides itself on boosting women up the career ladder. It wasn't always that way; a group called Women of Merck was organized in the 1970s to protest the lack of day care and promotions, among other issues. But two CEOs, John Horan and Roy Vagelos, put some effort into opening the career track, and ever since the mid-1980s Merck has been a regular on all the "best companies for women" lists. By 2002, 2 women (Judy C. Lewent, the CFO, and Wendy L. Yarno, the senior vice president for human resources) ranked among Merck's top 12 executives. According to *Working*

Mother's listing that year, 26 percent of all executives and 35 percent of the top earners at Merck were women, and Lewent came in 21st in *Fortune*'s ranking of the 50 most powerful American businesswomen.(However, she was beaten out by Pfizer executive vice president Karen L. Katen, number 7.)

What's especially interesting about Merck is *where* its female staffers are. As Joanne Cleaver outlines it—she's the project editor for the National Association for Female Executives' rating of the top 25 companies for executive women—"in the pharmaceutical industry, women can find it easy to get segregated in the lab. There are long-term projects, predictable hours, relatively low-stress jobs." That may be ideal for mothers with young kids, but the trouble with those jobs is that there's no real career track, and not even much glory. (The company gets the patent for any drugs discovered by the women—and men—in its labs.) Merck, though, "tries to cycle high-potential women, give them other opportunities in business operations, marketing, finance. It tries to include them in the marketing team of the product they develop, for instance. That's imaginative." The worldwide business strategy teams devised by Gilmartin are a help here, because they regularly bring together the lab researchers with people from other disciplines. Also, every corporate division has its own women's network, which is smart, Cleaver says, because that makes it easier to set up mentoring programs for women.

The story for African-Americns is more mixed. They, too, organized an advocacy group in the 1980s—Black Employees at Merck—and, again, CEO Horan set in motion a flurry of affirmative action. The company has made the rounds of "best" rankings for minorities. In fact, there are more minori-

ties than women among its top 12, most notably Bradley
T. Sheares, the president of U.S. human health at Merck
(named one of "the fifty most powerful black executives in
the United States" by *Fortune* in 2002) and General Counsel
Kenneth Frazier. Still, Merck has been sued for racial discrimination and harassment at a couple of plants.

For the ultimate proof of what Merck is like as a task-
master, look at its labor-management relations. In half a
century, there have been only three strikes, the last in 1984.
The company doesn't show up on the radar screen of the
Washington, D.C.-based Pension Rights Center, which helps
workers who have been deprived of pension benefits, or that
of the Council of Institutional Investors, which looks at corporate governance issues like executive pay and board oversight. Labor relations are so smooth that when I went to
Rahway to meet with Fleming and other union officials, they
insisted that I interview the plant management.

Flexibility isn't the only benefit people get from Merck in
exchange for their hard labor. The work-life trade-off goes
something like this: By agreeing to virtually any perk that
employees request, from day care to dry cleaning, "Merck
answers every need so that they can work a longer day. It's a
double-edged sword," says Stein of *Working Mother*. Or, as
Steve Darien, the former HR chief, puts it, "My wife used to
joke that they were trying to make sure I never came home."
You name it, and Merck does it—usually before anyone else.

The company is probably most famous for its four child
care centers, all located on or right near its facilities at

Rahway, Whitehouse Station, and two in Pennsylvania. It wasn't Merck management's initiative; the idea came from a group of research employees at Rahway back in the 1970s, who couldn't find good child care in the area. Merck agreed to provide some funding to set up a center in the basement of a local church, and over the next 20 years it slowly added the other centers and replaced the one at Rahway. And we're talking quality babysitting: The centers are open roughly 12 hours a day, with a high caregiver-to-kids ratio and an onsite nurse, and mom and dad can watch their offspring online via streaming video. The 17,000-square-foot center at White-house Station, about a block away from the corporate head-quarters, is a one-story, kelly-green building with skylights, a sizable outdoor playground, and room for 120 children.

Of course, all that's still not enough. Even though the company subsidizes nearly 20 percent of the cost, employees have to pay around $1000 a month (the fee varies with the child's age). The centers are no good for people who work night or swing shifts, which leaves out most of the union members, nor for those based at Merck sites in other states. Nevertheless, there are long waiting lists.

What else? Merck provides six months of maternity leave—decent but not radical—plus lactation rooms for nursing moms. A 14,000-square-foot fitness center at Rahway, at $30 a month, has several dozen Stairmasters, treadmills, rowers, and assorted other muscle-building equipment in a bright, airy room with a floor-to-ceiling window view of industrial pipes. One of the most unusual perks is a daily two-page "newspaper," called *The Daily*. (Sample: An article on the Bush policy on Medicare drug coverage, another one updating the status of a new drug application, and lots of classified ads.) "I don't know of any other company in that industry that communicates as well. If there's any news, they make sure the employees know it first, before the press, before the analysts," says Milton Moskowitz, the veteran business writer who started probably the first "best places" list in 1984. Like many big companies, Merck still offers old-fashioned indemnity health insurance plans as one of several choices, albeit at a higher cost to employees than the managed care versions. (PACE officials say the medical and retirement coverage are a little better than at other chemical and pharmaceutical companies.) Employees can join the Merck softball team, skydiving club, scuba diving club, singles club, black employees club, gay and lesbian club, Chinese Christian Bible study group, and a score more. Twice—before it became popular in the business world—Merck extended stock options to the entire workforce.

According to Darien, Merck was one of the earliest to post in-house job openings—which might seem pretty ordinary now, but years ago "it was considered radical. Division heads hated it. They said, 'That means someone could leave my division and go to another.'" Darien also says he thinks Merck was the first company in the United States, back in the late 1980s, to decree all of its property smoke-free. Again, this may seem an obvious move for a company that, after all, runs factories using lots of flammable chemicals. However, it was actually a tough negotiation with the PACE union. Fleming recalls that Roy Vagelos walked over to him in the Rockway cafeteria at one point to ask, "Why was I against it, didn't I know it killed you? My feeling was, people have a right to smoke." Ultimately, Merck gave its workforce one year's notice and paid for quitting-smoking classes for staffers and spouses.

For Charles Hyman and for Gordon Douglas, coming from the public sector and academia, respectively, the largesse in terms of supplies and support staff was overwhelming. "If you needed something, you got it," Dr. Hyman recalled, still half-amazed, years later. "My second day on the job, my secretary asked me, 'What do you need?' I was used to asking for 15 times what I needed, then add my Social Security number, and maybe I'd get a third of that." So that's what he requested, more or less, at Merck. But this time, "lo and behold, I come in the next day, and my desk was covered.

"'What is this?' I asked.

"'Well,' she said, 'we thought there was a lot, but we figured you were going to work hard.'"

The move to Whitehouse Station brought even more perks—though not enough to make up for the general dislike of the place. "Whitehouse Station is a little isolated," Darien explains. So the HR department asked people, "What makes sense in terms of making employees' life easier? We don't want people running out every day to get their cleaning." They ended up, both at Whitehouse and at some of the other facilities, with a dry cleaning service that picks up and delivers twice a week; take-home packaged dinners; a bakery where birthday cakes can be ordered; a company called "Dukes of Oil" that changed the oil in employees' cars; convenience stores (Rahway's is called Pharmer's Market) that sell, among other things, greeting cards, coffee mugs, and

Merck teddy bears and T-shirts—and more. Ken Merkin, who operated the dry cleaning service for years with his wife, says that other vendors would be allowed in from time to time to sell things like watches and clothes in the lobby.

Merck also tried to make it easier for employees to get to the new location. "They went to extraordinary lengths with the workforce," Milt Moskowitz says. "If you had to sell your home and move, they paid all the costs. They arranged trips to visit there. They consulted employees as to what kind of building they would like to work in." Because Whitehouse Station has basically no public transportation, Merck runs a van between there and Rahway

When Merck bought the pharmacy benefits manager Medco, it carried over its benefits philosophy, says Sean Brandle, the former Medco finance director who switched to benefits consulting at the Segal Company. Thanks to the Merck influence, Medco established a child care center across the street from its headquarters in suburban Franklin Lakes, New Jersey. It adopted the so-called "six sigma" management philosophy, which is essentially a statistics-based approach to quality control. "I think [Medco's] service got a lot better," adds Brandle's Segal colleague, vice president Ed Kaplan. Before Merck took over, "we had [Medco] clients complaining that they had the wrong plan design in place."

If prediction by PricewaterhouseCoopers, in a report in the summer of 2001, are on target, Merck's kind of employee relations will become even more important to the pharmaceutical industry over the next few years, as the labor pool shrinks and people with a science background become especially hard to find. More flexible working arrangements are one of a handful of solutions the report proposes, specifically citing Merck as an example. (Alternatively, the report says, drug companies could move more research work to Asia, hire more non-Americans, or do more online R&D.)

Darien says he can hardly think of anything employees asked for, during his time there, that wasn't granted. The big "no" was the limit placed on the child care subsidy at Whitehouse Station, wherein Merck agreed to finance the capital cost but employees would have to cover most of the operating expenses. "There can be an unending demand for services in a facility like that. We said, 'If you want a Montessori education, fine, but you have to pay for it.'" Beyond that, Merck—like most companies—increased the employees' copayments for health insurance, Darien says. Also, Dr. Douglas notes, there was a strict policy of no free take-home medicine.

The only time Merck has been really stingy, many people say, is when it comes to executive perks. The limo that Guy Fleming uses for chauffering Ray Gilmartin and other brass is a sedan-size Cadillac DeVille that seats five tightly, with no bar or TV. The company chartered a couple of planes rather than buying them outright, says the 15-year former executive, and they were used only to fly among Merck's U.S. plants, not to jaunt to Europe. For that matter, the executive makes a point of noting, top managers like Dr. Scolnick didn't have a helicopter or plane assigned specifically to them, at least when he was at Merick in the 1980s and 1990s.

There is one more place where Merck may pinch pennies, and that's the most important benefit of all: the paycheck.

On the outside, among the rankers, Merck has a reputation for generosity. Moskowitz says flat-out that "they still are known as the highest-paying for most jobs" in pharmaceuticals, and its liberal salary scale for research scientists was a key reason why Merck was the only Big Pharma chosen for the original Domini 400 Social Index in 1990 (the index screens for socially responsible factors like employee relations, ethnic diversity, and environmental sensitivity). Under both Vagelos and Gilmartin, the salary target has been to rank in at least the top quartile of the industry's pay grid.

Yet some blue-collar workers and middle managers increasingly gripe that the pay isn't competitive any more, if it ever was. The complaints are anecdotal, so it's hard to generalize. On the Merck message board at the Vault.com job search web site, postings have complained about taking a pay cut of $12,000 to come to Merck, or getting a new job elsewhere for a 20 percent raise. The PACE union says its pay scale—$19 an hour on average, with mechanics, at the top, getting around $26—is probably on a par with those of other pharmaceutical companies. But several Rahway mechanics say their paychecks have gone from being high to average for the industry.

Clearly, one problem is that a significant part of managers' compensation depends on how the company has performed, and when earnings suffer, so do their pay and stock options. To determine employee bonuses, Merck traditionally used a series of quantitative measures on a two-part grid. On the individual side of the grid would be the person's success at meeting personal goals—say, launching a new product on time. On the unit or divisional side would be the group's performance in areas such as cost management, asset growth, and sales growth. For each measurement, the employee gets a particular number of points.

To give Merck credit, if it does skimp with its middle managers and blue-collar labor force, it seems to be no more generous with its top brass. Gilmartin tends to come out in the low to middle end of the industry in the executive compensation rankings done by *Forbes, BusinessWeek,* and *The Wall Street Journal,* typically well below Pfizer.

But there's also a certain arrogance toward the issue, an attitude that says, we don't have to pay well, because we're Merck. "Pay is not the only thing. Benefits are not the only thing," Darien tosses off. "You've got to be competitive, but what excites people is the work they are doing and the opportunity to make a contribution." Adds Dr. Douglas, "I don't think Merck bought people from other companies. They had an advantage because there was this perception that Merck is better."

Then again, maybe Darien and Dr. Douglas are right.

Employees stay for decades—even generations. When Merck hosts its annual party for 25-year veterans, "there might be two or three people from the same family," Finnigan of *Working Mother* notes. Elliston, the ex-bioinformatics chief, says that after being at the company for a decade, "I was seen as a short-termer."

Merck staffers are fiercely loyal and extraordinarily close-mouthed when it comes to talking to the press, proud of their company's reputation for research and ethics, even years after they've left. They constantly say things like, "These are the smartest people I've ever worked with." Sooner or later, just about everyone will bring up George W.'s motto.

"We're not a company that looks to see how others do it. We set the standard. We were the ones asking the questions," explains Dr. Hyman, who ultimately quit his job in the summer of 1999 in order to return to clinical medicine. Sitting at the kitchen table in his brownstone row house in Brooklyn, still youthful looking despite graying hair, he searched for the right image. "It's like walking into a field of freshly fallen snow," he finally decided. "Merck's footsteps were the first ones."

The flip side, though, is that it can be very hard for an outsider to break in. One participant on Vault.com warned others in the summer of 2002, "Unless you grew up in this culture you will be treated badly....You will not be trained, you will not get answers to your questions and you will be made to feel inadequate because you came from the outside." While the company might bring in scientists at high levels from universities or the NIH, "Merck had a tradition of growing its own marketing, sales, and business types," notes Dr. Douglas—who himself was hired from Cornell University's Medical College as a senior-ranking scientist in 1990 and then, as he puts it, "migrated" to management to run the new vaccine division in 1991.

Ed Scolnick, the longtime head of research until he stepped down at the end of 2002, is in many ways the archetypical Merck employee. The first thing most people say about him is how brilliant he is. The second is how intimidating.

A graduate of Harvard University, Harvard Medical School and the ultra-high-achiever high school, Boston Latin School, Dr. Scolnick came to Merck from the National Cancer

Institute's Laboratory of Tumor Virus Genetics in 1982 with a string of scientific awards behind him. At Merck, he was one of the driving forces behind Mevacor and Vioxx. His authority burgeoned under Ray Gilmartin, as he became the scientific eyes, ears and brain of a CEO who lacked a scientific background himself and also lacked his predecessor's opportunity to mingle with researchers at the Rahway cafeteria. Within the drug world, he's probably as well known as the CEOs of smaller companies.

Tall and slightly stooping, with fierce dark eyebrows, he has been known to terrorize staff scientists even as he looms over them. As one senior-level Merck scientist recalls, a first-year scientist was making a presentation at a meeting about cholesterol research back around the late 1980s, discussing a novel way of isolating fungi. Dr. Scolnick dramatically slapped his hands over his face in ostentatious disbelief. Another time, at a monthly review of AIDS research, Dr. Scolnick lit into a researcher who was describing some tests that were under way, the senior-level scientist says. He threw question after question at the researcher—How many assays (tests) were being run? Why was the progress so slow?—until Emilio Emini, who was in charge of the project, ran out a door at the back of the room, ran in another door at the front, and demanded of Dr. Scolnick, "Why don't you get in the lab and do it yourself?" Ah, Dr. Scolnick quickly came back, defusing the tension, "you have to be careful of these volatile Italians."

By various accounts, he has micromanaged the scientists' independent research in ways they weren't used to. His former deputy, Roger Perlmutter, quit after ongoing fights. When someone goes to present research to Dr. Scolnick, says the middle manager who left in the early 2000s, "You'd better be prepared. He has very high standards."

Yet who would want anyone in charge of research who wasn't brilliant, demanding, perfectionist, intense—who might, in other words, let a dangerous drug slip by? When an FDA official, at a meeting of the FDA advisory committee on Zocor, raised a slew of unexpected questions about Merck's application, Dr. Scolnick saved the drug, says Al Alberts. It was coming up on lunchtime, so the research chief asked for some extra time in the afternoon to respond. While the others ate, he disappeared. After the session resumed, he proceeded to expound for 30 minutes or so, batting back questions, explaining the data. "He came up there and turned the whole thing around." And the committee unanimously voted to approve Zocor.

Dr. Scolnick's really not so bad, Darien insists. The former HR chief admits that Dr. Scolnick "challenges people on the issues, he's very bright; that intimidates people. But," Darien goes on, "I see him sitting with some young scientists, very encouraging, opening their eyes to things. Whenever he and I talked, the attitude was always, how can we develop people? How can we make the environment better for science?"

Pretty much any big company knows it has to write checks to the local arts center, the Little League stadium, or a college endowment if it wants to keep up its good image. Similarly, big drug makers donate medicine to worthy causes, including antibiotics for epidemics and, after the World Trade

Center attacks, drugs to treat anthrax. Merck is probably no more generous with its checkbook than anyone else. However, it often finds innovative ways to spend that money and will get down into the trenches to do so. It likes to be first. In other words, Merck treats its community service the same way it treats its day job.

Its most dramatic and unprecedented philanthropic gesture, of course, is its open-ended commitment to manufacture and distribute Mectizan, the river blindness drug it discovered, for free, forever, to millions of sufferers in Africa, Latin America, and other impoverished areas. There's also nothing like its hands-on involvement in training science teachers and revamping the science curriculum in the four local school districts. In another unusual move, Merck selected four groups—the Catholic Medical Mission Board, Interchurch Medical Assistance, Project HOPE, and MAP International—as the main conduits for its philanthropy. These groups get to order whatever medicines they want from Merck's production lines, up to a specific annual maximum (neither side will say how much). Other drug makers later copied this approach.

"Merck has wonderful attitudes [toward philantropy]— it's how they do R&D. You see what went wrong, and try again," says Tom Corcoran, codirector of the Consortium for Policy Research in Education at the University of Pennsylvania, a group of five universities that works on state and local education policy for the U.S. Department of Education. In particular, Corcoran has been evaluating Merck's science education project in the New Jersey and Pennsylvania schools. The company made some mistakes in the beginning, bypassing the school principals and rushing the selection of which teachers to train as "leader-teachers." But, he adds, Merck learned its lesson, and it ultimately made sure to involve the principals and to expand the special training.

Nancy Collins, director of procurement at International Aid (a Christian relief and development organization that works in Ghana, Honduras, Kosovo, and the Philippines), says the Merck rep who works with her "is always examining things, coming up with ideas, looking at situations differently—I think of her as a kind of leader." For instance, the rep spearheaded an effort to develop best-practices guidelines for organizations seeking pharmaceutical donations. (In terms of hard cash, Merck was more generous than others until around 2000, Collins says. Then it switched priorities to disease eradication, which International Aid doesn't do.)

At the New York Business Group on Health, a trade group representing 150 employers and health care providers in New York City, executive director Laurel A. Pickering wanted to raise $11,000 for a needs assessment survey of her members in 2001. Knowing she could count on Merck's desire not to be outdone, Pickering decided to ask only Merck and one other drug company to split the cost. She needn't have bothered with Number Two; Merck ponied up the entire $11,000 itself.

Pickering, too, raves about her Merck rep. It may seem like small stuff: If several pharmaceutical reps get together, the Merck rep is the only one who worries publicly whether this might be some sort of violation of antitrust laws, collusion or something.

Of course, all this community activity is not pure altruism on Merck's part. The advantages go beyond the obvious tax breaks and good PR. By funding the whole cost of the New York business group's survey, Merck got exclusive access to the answers, which provided some insight into what kind of health insurance information the member companies were looking for. By improving science education in New Jersey, Merck hopes to create a pool of skilled potential employees, thus helping to ease the science worker shortage that the PricewaterhouseCoopers report warns about. Roy Vagelos, in setting up the schools program, "knew his company was having trouble hiring people who were American citizens who had this knowledge and skill," Corcoran notes. And one more thing: There is a core of small, loyal investors who know Merck and own its stock mainly because of Mectizan.

But the old Merck was slowly eroding. By the late 1990s, the whole business world had become less family-friendly and more corporate. Even drug research was more like an assembly line, with the growing use of robotics for screening. Merck's CEO no longer recognized every manager he might see in the elevator; the Rahway cafeteria lost its sociological mix.

The already ponderous bureaucracy piled on more levels. To put in a business proposal in the Vagelos era, "you had to write up all the detailed criteria with alternative approaches, go up through at least two levels of committees, have functional sign-offs from finance and legal, and then get approval of the Operating Review Committee and Vagelos," Simon

Benito recalls. Gilmartin eliminated a lot of the paperwork, but that, Benito says, didn't really improve the situation because instead he introduced all sorts of other committees and processes, which probably had a more paralyzing effect on the organization. "People felt that they needed to get someone's written approval to make sure that the top management was on board. At least under Vagelos, they already had the sign-off."

Marketing, too, got more bureaucratic with the addition of a level of management called health science associates, says Casey Webber, the longtime rep who left in the early 2000s. More approvals became necessary for coddling the special physicians known as "thought leaders," who conduct cutting-edge research. In a move that puzzled some old-timers, some Asian marketing was put under the CFO's purview. Gilmartin's personality and management style also had the effect of slowing things down. Because Vagelos was so accessible at Rahway, it was easier to get an informal approval for a business proposal. "You would see him almost every day in the cafeteria and may have joined him for lunch, during which he would let you know how he felt about your project," Benito points out. "If he said okay, you knew you could go ahead." But Gilmartin doesn't hang out at the cafeteria. "Employees seldom see him and therefore feel that they do not know him—and may indeed be afraid of what they don't know," Benito says. "Consequently, they are afraid of taking risks in case they make a mistake."

Turnover has reportedly doubled from the 3 to 3.5 percent under Vagelos. A lot of people, especially, went to Aventis and Schering-Plough in 2001, according to current and former staffers. With the stock price sinking steadily through that year and much of 2002, Mother Merck tightened her belt in small ways, even eliminating the coffee and pastry that used to be served at monthly steering committee meetings, the PACE members say. For the 2002 company picnic, the food was less elaborate, and there was no band.

"People are worried that business won't turn around," Robert Watkaskey, the union's full-time international representative, said in June of 2002, when the stock was in the 50s. "The people see it in their everyday jobs, this week we're working overtime, next week no overtime, next week we're going to be bumped out." Vioxx production moved to Singapore, and the Arcoxia line that the union was counting on was delayed, although there was supposed to be an increase in the Cozaar run. Within the plant at Rahway, the talk was of how much better the pay used to be and how many people were leaving.

Bad as that was, it was nothing compared to the morale the week after July 4, 2002, after *The Wall Street Journal* reported that Merck had booked $12.4 billion in revenue from its Medco subsidiary over the prior three years that it hadn't actually received. Coming on top of months of corporate scandals, the news sent Merck stock—as well as the Dow Jones Industrial Average, the Standard & Poor's 500 stock index, and even the Nikkei Stock Average in Japan—plunging. Merck shares toyed with a five-year low, and the initial public offering of Medco was postponed, then withdrawn.

Ray Gilmartin quickly got on a video hookup to Merck's farflung U.S. plants, held at least one big meeting with employees in person, sent an e-mail to the staff, and drafted a letter to shareholders to put out the message: *Merck did nothing wrong. It wasn't really inflating profits, because it was subtracting the same amount on the other side of the ledger as an expense. The accountants and the SEC all said it's okay.*

Executives and former executives rallied around the message to a certain extent. For the most part, they agreed with the official line that there really wasn't anything scandalous in the way Medco's profits were accounted for, and they were annoyed that the outside world had the temerity to put Merck's name alongside those of Enron and WorldCom, the poster children of corporate malfeasance. But some of the executives were also annoyed at Merck's own management: Even if the accounting was technically legal, didn't anyone realize it would look bad? What had happened to the company that prided itself on its ethics, that didn't stoop to fighting generics or giving doctors tickets to the opera, the kind of company whose reps would worry about violating antitrust laws if they simply chatted with competitors?

What made things really hurt was that this sort of mess-up was exactly what Merck's vaunted thoroughness and bureaucracy were supposed to prevent. Months before the Medco story made headlines, when former marketing executive Boyd Clarke was talking about the centralization and tortuous decision making that had driven him away from Merck, he also noted, in defense of that very bureaucracy, "The good news is that you always end up with the most senior and presumably most effective executive engaged in decisions that are important. Protecting against the lone wolf in the hinterland making some decision you were uncomfortable with." He couldn't imagine, he said, an Enron-type accounting scandal at Merck.

The fact that such a scandal now seemed to have in fact happened at Merck didn't change his opinion of the company's systems and controls, Clarke insisted, as the headlines swirled. "Merck had not only been using this accounting method, but disclosing it. There was no impact on earnings per share," he pointed out. "I don't think it would ever have been questioned," he added, "if you had not been in a time when any mention of the word 'accounting' was in a sentence that included the word 'scandal.'"

Other executives weren't as forgiving of the company that had demanded so much of them for so many years. "This was a company that was proud of its ethics," snapped one former high-level manager. "Now it's become a laughingstock, up there with WorldCom."

10

A Different Business Model

Adam Smith raised the issue of drug makers' prices and profits in *An Inquiry into the Nature and Causes of the Wealth of Nations* in 1776, back when the Mercks were still running a drugstore in Germany: "Apothecaries' profit is become a bye-word, denoting something uncommonly extravagant." But then he went on to defend high drug prices against the prevailing public opinion by citing the cost of R&D:

> This great apparent profit, however, is frequently no more than the reasonable wages of labour. The skill of an apothecary is a much nicer and more delicate matter than that of any artificer whatever, and the trust which is reposed in him is of much greater importance. . . . His reward, therefore, ought to be suitable to his skill and his trust, and it arises generally from the price at which he sells his drugs. But the whole drugs which the best employed apothecary, in a large market town, will sell in a year, may not perhaps cost him above thirty or forty pounds. Though he should sell them,

therefore, for three or four hundred, or at a thousand per cent profit, this may frequently be no more than the reasonable wages of his labour charged, in the only way in which he can charge them, upon the price of his drugs.[1]

It's been up and down in public opinion ever since, with the pharmaceutical industry alternately hated and admired. ("Where did we get all those [safe food and drug] laws?" points out Bill McCutchen of Baruch College.) The industry produced miracle drugs like penicillin, and horrifying drugs like thalidomide. In Sinclair Lewis's *Arrowsmith*, published in 1925 and taking place over the previous couple of decades, the idealistic Dr. Martin Arrowsmith is aghast when his medical school mentor goes to work for a pharmaceutical company: "Of all the people in the world! I wouldn't have believed it! Max Gottlieb falling for those crooks!"[2] Twenty years later, streptomycin was pouring out of Merck's production line at Rahway, and seven years after that George W. Merck was a hero on the cover of *Time* magazine—of course, with his ubiquitous motto.

The newest cycle of unpopularity probably began in the late 1990s, as Americans gradually realized that they were paying ever more for their prescriptions. That hit to their wallets, in turn, got the public noticing other nasty things about Big Pharma: The fact that the same drugs were a lot cheaper in Canada. The barrage of commercials on TV. The children suffering from AIDS in Africa while the drug companies fought to block generics and discounts. The reports, even in the United States, about people who had to skip their pills every other month because they couldn't always afford to pay for their prescription. After their bout against

HMOs earlier in the decade, Americans were primed to be suspicious of health care costs. And having forced the HMOs to backtrack, they fully expected to win again.

By the beginning of the twenty-first century, it may have seemed to the industry as though this was the worst period yet. The list of who hated the big drug makers was almost all-encompassing: doctors, patients, politicians, consumer groups, humanitarian groups, pharmacists, insurers, generic-drug makers, and basically every company in the United States that provided health insurance to its workforce.

The last to lose faith was Wall Street. It hung on for some of the very reasons all the others started to hate the drug makers—those fat profits, rolling reliably onward year after year and with a good 40 more years of Baby Boomers heading into the prescription heaven of old age to carry them through. But even Wall Street couldn't ignore the growing public animosity, which raised the possibility of increased government regulation and price controls. Moreover, the old 18 percent margins were eroding. Demographics weren't so reliable after all. By the spring of 2002, many of the big pharmaceutical stocks, which had briskly outpaced the S&P for most of the late 1990s and early 2000s, were tumbling faster than the market overall.

And Wall Street fell out of love with Merck.

It's pretty easy to date when that happened: sometime between June and December of 2001, starting with Merck's first warning that earnings growth would be lower than forecast that year, quickly followed by the article in the *Journal of the American Medical Association* about the cardiovascular risks of Vioxx and other COX-2 inhibitors, finally hitting a crescendo at the company's annual meeting with analysts. In fact, it can be dated even more precisely—after lunch at the analysts' meeting.

During the morning session of the all-day gathering at Merck's serene, rustic headquarters, several dozen analysts listened with interest to the newest plans for the cholesterol drug Zetia and the defense of Vioxx. They asked about Vioxx's cardiovascular problems, about the upcoming trial over the Prilosec patent, about Singulair's potential use in allergy treatment, and about progress on the substance P antagonist for depression—the kinds of questions they had come expecting to ask. They were worried, of course, with five of Merck's biggest sellers scheduled to go off patent, no blockbuster apparently ready to replace them, and Vioxx, which was supposed to have been the big replacement, plagued by the heart condition warnings. Still, by and large, Wall Street had faith in Merck. These were the smartest people in the business. Many analysts emerged from the morning session fairly optimistic about the future-product pipeline. A couple of fund managers even considered the stock a buying opportunity, down from the 90s to the high 60s. They ate tuna sandwiches and chocolate chip cookies in the cafeteria.

Then all hell broke loose, as Ray Gilmartin and CFO Judy Lewent unexpectedly announced that, not only had Merck already missed the earnings forecast for this year, but they expected earnings to be flat for the next year, at $3.12 to $3.15 per share, rather than the $3.40 or so that analysts had been predicting. "Certainly," Gilmartin said, "the guidance [early forecasts] we gave you for this year is not competitive and the guidance for next year is not competitive. We don't take lightly the fact that we've had to make these revisions. We do not give out numbers that we don't intend to make. This year, next year, we did not make it."

Merck stock plunged almost 10 percent. For that matter, the Dow Jones Industrial Average and the S&P 500 stock index also slipped a little, and some observers blamed Merck in part for those drops. Analysts do not like to see numbers fall below what they've counted on. And they especially do not like surprises about falling numbers.

The bad news only continued over the next 10 months: the withdrawal of the application for Arcoxia, which was supposed to be the next-generation COX-2 inhibitor after Vioxx; the revelation that Merck had booked $12.4 billion in revenue from its Medco subsidiary that the firm never actually got; the delay after delay on spinning off Medco through an initial public offering. In the brief tempest over Medco's accounting, analysts and professional money managers generally sided with Merck, arguing that there was nothing wrong with booking the revenue the way the company did and that the public was overreacting. But added to the accumulation of other problems—especially the sense that the company seemed to be constantly hiding things—the accounting dispute chipped away at Merck's image. First Merck gave one reason for withdrawing Arcoxia, then another. All along it had been saying that Medco didn't favor Merck drugs; now it turned out that Medco did. Couldn't a big company like Merck at least get the timing right on its IPO—after three tries?

Worth magazine, in a roundup of pharmaceutical stocks in February 2002, rated Pfizer and GlaxoSmithKline both a "buy," Johnson & Johnson a "hold," and Merck a "sell." Richard Stover of Arnhold and Bleichroeder had already lowered his rating to "sell" back in May of 2001, as soon as he saw the first signs of heart trouble in a big study of Vioxx. Viren Mehta, the money manager and analyst, went from "neutral" to "negative"; Merrill Lynch downgraded from "buy" to "neutral"; UBS Warburg, from "buy" to "hold"; Raymond James from "strong buy" to "market perform." *Barron's* senior editor Andrew Bary in July called Merck "one of the weakest stocks in the Dow." According to published reports, Janus mutual funds liquidated their Merck holdings.

Two years earlier, if Richard Evans of Sanford Bernstein was too pessimistic, "people would say, 'Come on, it's Merck.'" Now, he was having trouble getting portfolio managers interested in the Medco spinoff. "Probably the biggest problem is that Merck still sees itself in that role [as the industry leader]. A dramatically shrinking number of external contractors see it that way," Evans says.

About the most supportive thing anyone could say about Merck was that it was undervalued and reliably paid a dividend—a heck of a comedown for "the miracle company."

You could read the change in the headlines. In January 2001, in *The Wall Street Journal*, it was: "How Merck Survived While Others Merged—Drug Maker Relied on Inspired Research." In July 2002, in *Fortune*, it was now a question: "Will R&D Make Merck Hot Again?"

To some degree, Merck was just sharing the problems facing the whole industry. Others reported even worse earnings and similarly strong patent challenges. Moreover, Merck's stock did perk up a bit when Zetia was approved and when the company announced the encouraging test results for its human papillomavirus vaccine in late 2002. Still, investors clearly favored certain pharmaceutical companies more than others, and probably the favorite of all was Merck's archrival Pfizer. It had eight certified blockbusters bringing in at least $1 billion in sales apiece, a decent pipeline, no imminent patent threats, probably the most aggressive sales force in the industry, and, as Merck could never forget, the Number One drugs for cholesterol and arthritis over Merck's own offerings. Moreover, by gobbling up Warner-Lambert in a hostile takeover in 2000 and then announcing plans in 2002 to acquire Pharmacia, Pfizer had pumped itself into a giant far and away the biggest in the industry, more than twice as rich in terms of market capitalization as Number Two GlaxoSmithKline or Number Three Merck. It was like Ursula the sea witch toward the end of the Disney cartoon of "The Little Mermaid," the towering figure in the ocean, seemingly far too big to challenge.

Small shareholders hung on to Merck longer, but when the Medco mess broke out, even they began to waver. Ronald Emma, a New Jersey salesman specializing in equipment leasing, had started buying Merck in 1992 because "I knew drug companies were very profitable. My philosophy was, pick a few key industries, and pick the top company in each field—which I felt Merck was." He added to his holdings during the height of the Clinton health care reform drive, figuring that the stock was underpriced, and eventually ended up with 500 shares. He even uses Vioxx himself for arthritis and a bone spur in his shoulder and calls it "a wonder drug."

A couple of weeks after the December analysts' meeting, he admitted, "I'm less confident than I was six months ago." Still, he wasn't bailing out. For one thing, the stock had slid from 90 to the high 50s, and while he didn't expect to see 90 again, he wanted to wait until it climbed back up a little—which he was sure it would. "It's not a $60 stock. I am confident they will come back. It's always going to be a leader in an industry that's a cash cow."

Seven months after that, with the stock down in the 40s, Emma was still holding on to his Merck shares. But it wasn't based on faith so much any more. The price was just too low now—in fact, the entire market was too depressed—to do any selling. With Pfizer's new merger, "I think Merck is going to get left behind rather quickly. I don't know what their strategy is. If I was going to buy anything in the pharmaceutical industry, I'd buy Pfizer."

Can Merck ever be Merck again, the industry leader?

Experts and kibbitzers alike have lots of advice, but in a nutshell it boils down to the fact that Merck needs new blockbusters: An R&D shot in the arm. The big debate is over how to get that shot.

To many on Wall Street, the answer is obvious: Merge, or acquire another major drug company and grab its pipeline. It is, after all, what almost every other company has done. That's where those long strings of names came from: Glaxo-SmithKline is the product of combining Glaxo Wellcome and

SmithKline Beecham, which are themselves the results of earlier linkups between Glaxo and Burroughs Wellcome, and SmithKline Beckman and The Beecham Group (and many other mergers), respectively. Or those strange, invented names like Novartis and Aventis, which were plucked from the air to encompass the marriages of Ciba-Geigy and Sandoz, and Hoechst and Rhône-Poulenc. Pharmacia merged with Upjohn, Monsanto bought G. D. Searle, Pharmacia bought Monsanto, and then Pfizer announced plans to buy the whole caboodle.

For that matter, in an era that has seen the creation of such behemoths as Exxon Mobil in oil, DaimlerChrysler in autos, and AOL Time Warner in media, it's the way of the business world in general. "Mergers are a natural evolution for any industry," says Hemant Shah, perhaps the most-quoted of pharmaceutical analysts.

The Pfizer-Pharmacia hookup tightened the external pressure on Merck. At the least, urged Simon Benito—who, among his many jobs at Merck through the years, oversaw the integration and expansion of Merck's Japanese subsidiary, Banyu Pharmaceutical Company—the new development should prompt Merck to go through its merge/don't merge analysis again, even if just "to reconfirm our initial belief." Maybe this time, some potential acquisition candidates would look better than they had six months before.

There are three basic arguments in favor of a merger or acquisition. First is a variation on the argument for doing more licensing and joint ventures—that no company, not even a big one like Merck, can expect to do everything itself or have a monopoly on great ideas. Even joint ventures aren't a solution, experts like Columbia professor Frank

Lichtenberg say, because "you're basically writing a contract with another entity, and it's difficult to write a fully specified contract that is going to cover every possible contingency, that gives everyone the right incentive." Moreover, the sides have to share the profits in a joint venture, which doesn't do all that much for the bottom line.

This reasoning works only if the acquirer buys a company with a solid pipeline or at least a well-regarded R&D staff. Some people narrow the criteria even further to say that it works only if both companies already have a joint stake in a drug, as Pfizer and Warner-Lambert had with Lipitor, or Pfizer and Pharmacia had with Celebrex. In Merck's case, that leads most merger advocates to suggest a pairing with Schering-Plough, because of their partnership in developing the cholesterol drug Zetia.

Presumably, too, mergers save money, through layoffs and economies of scale, that can then be used for more research. "You fire the blue-collar people, close plants, it buys you two years, maybe three," sums up Evans, the Sanford Bernstein analyst. Pfizer expected to book $270 million in savings from its acquisition of Warner-Lambert and a further $2.5 billion from Pharmacia. Even before the Pharmacia deal, its R&D budget was almost double Merck's; with Pharmacia, it would be spending over $7 billion, versus less than $3 billion for Merck. Standing alone, Merck didn't have a prayer of coming close.

After R&D, perhaps the advantages are most pronounced in marketing, since each sales rep can now carry more products. With more variety in the sample case, the rep has more hope of enticing the doctor to open the door. You're not

interested in a beta-blocker? Okay, how about an anticholesterol statin? "It's going to be difficult for a physician not to
see a Pfizer rep, because the rep is going to have lots of different products," Benito points out.

Casey Webber, the longtime Merck detailer, points to a
more subtle marketing advantage: A merged company is less
likely to annoy the physician. That's because, at least until the
company finishes consolidating, the reps often continue to
use their old affiliations. So one rep will show up in Doctor
A's office saying he or she is from Glaxo, then another the
next day from Burroughs Wellcome, and then a third a day
later from SmithKline Beecham. The doctor will think he or
she is meeting marketers from three different companies,
rather than three from the same combined company (Glaxo-
SmithKline), and won't consider it overkill. "Merck was the
only one that had one name," Webber laments. "Merck
caught a lot of flack, because it looked like they had more
reps" constantly bothering the same doctor.

During his tenure as CEO, Roy Vagelos says, "we certainly
considered mergers," though he won't say which companies
he looked at or why none were carried through. "As CEO,
you always consider various strategies," he adds. With its
stock (both literal and figurative) so strong, Merck could
almost have bought any company it wanted; supposedly,
Pfizer and Lilly were potential candidates. The high-level
executive who spent more than 15 years at Merck before,
during, and after the Vagelos era—and who believes Merck
should do a merger now—suggests that none panned out
because "the company was doing well, it didn't want to dilute
the stock, people didn't want to take risks." But Benito says

that "Vagelos seemed really determined to make a big acquisition. And in the end he did—he acquired Medco."

There is strong opposition to this conventional promerger wisdom—starting with the present-day Merck itself. Regardless of what Vagelos may have wanted or tried, Ray Gilmartin insists—at every forum he can find, at the analysts' meeting, in interviews—that Merck's not merging. It will stand on its own. It will make its fortune on its research alone. The company has done small acquisitions, such as its much-touted 2001 purchase of Rosetta Inpharmatics, which develops software for genetic analysis. But not since its troubled pairing with Sharpe & Dohme in 1953 has Merck tied the knot with another sizable company in its own industry. "Gilmartin's presidency will be evaluated on whether Merck can develop its own breakthrough drugs in a timely way, and on how he reacts to the merger issue," predicts Boyd Clarke, the veteran Merck marketer.

Merck is not alone in having doubts about mergers as the grand solution to a company's problems. During the same summer that Pfizer announced its purchase of Pharmacia, other once-vaunted alliances were coming apart at the seams. AOL Time Warner's stock had dropped something like 75 percent since its merger and its chief operating officer, Robert W. Pittman—one of the biggest cheerleaders for the deal's supposed synergy—was forced out. Vivendi SA acquired Seagram in 2000; two years later, with its share price plummeting, its credit rating downgraded to junk, and a $12 billion first-half loss, it ousted Chairman Jean-Marie Messier and began unloading some of his acquisitions. In a study of 302 mergers from 1998 to 2001, *BusinessWeek* in October 2002 found that after a year together, the merged companies' average returns lagged both the S&P index and their industry peers. Nor are all the drug mergers seen as winners. A lot of skepticism haunts the hookups between Pharmacia and Monsanto, Bristol-Myers Company and Squibb Corporation, and various parts of the Glaxo chain.

In some cases, companies jump into marriage too quickly without considering other alternatives. "Very often it's more a function of attention deficit disorder, multitasking impatience," quips Nell Minow, a longtime shareholder activist and editor of The Corporate Library, a research firm and web site that track board effectiveness. It can be so boring and difficult to delve into the nitty-gritty of operations in order to find cost savings. So, "The CEO comes to the board and announces, 'I've got a super idea. All we need is that synergy'" with a merger partner.

However, synergy is not so easy to create, it turns out. Twice the R&D staff does not lead to twice the drugs, unless the staff is already working on something promising. Although economies of scale can be achieved, and bigger is better to some degree, no one is quite sure where that degree ends. Merck says it's already there; how much bigger do you have to be than $48 billion in sales? "I haven't seen that innovation necessarily comes from these leviathan organizations," cautions Edward Pittman, the pharmaceutical analyst with the New Jersey state pension fund (though he says he's not intrinsically against Merck's "trying to generate some growth from the synergy" of a merger).

But it's easy to predict the negative effects of increased size; more bureaucracy and pressure for bigger blockbusters. If it takes a $500 million pill to have any impact on a $32 billion bottom line, what will it take to move a $50 billion one?

And the cost-cutting and uncertainty that inevitably accompany a merger can hurt staff morale as people await the ax. Milton Moskowitz, the pioneer in ranking "best places to work," says one reason Merck keeps placing so high on these lists is that it has adamantly refused to merge. "People feel, if they do well, they'll move up. They won't be displaced by someone from another company," he notes.

For that matter, what happened to all the predictions that the future lies with flexible little biotechs and targeted gene-based drugs aimed at niche markets? If that's the case, then getting bigger will simply mean a bigger disadvantage.

Some people bring up practical reasons why Merck shouldn't do a merger in the foreseeable future, not that they necessarily think it's a bad idea in general. With the stock so far down, "the currency is pretty diluted," Evans of Sanford Bernstein points out. The company doesn't have the wherewithal for a shopping spree. And even if it did, who's available to merge with? The days when Merck could consider acquiring Pfizer are, of course, a bitter memory. Schering-Plough, the obvious partner, had some serious manufacturing problems that cost it a $500 million fine—a record for the industry—and was being socked by the end of

Claritin's patent exclusivity. Its CEO retired under fire in late 2002. So it's not clear how much trouble Merck would be buying, along with full rights to Zetia.

To Wall Street, the drug companies may be another potential investment, to be analyzed on the basis of synergy and earnings per share. But to the public, they're much more than just a business. They represent health, youth, physical prowess, long life—the ability to cheat death.

Which explains why the public is so unforgiving when the cycle turns negative, and which puts all the controversies over prices, regulation, generics, and advertising into a vastly wider context. Should Merck and the other drug makers be treated as businesses, or as a public good?

"We still have not, as a country, decided whether health care is a social service," says Paul Reitemeier, the health care ethicist. "If it were, we would guarantee access to it, as we do education and food stamps." Okay then, so the public considers the drug industry a business. But that's not quite true either. "Consumers lose sight of the fact that the pharmaceutical industry is proprietary, not altruistic. They're [drug companies] not in the health care business; they're in the business of providing tools. But because it's health care, they get the halo effect."

Uwe Reinhardt, the Princeton economist, starts his analysis from the opposite direction but ends up with the same contradictory public opinion. "Americans want the drug industry to be competitive and price-oriented. But every time it actually behaves that way, we wring our hands and say, 'How come you're not behaving like a Catholic non-profit hospital?'"

Even the drug companies themselves send a mixed message. Sure, they want to be treated as a business when the issue is freedom to maximize their returns. But they are quick to cite their perceived special role in society when it suits them—for instance, in arguing that their prices aren't so high once you consider how much risk they take on, how many years they struggle, to develop these products that *save people's lives.* "I don't think that anybody in the general public fully understands just how many lives have been saved by innovative therapies discovered and developed by drug companies and how much risk they take financially," Simon Benito says, typically. "What people see is how much a prescription costs, and politicians ride the waves of public opinion by constantly accusing us of being a bloodthirsty industry."

"How do I want people to know us?" PhRMA's president, Alan Holmer, asked rhetorically at the trade group's annual meeting in 2002. He answered himself: "By the essence of who we are: our legions of doctors, scientists and researchers dedicated to the defeat of disease and the celebration of life." Oh, and by the way, we also make money for our shareholders by manufacturing pills.

Or, as Adam Smith put it, "the trust which is reposed in [the apothecary] is of much greater importance" than for any other business.

To the employers who have to pay the rising prescription drug costs in their health care plans, Big Pharma is a business, all right—too much like a profit-making business.

"They recognize the pharmaceutical manufacturers are business people, just like they are. Our clients [large employers] price their products at what the market will bear. They know the pharmaceutical manufacturers will do that as well," says Barbara Hawes, the consultant at Towers Perrin. And yet: "Having said that, there are plenty of them that will speak out against the pharmaceutical manufacturers. They see DTC ads as sort of feeding the demand. The brand-name drugs that are being advertised are driving their incremental costs. Are the pharmaceutical manufacturers the bad guys? I don't want to give an outright 'yes,' but they are blamed to a certain extent for the increasing costs." In other words, how dare the drug makers act like other businesses by advertising and driving up demand for their products?

By the same token, consumer advocates say that it's okay for Big Pharma to make a profit, but it shouldn't make too much profit, because what it produces is so crucial to their lives. (A corollary to that argument is that the industry doesn't need big profits to cover the cost of research, because its research doesn't really cost the $800 million per drug that it claims.) "None of us expects drug companies to become philanthropic organizations," begins Mark Milano, the AIDS activist. Then comes the "but": "Make a profit, not an obscene profit. They don't need profits four times that of other industries. If they want to be ethical—that's what Merck says, 'we're the ethical drug company'—drug companies should fight to keep their profit margins as low as possible. When I buy a cell phone, I can buy Nokia, Ericsson. When you're buying drugs, you often don't have a choice. 'You take my drug or you die.'"

Some consumer activists, in fact, argue that the industry is such a social service that it ought to be doing more public health work even at no profit, the way a public hospital has to take in every patient who comes in the emergency room, regardless of ability to pay. Thus, the pharmaceutical companies should be developing drugs for epidemics like sleeping sickness or malaria that afflict and kill millions of people in the developing world, says Daniel Berman of Doctors Without Borders. "I think there is something fundamentally different [about the drug industry]," he explains. "Considering their profitability, if you think of health care as a right, they can contribute to some of the solutions because they're in the health business."

Pretty much the only ones who don't want to be seen as special are the generic drug makers. They don't discover great cures, and they don't expect any credit for that. "The innovators are often the ones that claim such privileges," Clay O'Dell of the trade association says airily. "The generic companies have one thing in mind: competition, competition, competition. Treat us just like any other industry."

And they're all right.

The pharmaceutical industry isn't just another business.

It's a business that provides a vital public good. Its products keep people alive but can kill if not properly regulated. Patients desperately need its products but can't afford them.

Yes, it is a business, and therefore, like all businesses, it has an obligation to turn out a profit for its shareholders. But it is also, perhaps uniquely, a profit-making social service. And therefore, like it or not, the drug industry is answerable to the public in ways that other businesses aren't. Although it's not regulated to the degree that the phone companies or the airlines used to be—it doesn't need government authorization to raise prices or change the mix of its products—no other industry's ads have to go through the kind of approval process or include the kinds of warnings that drug ads do. The buying public doesn't complain when other industries advertise on TV.

This oversight is only going to increase, as it has in the hundred-plus years since George Merck came to America to protect the integrity of his family company's labels. In the 1930s, George Merck's company learned to live with the FDA. Since the late 1990s, Big Pharma has been getting a taste of increased public pressure, first in the outcry over AIDS drug pricing, then in the furor over drug prices in the United States and the related issues of generics, advertising, and drug shopping in Canada. Now, whether the federal government dictates it via Medicare, the states do it through their Medicaid buying clout, or the HMOs do it with their formularies, many experts predict that the pharmaceutical makers are ultimately going to have to live with price controls and lower profits. There will probably be tighter rules, too, on patent extensions, marketing, and clinical trials.

Sean Maguire, the Watson Wyatt consultant, is one of the experts who foresees more controls. "I feel for the manufacturers," he says. "They're in a lose-lose situation. They have to keep shareholders happy, and simultaneously keep government out of the backyard. Other industries don't face this pressure. Should they be limited to what they should be allowed to make? That doesn't sound like the American market to me." "Industry will have to adapt" to increased regulation, says Simon Benito.

Along with the regulation, though, comes an extra dose of benefits from the government. The main one is the basic scientific research done by government labs. Bernadette Healy, a former head of the National Institutes of Health, told the ABC News special report on prescription drugs that her erstwhile agency contributes 50 to 60 percent to the development of major drugs. It did crucial testing on AZT, the first AIDS drug, and funded research into more AIDS treatments. Its National Cancer Institute did the preliminary discovery and Phase I testing of what became the cancer drug Taxol. Other drugs—all blockbusters—that have gotten significant help from government research are the antidepressant Prozac, the ulcer drug Zantac, and Merck's Vasotec for high blood pressure. Add to all that the patent protection under the Hatch-Waxman Act, the laws against reimportation, and the orphan drug tax credits.

To underscore Big Pharma's reliance on Big Government, Uwe Reinhardt compares the drug companies to General Motors Corporation: "Which industry could exist without government? GM could. They could make cars that could drive, though they might not be as safe as they are [now]. Could the pharmaceutical industry exist without government? It couldn't make it through a month."

Still think it's just a business? Then imagine Merck announcing, as the retail chain Montgomery Ward did in 2000, that it's shutting its doors. That's it, no more Zocor.

The world that faces Merck plays in some ways to its strengths. True, Merck bet wrong once before in predicting an increased government role in health care, back in 1993 when it bought Medco. But this time, it doesn't need to take any extraordinary steps to accommodate stronger public oversight and government involvement. It only needs to keep doing what it's already gained a reputation for, as the "good" drug company that signed on early to the idea of having Medicare cover prescription drugs, that doesn't fight nasty against generics, that stopped plying doctors with extravagant freebies—that saved Jules Levin's friends' lives by speeding up access to the AIDS drug Crixivan. The companies that have tried hardest to block the generics or that have relied most on courting doctors with fancy meals are going to have a much harder time adapting. Merck has already been preparing to live in this new kind of world by focusing on breakthrough research instead of patent suits and by building relationships with doctors that don't require theater tickets. It's still a drug company; to the public, it still carries with it a cloud of suspicion. But when it goes to lobby Congress, it comes with a better reputation than, say, PhRMA.

Moreover, if Viren Mehta of Mehta Partners is right, marketing will be less important in the future. Armies of sales people, he says, won't be necessary for the kinds of niche drugs that everyone is foreseeing, because the patient markets simply won't be that big. "If you have targeted drugs, they have their own channels. The drugs can theoretically sell themselves on the Web." In which case, it won't matter so much if Merck laid off too many salespeople back in the 1990s or if its DTC advertising is mediocre. It won't do Pfizer much good to be the most powerful marketing force in the industry. The focus will be back where Merck says it wants it—on R&D.

In that case, can Merck be Merck, the industry leader, again?

That won't be as easy. It comes down to the drugs Merck can produce. Thus, it depends more on the white coats in the labs at Rahway than the suits in the headquarters at Whitehouse Station; more on whether Zetia is a significant improvement over the older cholesterol drugs on the market than whether Merck merges with Schering-Plough in selling Zetia; more on whether Arcoxia can significantly ease pain without causing risk to the heart, than whether Ray Gilmartin misled investors about Arcoxia's problems. To be a successful drug company, Merck will need blockbusters. But to be Merck, it will need blockbusters that are also significant scientific leaps forward.

Merck likes to brag that (in the oft-repeated words of its 2001 annual report) it "anticipates filing or launching 11 new medicines and vaccines by 2006," which is indeed a sizable number. Looking into that pipeline, some observers are more pessimistic than others. Of the best-known candidates, Zetia and the Zetia-Zocor combination could be genuine breakthroughs in cholesterol treatment as well as big sellers. Vaccines for HPV (the sexually transmitted human papillomavirus) and rotavirus (the cause of infant diarrhea) are potential innovations, too, since there are no successful vaccine approaches to those widespread diseases now. However, Merck has competition from GlaxoSmithKline and Roche, and one- or two- or three-shot vaccines are inherently less profitable than an ongoing medication—especially in the case of rotavirus, which hits the developing world harder than the health-insured West. For its part, the HPV product would face the tricky marketing problem of asking parents to vaccinate their daughters just in case they became sexually active. Still, with a market of potentially evevy adolescent and preadolescent American girl—if not every girl in the world—an HPV vaccine could be a billion-dollar product, says Gordon Douglas, who oversaw the beginning of that research when he headed Merck's vaccine division. Meanwhile, Arcoxia—even if it works—will be merely the second drug in the second generation of a category of painkillers that many people say isn't needed anyway. Then there's substance P for depression, which would be a great new approach if it succceeded, but its mixed history has to raise doubts. Other near-term filings are simply additional uses for existing drugs, like Singulair for hay fever. Further down the road, the prospect of an HIV/AIDS vaccine sounds like the good old Merck—a pathbreaking approach to a dreadful problem.

This list isn't a bad one. There are some intriguing new approaches, especially for cholesterol, AIDS, cervical cancer and depression. For the rest, Merck can hardly be expected to have a pill for every ill or a breakthrough in every pill. It's probably not the best lineup in the industry.

But can Merck actually produce this pipeline? For most of the list, it's simply too soon to predict—even if we knew all the details of what's going on in Merck's lab. The only thing that can be said for sure is that some candidates will never make it to market. AstraZeneca's setback with its cancer drug Iressa, Pfizer's abandonment of its $71 million "youth drug," and Merck's own back-and-forth hopes for substance P are all case studies of the high risks of pharmaceutical research that the industry keeps warning about.

Merck still has a talented pool of scientists, though it's obviously lost a lost of brainpower. It still has the exasperating combination of freedom and bureaucracy in its labs. And it's still got the aura. Maybe it's only living off past glory, as many observers suggest, but it still gives investors hope and pulls at people who have been gone for years. It's an aura born of long hours of camaraderie with brilliant colleagues, the thrill of glowing headlines, a memory, a slogan.

"I have a child," begins Alaina Love Cugnon, the former Pepcid researcher and HR manager. This is eight years after leaving Merck, two years after her husband left, and she's not happy with what's happened to the management or her Merck stock since then. She's living in a completely different world now, in Virginia, far removed from the pharmaceutical industry—consulting on leadership development; importing, breeding, and training Lusitano horses from Portugal; and manufacturing and importing horse-care products. She is pretty and vivacious, younger-looking than her résumé would indicate, with wavy, shoulder-length dark hair and a large diamond ring. "If I had a choice between a Merck product and another company's for the treatment of my child," she continues, "I would choose Merck's."

"You have to understand," she adds, "the care and research Merck puts in. There are so many smart people, they'll figure out how to bring it back."

Roy Vagelos has been gone from Merck about as long as Cugnon. Of course, he might be expected to feel tremendous loyalty to a company he ran for 9 years and worked at for 19. Still, by his own admission, "I severed my ties" to that life. He rarely sees anyone from Merck socially, he's not on the board, he's not consulted. Instead he's very involved now with two biotechs whose boards he chairs. His former company is being run by someone he did not select. He is free to criticize.

For all that, Vagelos ends his interview: "Say good things about Merck."

Chapter 1: In the Bull's-Eye

1. Werth, Barry, *The Billion-Dollar Molecule*, Touchstone, 1994, p. 271 (paperback edition).

Chapter 2: From Little Pharmacy to Big Pharma

1. *Time*, August 18, 1952, p. 43.
2. *Values & Visions: A Merck Century*, Jeffrey L. Sturchio, ed., Merck & Co., 1991, pp. 29–30.
3. Ibid, p. 28.

Chapter 3: Off the Cutting Edge

1. *The New Republic*, "Drug Abuse," Nicholas Thompson, October 7, 2002, p. 18.

Chapter 4: The Drugs of Tomorrow

1. Berkow, Robert, M.D. (editor-in-chief), *The Merck Manual* (home edition), Merck & Co., Inc., 1997, p. 681.

Chapter 7: "It Is Not for the Profits," Part One: Prices and Politics

1. Callahan, Daniel, *The Research Imperative: What Price Better Health?*, University of California Press. In press.

Chapter 8: "It Is Not for the Profits," Part Two: The AIDS Debacle

1. *The Wall Street Journal*, Elyse Tanouye, November 5, 1996.
2. Galambos, Louis and Sewell, Jane Eliot, *Confronting AIDS: Science and Business Cross a Unique Frontier*, Merck & Co., p. 48.
3. Ibid, p. 23.
4. Ibid, p. 22.
5. *The Asian Wall Street Journal*, "AIDS—Drug Makers Escalate Price War—Treatment Price Plunges for Poor Nations," Mark Schoofs and Michael Waldholz, March 8, 2001, p. N1.

Chapter 10: A Different Business Model

1. Smith, Adam, *An Inquiry into the Nature and Causes of the Wealth of Nations*, Book I, Chapter 10.
2. Lewis, Sinclair, *Arrowsmith*, New American Library, p. 132 (paperback edition).

Bibliography

Books

Bauman, Robert P., Jackson, Peter, and Lawrence, Joanne T., *From Promise to Performance: A Journey of Transformation at SmithKline Beecham*, Harvard Business School Press, 1997.

Blumberg, Baruch S., *Hepatitis B: The Hunt for a Killer Virus*, Princeton University Press, 2002.

Boyer, Paul, *The American Nation*, Holt Rinehart and Winston, 2001.

Callahan, Daniel, *The Research Imperative: What Price Better Health?*, University of California Press, 2003.

Cohen, Jay S., M. D., *Over Dose: The Case Against the Drug Companies*, Jeremy P. Tarder/Putnam, 2001.

Collins, James C., and Porras, Jerry I., *Built To Last: Successful Habits of Visionary Companies*, HarperBusiness, 1994.

Galambos, Louis, with Sewell, Jane Eliot, *Networks of Innovation: Vaccine Development at Merck, Sharp & Dohme, and Mulford, 1895–1995*, Cambridge University Press, 1995.

Giniat, Edward J., and Libert, Barry D., *Value ℞ for Healthcare*, HarperBusiness, 2001

Glynn, Alan, *The Dark Fields*, Bloomsbury, 2001.

Griffenhagen, George, *150 Years of Caring*, American Pharmaceutical Association, 2002.

Kramer, Peter, *Spectacular Happiness*, Scribner, 2001.

Le Carré, John, *The Constant Gardener*, Scribner, 2001.

Lewis, Sinclair, *Arrowsmith*, Harcourt, Brace & World, Inc., 1925.

Lossky, Andrew (editor), *The Seventeenth Century* (Sources in Western Civilization series), The Free Press, 1967.

Nanus, Burt, *Visionary Leadership: Creating a Compelling Sense of Direction for Your Organization*, Jossey-Bass Publishers, 1990.

Palmer, R. R., and Colton, Joel, *A History of the Modern World*, third edition, Alfred A. Knopf, 1965.

Possehl, Ingunn, *Modern by Tradition: The History of the Chemical-Pharmaceutical Factory*, E. Merck Darmstadt.

Sturchio, Jeffrey L. (editor), *Values & Visions: A Merck Century*, Merck & Co., 1991.

Werth, Barry, *The Billion-Dollar Molecule*, Simon & Schuster, 1994.

Reports

Cockburn, Iain M., Henderson, Rebecca M., and Stern, Scott, "Untangling the Origins of Competitive Advantage," *Strategic Management Journal*, Fall 2000.

DiMasi, Joseph A., "Risks in New Drug Development: Approval Success Rates for Investigational Drugs," *Clinical Pharmacology & Therapeutics*, May 2001.

DiMasi, Joseph A., Hansen, Ronald W., Grabowski, Henry G.; and Lasagna, Louis, "Research and Development Costs for New Drugs by Therapeutic Category: A Study of the U.S. Pharmaceutical Industry," *Pharmacoeconomics*, February 1995.

Galambos, Louis, and Sewell, Jane Eliot, "Confronting AIDS: Science and Business Cross a Unique Frontier," Merck & Co.

Guilloux, Alain, and Moon, Suerie, "Hidden Price Tags: Disease-Specific Drug Donations: Costs and Alternatives," Médecins Sans Frontières Access to Essential Medicines Campaign, 2000.

Henderson, Rebecca, and Cockburn, Iain, "Measuring Competence? Exploring Firm Effects in Pharmaceutical Research," *Strategic Management Journal,* Winter 1994.

Henderson, Rebecca, and Cockburn, Iain, "Scale, Scope, and Spillovers: The Determinants of Research Productivity in Drug Discovery," *RAND Journal of Economics,* Spring 1996.

Lichtenberg, Frank R., "Are the Benefits of Newer Drugs Worth Their Cost? Evidence from the 1996 MEPS," *Health Affairs,* September–October 2001.

Lichtenberg, Frank R, "The Benefits to Society of New Drugs: A Survey of the Econometric Evidence," presented at the Federal Reserve of Dallas, April 2002.

Lichtenberg, Frank R., "The Effect of Changes in Drug Utilization on Labor Supply and Per Capita Output," March 2002.

Tollman, Peter; Guy, Philippe; Altshuler, Jill; Flanagan, Alastair; and Steiner, Michael, "A Revolution in R&D: How Genomics and Genetics Are Transforming the Biopharmaceutical Industry," The Boston Consulting Group, 2001.

"Consumer Use of Dietary Supplements," *Prevention* Magazine.

"Enough To Make You Sick: Prescription Drug Prices for the Elderly," Families USA, 2001.

"Fatal Imbalance: The Crisis in Research and Development for Drugs for Neglected Diseases," Médecins Sans Frontières Access to Essential Medicines Campaign and The Drugs for Neglected Diseases Working Group, 2001.

"The Future of Pharma HR," PricewaterhouseCoopers, 2001.

"International Survey on Wellness and Consumer Reaction to DTC Advertising of Rx Drugs," *Prevention,* 2000–2001.

"Key Issues Facing the Pharmaceutical and Health Care Products Industry," PricewaterhouseCoopers, 1999.

"Pharma 2005: Marketing to the Individual," PricewaterhouseCoopers, 1999.

"Prescription Drugs and Intellectual Property Protection," National Institute for Health Care Management, 2000.

"Prescription Drugs and Mass Media Advertising, 2000," National Institute for Health Care Management.

"Prescription Drug Expenditures in 2000: The Upward Trend Continues," National Institute for Health Care Management.

Newspaper and Magazine Articles

For this book, I read literally hundreds of newspaper and magazine articles, mainly from *The New York Times, The Wall Street Journal, BusinessWeek, Fortune, Forbes,* the Associated Press, *Time, Newsweek, Money, Barron's,* theStreet.com, and Dow Jones News Service. There are far too many to list, but I do want to mention some of the most useful:

Abelson, Reed, "Out of the Merger Rush, Merck's on a Limb," *The New York Times,* August 4, 2002.

Barrett, Amy, with Arndt, Michael, "No Quick Cure," *BusinessWeek,* May 6, 2002.

Byrne, John A., "The Miracle Company," *BusinessWeek,* October 19, 1987.

Clifford, Lee, "Tyrannosaurus Rx," *Fortune,* October 30, 2000.

Greenwald, John, "Rx for Nosebleed Prices," *Time,* May 21, 2001.

Harris, Gardiner, "As a Patent Expires, Drug Firms Line up Pricey Alternative," *The Wall Street Journal,* June 6, 2002.

Harris, Gardiner, and Adams, Chris, "Drug Manufacturers Step up Legal Attacks That Slow Generics," *The Wall Street Journal,* July 12, 2001.

Harris, Gardiner, "How Merck Survived While Others Merged— Drug Maker Relied on Inspired Research," *The Wall Street Journal,* January 12, 2001.

Harris, Gardiner, "Merck To Shed Medco, Its Drug-Benefits Unit, in Bid to Boost Stock," *The Wall Street Journal,* January 29, 2002.

Harris, Gardiner, "Why Drug Makers Are Failing in Search for New Blockbusters," *The Wall Street Journal,* April 18, 2002.

Langreth, Robert, "Betting on the Brain," *Forbes,* January 7, 2002.

McLean, Bethany, "A Bitter Pill," *Fortune,* August 13, 2001.

O'Reilly, Brian, "There's Still Gold in Them Thar Pills," *Fortune,* July 23, 2001.

Simons, John, "Will R&D Make Merck Hot Again?" *Fortune,* July 8, 2002.

"What the Doctor Ordered," *Time,* August 18, 1952.

Index